DATE DUE

MAY 2 9 2010			

Governors State University
Library Hours:
Monday thru Thursday 8:00 to 10:30
Friday 8:00 to 5:00
Saturday 8:30 to 5:00
Sunday 1:00 to 5:00 (Fall
and Winter Trimester Only)

Kept 12/2013

INTEGRATED HEALTH CARE DELIVERY

Integrated Health Care Delivery

Leonie A. Klein and
Emily L. Neumann
Editors

Nova Science Publishers, Inc.
New York

Copyright © 2008 by Nova Science Publishers, Inc.

For permission to use material from this book please contact us:
Telephone 631-231-7269; Fax 631-231-8175
Web Site: http://www.novapublishers.com

NOTICE TO THE READER

The Publisher has taken reasonable care in the preparation of this book, but makes no expressed or implied warranty of any kind and assumes no responsibility for any errors or omissions. No liability is assumed for incidental or consequential damages in connection with or arising out of information contained in this book. The Publisher shall not be liable for any special, consequential, or exemplary damages resulting, in whole or in part, from the readers' use of, or reliance upon, this material. Any parts of this book based on government reports are so indicated and copyright is claimed for those parts to the extent applicable to compilations of such works.

Independent verification should be sought for any data, advice or recommendations contained in this book. In addition, no responsibility is assumed by the publisher for any injury and/or damage to persons or property arising from any methods, products, instructions, ideas or otherwise contained in this publication.

This publication is designed to provide accurate and authoritative information with regard to the subject matter covered herein. It is sold with the clear understanding that the Publisher is not engaged in rendering legal or any other professional services. If legal or any other expert assistance is required, the services of a competent person should be sought. FROM A DECLARATION OF PARTICIPANTS JOINTLY ADOPTED BY A COMMITTEE OF THE AMERICAN BAR ASSOCIATION AND A COMMITTEE OF PUBLISHERS.

LIBRARY OF CONGRESS CATALOGING-IN-PUBLICATION DATA

Integrated health care delivery / Leonie A. Klein and Emily L. Neumann (editors).
    p. ; cm.
 Includes bibliographical references and index.
 ISBN 978-1-60456-851-6 (hardcover)
 1. Continuum of care. I. Klein, Leonie A. II. Neumann, Emily L.
 [DNLM: 1. Delivery of Health Care, Integrated. W 84.1 I607 2008]
 RA644.5.I577 2008
 362.1--dc22
                          2008023303

Published by Nova Science Publishers, Inc. ✦ *New York*

CONTENTS

Preface   **vii**

Chapter 1   A Brief Description of the Limitations of the Current Health Care
                 System in the United States, and a Program Response to the
                 Complex Issues of Many Individuals Who Are Confronted with
                 Multiple, Chronic Conditions   **1**
                 Christina Miles Krause, Maria E. J. Kuhn
                 and Katja Kremer Wolfe

Chapter 2   A Comparison of Integrated Dual Diagnosis Treatment Service
                 Delivery Models on Fidelity and Client Outcomes at 1- and 2-Year
                 Follow-Ups   **19**
                 Laurel F. Mangrum, Richard T. Spence and Molly Lopez

Chapter 3   Operating Room Costs and Resource Utilization in Lumbar Fusion
                 with Instrumentation Procedures: Integrated Delivery System Is
                 Implicated   **35**
                 Wei-Ching Chung, Herng-Chia Chiu and Dong-Sheng Tzeng

Chapter 4   Social Capital and Partnership Opportunities: Management
                 Implication in Integrated Healthcare Networks   **49**
                 Blossom Y. J. Lin and Thomas T. H. Wan

Chapter 5   Integrated Care for Patients with Chronic Diseases   **67**
                 Mariëlle M. M. T. J. Ouwens, Rosella R. P. Hermens,
                 Marlies M. E. Hulscher, Henri A. M. Marres,
                 Richard P. and Hub J. Wollersheim

Chapter 6   A Case Manager Model for Integrative Healthcare Delivery:
                 Orchestrating Delivery with an Information Management System   **93**
                 Curtis H. Jones

Chapter 7   Integrated Care Delivery: Process Redesign and the Role of Rules,
                 Routines and Transaction Costs   **115**
                 A. J. A. van Raak, A. T. G. Paulus and S. Groothuis

Chapter 8   Whys and Wherefores of Integrated Health Care   **137**
                     Bengt Ahgren

Chapter 9   Image Exchange between a Major Health System and a Private
                     Radiology Group Using a Shared Image Server   **151**
                     Linda Womack

Index   **157**

PREFACE

In an integrated health network, various types of organizations are connected along a continuum of care through horizontal and vertical integration. Integrated health network has several interchangeable terms such as integrated health system, integrated delivery system (network), integrated care system (network), organized delivery system, community care network, integrated health care organization, integrated service network, population-based integrated delivery system, and so on, which all emphasize as a multi-organization form characterized by serving a defined population across multi-disciplines, including professionals, units, or service-lines of primary care, acute care and long term care. This book provides leading-edge issues on this field from around the globe.

Chapter 1 - This chapter describes an innovative, theory-driven, multidisciplinary intervention program designed to a) improve the health and health care of individuals who are dealing with multiple chronic health conditions, and b) help these individuals learn to manage their health care by means of an empowerment process through modeling, education, and decision support by a collaborative, multidisciplinary team (a nurse, a physician, and a psychosocial specialist). The focus of the intervention is to empower participants to be responsible for their health care through a gradual process of increasing personal involvement in the health care decision-making process. The program addresses the physical, social, psychological, spiritual, financial and vocational well-being of an individual, and was designed to eliminate the traditional "departmental-like" walls that impact patients with chronic care needs, as well as their providers. The on-going team process involves: a comprehensive assessment of all available previous health care records; collaborative on-going meetings with their Advocacy Team, the participant, his/her providers, and other significant individuals (e.g., family members, friends, etc.) to determine, and revise when appropriate, plans for treatment; assisting the participant's primary provider by providing a comprehensive summary of previous health care issues, tests and treatments; and providing avenues for communication between providers regarding an individual's treatment goals. The Advocacy Team's goal to remove the traditional barriers that have interfered with the participant's achievement of best possible health (e.g., restrictions on mental health care appointments, prohibitive co-payments on prescriptions, transportation to appointments, etc.) is described. The team process of identifying the participant's current social network, the process of helping the individual to develop other relationships to address spiritual, employment, physical, mental, and other issues are clarified. Another goal of the program is the effective use of health care dollars. The literature review explains the reasoning behind the goals of this program. A description of information learned through the research data collection process is described, and conclusions are presented.

Chapter 2 - The measurement of treatment fidelity is an important, yet often omitted component in examining the efficacy of various treatment models. Although the measurement of fidelity is often complex, the potential benefits of including fidelity measures in studies of treatment models are numerous. Fidelity measures are useful in evaluation studies as a means of documenting appropriate implementation and adherence to the model under study, as well as confirming treatment differentiation in research designs that include control groups. Further, fidelity measures provide a potential method for determining critical ingredients in treatment models that are most strongly associated with client outcomes. Despite these important benefits, studies of the relation between fidelity and client outcomes are limited. The current study in this chapter compares two integrated dual diagnosis service delivery models on fidelity and 1- and 2-year psychiatric hospitalization and arrest outcomes of clients with severe mental illness and substance use disorders. Two modes of implementation, the integrated treatment ($n=3$) and adjunct service ($n=3$) models, were identified through qualitative process evaluation of six pilot sites participating in an integrated dual diagnosis treatment demonstration project. The integrated treatment and adjunct service models were contrasted on the Texas Integrated Treatment Integrity Scale (TITIS) to explore potential differences in implementation of specific components of integrated dual diagnosis treatment. Psychiatric hospitalization and arrest outcomes of 256 clients were compared between the implementation models at 1 and 2 years post treatment entry. On the TITIS subscales, the integrated treatment model achieved higher fidelity scores on the Staffing and Treatment Team Structure scale but no differences were found on the Treatment Program Structure and Services, Integrated Treatment Documentation, or Overall Fidelity scales. Although the comparison of hospitalization days 24 months pre- and post-baseline indicated greater reduction in hospitalization for the integrated treatment group, two other models analyzing 12 months pre- and post-baseline and contrasting 12-month baseline, year 1, and year 2 hospitalization days and arrests did not reveal significant differences between the service delivery models. The overall results of this study indicated that the two service delivery models achieved comparable fidelity ratings and outcomes at 1 and 2 years post treatment entry. These findings suggest that mode of service delivery may be a less essential component of the integrated dual diagnosis treatment model relative to other elements of the framework, such as program structure, service array, and documentation. Future studies of this nature are needed to assist in isolating critical components of integrated treatment to inform technology transfer of this evidence-based practice into community settings.

Chapter 3 - Very few studies have addressed the magnitude of hospital costs in lumbar fusion with instrumentation in Asian countries. The objectives of the study were to analyze and compare lumbar fusion with instrumentation operating room (OR) costs between two hospitals.

Patients who underwent lumbar fusion with instrumentation in 2004 at one medical center and one public teaching hospital were invited to participate. Patient demographics and clinical information were derived from patient charts. Cost information was obtained from detailing billing charges and the hospital financial accounting divisions. In the linear regression analysis, significant differences in age and severity were observed between the two study hospitals in terms of total costs.

There were significant differences in patient demographics and disease severity at the two hospitals (p=0.000). The case mix in the medical center was 1.76, and in the public teaching hospital, 1.05. The medical center consumed more resources than did the public teaching hospital (NT$106,462 vs. NT$87,643). A difference was found in direct materials costs (p=0.000~0.199), direct professional costs (p=0.000~0.342), and indirect costs in the two study hospitals (p=0.000). Patients who scored higher in the American Society of Anesthesiologists physical status index incurred significantly higher costs and longer hospital stays (p=0.011) than did patients with lower scores (p=0.000).

The knowledge and experience of surgeons and hospital management are equally important to maintain a hospital's competitive position. These results showed the different patient severity referred to different care provider, different resource utilization from different health care delivery system which are critical factors in care management. A vertically integrated health care delivery system would be a suitable model to cover the demands of patients when providers face the cost considerations of National Health Insurance.

Chapter 4 - Social capital as a multidimensional construct measurable from a spirit of trust, cooperation, and commitment could be considered integral to understanding how health care organizations may enhance their survival and growth potential in networks. The organization and dynamics of Taiwan's primary community care network (PCCN) could serve as a good example to illustrate the role of social capital in establishing partnership opportunities. This chapter employs integrated health networks as a framework to identify the importance of social capital and to explicate managerial issues related to health care network management. Analytical issues pertaining to social capital were raised and relevant arguments were reviewed. Finally, using Taiwan's primary community care network (PCCN) as a thinking model, the authors propose several indicators to study the nature of social capital from three domains: structural, relational, and cognitive. The principles of social capital applicable to network management in the health care sector were discussed.

Chapter 5 - Chronic diseases such as cancer, heart disease, stroke, arthritis, diabetes mellitus, mental illness and obstructive pulmonary diseases are now the leading causes of illness, disability and death. Meeting the complex needs of a growing group of patients with chronic diseases is one of the greatest challenges that health care faces today. New models of health care delivery are needed and integrated care programmes or disease management programmes have begun to receive greater support as approaches to improve quality of care for these groups of patients. This chapter shows that the aim of these programmes are usually very similar, namely to reduce fragmentation and improve continuity and coordination, but that the focus and content of the programmes differ widely. Based on these findings it is concluded that integrated care is based on five principles: patient-centredness, multidisciplinary care, coordination of care, evidence-based medicine and continuous quality improvement. The first three principles are considered as being the main principles of integrated care, the other two are general principles for delivering high quality of care. Interventions mentioned that sustain these principles focus on health care providers and/or the organization of care, while patient education had often been added. To improve integrated care, actual care should be measured and successful integrated care interventions should be implemented. In the presented examples on measuring and improving integrated care for patients with head and neck cancer and patients with lung cancer it is demonstrated that there is much room for improvement and that a multi-component programme can lead to relevant improvements.

Chapter 6 - This chapter makes the case that the delivery of integrative healthcare would be well served by developing an information management system operated by a Case Manager to reduce the amount of preliminary information about patients the practitioners need to gather. Integrative healthcare (IHc) has been defined in a variety of ways [1]. In this chapter integrative healthcare is understood as "combining of CAM therapies, at times with conventional medicine, and having patient-centeredness as one of its goals."

A Case Manager model would require: 1) an overview of all possible therapies, CAM and conventional, based on a comprehensive organizing principle, see Table I; 2) a Case Manager that facilitates the process of IHc delivery, while not supplying treatments; and, 3) expansion of the definition of 'patient-centeredness' toward increasing patient-input into the treatment selection process, with the goal of inducing the patient's healing response.

The Case Manager (CM) model described here is a delivery system that will deeply honor patient-centeredness, make treatment selections from a broad range of options, account for research on CAM efficacy, and create efficiency in clinical decision-making and practitioner communications. The CM model is an information management system that assists practitioner decision-making in IHc by managing information flow and maintaining the patient-centeredness in the clinical decision-making process. Also, the CM model is scalable, meaning it can be reproduced widely independent of practitioner expertise, which is necessary for the broad dissemination of integrative healthcare.

Chapter 7 - In many countries, managers are making efforts to organize integrated health care and social care. The managers need information from research that they can use in order to understand the situation they are facing and to make decisions about the implementation of integrated care. In this chapter, the authors present an approach that, when applied by researchers, will provide this information. The approach covers four parts: a *systematic analysis* of the existing care delivery processes and the waste of resources that occur during these processes; the *redesign* of these processes into a tailor-made, optimized integrated care delivery process where waste is reduced; use of knowledge about *rules for actions* and *routines* (action patterns) of care providers, which rules and routines can hamper implementation of integrated care; use of knowledge about *transaction costs,* which occur during the implementation of integrated care, especially when routines of care providers must be changed. The authors illustrate the approach on the basis of data about care delivery to HIV/AIDS patients in Botswana (Africa). They selected this case because it concerns an illness that is widely spread across the continents, and therefore is recognizable for an international readership. In addition, cooperation among care providers in the case is in its infancy, and therefore brings to light the problems and challenges of redesigning and implementing integrated care. In the final section, the authors discuss how their approach might help managers to decide whether or not to initiate change towards integrated care.

Chapter 8 - The development of health care systems can be described in terms of an escalating differentiation of roles, tasks and responsibilities. There are three main forces behind this development: decentralisation, specialisation and professionalization. The outcome can, on one hand, be regarded as a success story. On the other hand, there is also a flipside of this development. The three driving forces, individually and together, have contributed to a state of differentiation, often described as fragmentation. This state can be divided into different categories, depending on the interaction between the three driving forces: organisational fragmentation, clinical fragmentation and cultural fragmentation, which, in turn, may lead to patients becoming lost in health care delivery systems. This phenomenon can metaphorically be described as a Patient Bermuda Triangle.

Integrated health care is an issue addressed in many countries. Furthermore, there are many different approaches and their scopes are quite different. Some approaches aim to eliminate professional and departmental boundaries and develop multiprofessional teams, while others have the objectives to integrate different sectors of health care, i.e., to link primary, secondary and tertiary health care. Integrated health care should therefore be regarded as a concept of organising between different health care providers. Moreover, the dominating motive for creating integrated health care is to bring order in the chaotic condition of a fragmented health care.

It seems possible to diminish the clinical and organisational fragmentation in health care organisations by developing clinical guidelines and an integrated health care network. However, the cultural fragmentation is probably the biggest challenge when creating integrated health care. It is proven to be difficult to change the values of health care professionals by top-down actions. Moreover, physicians tend to listen more to patients than to politicians or health care managers. A major breakthrough for patient empowerment may therefore imply that existing sets of professional values will be combined with demands emerging from consumer behaviour. Thus, political and top management rhetoric of integration will perhaps not be realised until articulated demands from patients and carers are channelled to health care professionals. By creating change bottom-up and also integrating the patients as resources and change-agents may thus increase the possibilities to diminish cultural fragmentation.

To conclude, the challenge of the future is to simultaneously promote integrated health care networks, clinical guidelines, patient empowerment, and change bottom-up, so as to ensure that the patients not are lost in a "Bermuda Triangle" of a health care system.

In: Integrated Health Care Delivery
Editors: Leonie A. Klein and Emily L. Neumann

ISBN 978-1-60456-851-6
© 2008 Nova Science Publishers, Inc.

Chapter 1

A Brief Description of the Limitations of the Current Health Care System in the United States, and a Program Response to the Complex Issues of Many Individuals Who Are Confronted with Multiple, Chronic Conditions

Christina Miles Krause[1], Maria E. J. Kuhn[2] and Katja Kremer Wolfe[3]

[1]Aurora University, 347 South Gladstone, Aurora, Illinois, 60506-4892, USA
[2]Benefit Performance Associates, LLC, 1 West State Street, Geneva, Il. 60134, USA
[3]Aurora University, 347 South Gladstone, Aurora, Illinois, 60506-4892, USA

ABSTRACT

This chapter describes an innovative, theory-driven, multidisciplinary intervention program designed to a) improve the health and health care of individuals who are dealing with multiple chronic health conditions, and b) help these individuals learn to manage their health care by means of an empowerment process through modeling, education, and decision support by a collaborative, multidisciplinary team (a nurse, a physician, and a psychosocial specialist). The focus of the intervention is to empower participants to be responsible for their health care through a gradual process of increasing personal involvement in the health care decision-making process. The program addresses the physical, social, psychological, spiritual, financial and vocational well-being of an individual, and was designed to eliminate the traditional "departmental-like" walls that impact patients with chronic care needs, as well as their providers. The on-going team process involves: a comprehensive assessment of all available previous health care records; collaborative on-going meetings with their Advocacy Team, the participant, his/her providers, and other significant individuals (e.g., family members, friends, etc.) to determine, and revise when appropriate, plans for treatment; assisting the participant's primary provider by providing a comprehensive summary of previous health care issues, tests and treatments; and providing avenues for communication between providers regarding an individual's treatment goals. The Advocacy Team's goal to remove the traditional barriers that have interfered with the participant's achievement of best possible health (e.g., restrictions on mental health care appointments, prohibitive co-payments on prescriptions, transportation to appointments, etc.) is described. The team process of identifying the participant's current social network, the process of helping the individual to develop other relationships to address spiritual, employment, physical, mental, and other issues are clarified. Another goal of the program is the effective use of health care dollars. The literature review explains the reasoning behind the goals of this program. A description of information learned through the research data collection process is described, and conclusions are presented.

INTRODUCTION

Health professionals and researchers indicate that costs related to chronic diseases, such as heart disease, arthritis, diabetes, and cancer, are causing an alarming escalation in health care costs in the United States (Anderson and Horvath, 2004). Chronic health conditions often necessitate expensive, long-term care, which may involve a number of medical specialties. Over 125 million Americans have at least one chronic health condition, and this number is expected to increase steadily in the future (Anderson and Horvath, 2004). Unfortunately, the current health care system is not equipped to address the numerous needs of these individuals with chronic conditions (Ostbye et al., 2005). In response to these expensive developments, a number of researchers have focused on finding ways to help prevent chronic diseases, as well as finding ways to improve the health status of individuals who are suffering from chronic diseases (i.e., disease management education programs).

The purpose of this article is to explain the inadequacies of the current health care situation in regard to the management of chronic conditions, and to introduce the Integrative Health Advocacy Program^{SM} (IHAP®), a unique and innovative intervention designed to address the numerous issues of individuals who are dealing with multiple chronic diseases. This intervention process involves a comprehensive assessment of the physical and psychosocial issues of patients, the development of appropriate treatment plans, monthly meetings of patients and their advocacy team, and tailored patient education sessions. The goals of the program are to build a true collaboration process between health care providers and their patients, to improve the quality of life, health, and health care of patients, to gradually empower patients to successfully manage their chronic diseases, and to use health care dollars more effectively. This paper will explain in greater detail the impact that care for individuals with chronic diseases has on our current health care system, as well as the inefficiencies of the health care system in terms of its impact on the wellbeing of individuals who are dealing with chronic diseases. Also, a brief overview of existing interventions will be provided, and then a response to the current state of health care will be provided by means of describing the Integrated Health Advocacy Program. Finally, we will describe the theoretical concepts that form the basis of IHAP, the key components of the intervention, the research methodology and a brief description of the information learned through the research data.

LITERATURE REVIEW

Chronic conditions are defined as long-term conditions (at least a year) that require continuous medical care and that may lead to disabilities/limitations of activities of daily living (ADL) (Anderson and Horvath, 2004). Cardiovascular diseases (e.g., coronary artery disease [CAD], and hypertension), diabetes, behavioral health disorders (e.g. depression, anxiety, posttraumatic stress disorder, and substance abuse disorders), osteoporosis, chronic obstructive pulmonary disease (COPD), cancers, asthma, and arthritis are some of the most prevalent chronic conditions that affect people's everyday lives (Center for Prevention and Health Services, 2005; Ostbye et al., 2005). Chronic disease management is currently the most urgent health issue, with an estimated $277 billion being spent on chronic disease treatment (Committee for the Study of the Future of Public Health, 1988, as cited by Center for Prevention and Health Services, 2005). A large part of health care spending, over 75%, is the consequence of approximately 125 million individuals who suffer from at least one chronic disease and more than 60 million individuals who suffer from two or more chronic conditions (Anderson and Horvath, 2004). The Center for Disease Control and Prevention (2005) found that the costs of cardiovascular diseases and arthritis in 2001 reached $429 billion and almost $82 billion, respectively, due to treatment costs and loss of productivity. Furthermore, behavioral health disorders, such as depression, anxiety, and substance abuse, cost employers approximately $17 billion every year due to a loss of workdays and a decline in productivity; these disorders are a major cause of long- and short-term disability in the United States and worldwide (Center for Prevention and Health Services, 2005).

Understandably, the escalating costs of health care are distressing employers and their employees as this country is experiencing a tremendous pressure "to reduce, ration and delay health services to contain health costs" (Bandura, 2004, p. 144). According to results of the 2001 Employee Benefits Study conducted by the U.S. Chamber of Commerce, "benefits cost an average of 37.5% of payroll [expenses] in 2000, or an average of $16,617 per employee" (as cited in Parmenter, 2003, p.60). Over 35% of benefit expenses are a result of insurance premiums. Furthermore, health care costs have increased dramatically since the publication of this report (Parmenter, 2003), and thus health insurance coverage has become even more expensive for employers and employees.

To restate an alarming prediction, experts agree that we should expect a considerable increase in the number of patients with chronic illnesses and their associated health care costs over the next several decades (Anderson and Horvath, 2004). Although this upward trend will be found in all age groups, there seems to be a worrisome rise in the prevalence of children and adolescents dealing with conditions such as asthma, and other conditions found historically in the adult population, such as type-2 diabetes, obesity, and high blood pressure. The development of chronic conditions at younger ages will no doubt impact future chronic disease costs. At the other end of the spectrum, Americans are also living longer and, as they age, they become more susceptible to developing chronic conditions (Bandura, 2004). In fact, approximately 85% of individuals 65 years or older have at least one chronic disease, and over 60% have two or more chronic diseases (Anderson and Horvath, 2004). Furthermore, we are on the verge of a population shift; that is, many "baby boomers" are reaching retirement age, and this population is at an increasing risk of developing multiple chronic illnesses. Some researchers predict that almost 50% of Americans will have at least one chronic illness in less than 20 years (Anderson and Horvath, 2004). As Albert Bandura clearly stated, "Demand is overwhelming supply." (2004, p. 144).

Compounding these issues is the fact that, unlike acute illnesses, chronic diseases are rarely ever curable and often progressive. However, our current health care system is based on an acute care model (Holman and Lorig, 2004). Under our acute care model, illnesses or injuries, even those known to be chronic or those that may eventually lead to chronic conditions, are treated as acute conditions. Furthermore, typically, the physician is the primary decision-maker, and the patient is expected to adhere to a previously established course of treatment without having much input (Anderson and Horvath, 2004; Bodenheimer, Lorig, Holman, and Grumbach, 2002; Holman and Lorig, 2004). For example, bacterial infections are treated with antibiotics and a broken bone is set and put in a cast while the injury heals. This model was effective in past centuries, when acute illnesses were very common and most people did not live long enough to develop chronic diseases. However, advances in medical treatments have made, and are continuing to make, diseases that were once considered fatal, survivable, and surviving a chronic disease over an extended period of time is far more likely today than it was even 20 years ago.

It is clear that chronic diseases require different types of treatment protocols than acute conditions. The treatment of chronic conditions is not only long-term, but also incredibly complex, as patients often require continuous, comprehensive and integrated care by a number of medical and behavioral health specialists (Schneiderman, Antoni, Saab, and Ironson, 2001). There is no "quick fix," and people with chronic conditions tend to experience a decline in physical health and mental health over time. These individuals often have to deal with "pain, functional impairment, social and emotional dysfunction, and premature loss of wage earnings" (Marks, Allegrante, and Lorig, 2005b, p. 148). Even though it is apparent that it would be helpful to attend to medical and psychosocial problems as part of routine health care to improve a patient's health, these issues are often not addressed in the current health care environment. One reason for not addressing these issues is that there is continuing pressure in primary care to limit visits and "there is a reported 18 to 21 minutes for office visits for most patients" (Ostbye et al., 2005, p. 210). Furthermore, patients with co-morbidities have more medications that need reviewing for potential side effects, have more compliance issues, and "these patients have been found to require more primary care physician visits and time than patients with fewer co-morbid conditions" (Schellevis et al., 1994, Starfield et al., 2003, and Westert et al., 2001, as cited in Ostbye et al., 2005, p. 211).

Another serious issue in today's current care environment is that a number of health care services that are necessary or helpful to an individual's recovery are not covered by some insurance providers (Holicky, 2008). For example, mental health coverage was separated from physical health coverage with the development of managed care, even though individuals with chronic conditions have been found to frequently develop one or more comorbid psychosocial issues (Center for Prevention and Health Services, 2005). Furthermore, some health care policies provide limited coverage of services related to hearing, vision, and speech problems; these limitations essentially interfere with an individual's ability to recover, or maintain, sensory and cognitive functioning, and limit an individual's recovery from a stroke, spinal cord injury, or traumatic brain injury.

Furthermore, there are social issues that appear to be associated with chronic diseases, such as social isolation, patients' and families' actual, or perceived, lack of emotional support, and the lack of support for informal caregivers (Krause and Kuhn, 2007) that physicians seldom address during regular appointments. The absence of these supp result in an individual developing long-term dependency on medical treatm

Another concern that is very much related to the issues of individ conditions, that further complicates chronic disease care and ma fragmentation of the U.S. health care system. For example, when an individual who is dealing with multiple chronic conditions is treated by different physicians, as is often the case, the lack of communication among the patient's health care providers may result in a failure to coordinate treatments and medication usage (Blendon et al., 2003). Blendon and colleagues (2003) found that Americans with chronic health conditions reported having appointments with three or more physicians during a two-year period. Berenson and Horvath (2003, as cited in Anderson and Horvath, 2004) found that Medicare beneficiaries with more than four chronic diseases see more than 10 different physicians, visit their physicians' offices almost 40 times a year, and fill up to 50 prescriptions a year. In their study Blendon and colleagues (2003) found that 20% of U.S. respondents who were suffering from chronic conditions indicated that they were prescribed duplicate medical tests or procedures by different health professionals, resulting in unnecessary health care expenditures. Consequently, medical resources are being wasted, and these unnecessary expenses add to the burden of the U.S. health care system. Furthermore, there is an increase in the risk of harm to individuals who see multiple health care providers. For example, Blendon and colleagues (2003) found that many American respondents reported receiving conflicting information regarding their health issues and medication usage from their health care providers. Additionally, although medications may cause serious side effects or interactions if taken with other medications, "30% of U.S. respondents indicated that their physicians had not taken the time to reevaluate their current medications within the last two years" (Blendon et al., 2003, p. 107). For individuals with multiple chronic illnesses, this failure to review medication usage may result in unnecessary and expensive emergency room visits, hospitalizations and/or nursing home stays.

Clearly, the current health care system in the United States is not prepared to manage the increasing numbers of individuals living with chronic conditions (Holman and Lorig, 2004), as it has not found a way to coordinate the extensive health care services that these individuals require (Blendon et al., 2003). In response to the current health care crisis, health professionals and health behavior experts have developed interventions that focus on providing education to promote healthy behaviors (e.g., public health campaigns to reduce drug, alcohol, and tobacco use and to promote healthy eating and exercise). Additionally, other interventions have focused on the management of a specific chronic disease, such as osteoarthritis (Groessl and Cronan, 2003; Osborne, Wilson, Lorig, and McColl, 2007), breast cancer (Lev, 2000), dementia (Fitzsimmons and Buettner, 2003), renal disease (Oppenheimer et al., 2003), pulmonary disease (Arnold et al., 2006), asthma, and diabetes (Newman, Steed, and Mulligan, 2004). The next paragraph will describe the specific goals of a few of these disease-specific interventions.

In a review of existing intervention programs for asthma patients, Newman, Steed, and Mulligan (2004) found that the interventions tend to focus on educating these patients to avoid the triggers that may lead to an attack and on making adjustments to medications as a preventative measure, and that little time is spent on psychosocial issues related to the disease. Also, researchers reviewing diabetes interventions found that most focused on promoting health behaviors and lifestyle changes (Newman et al., 2004). An intervention for heart disease, however, focused on improving communication skills with physicians and found improvements in psychosocial functioning, but not physical functioning (Clark et al., 1992). Each of these interventions had different measures of success; however, each of the interventions focused on treating individuals with only one specific disease. .

Today, there are many different types of chronic diseases, and it would be very difficult to have a specific intervention for each chronic disease. However, Lorig and colleagues (1999) recognized the need for a broader chronic disease intervention program. They developed an intervention for patients with different types of chronic diseases, with the goal of educating these individuals regarding disease self-management skills (e.g., cognitive symptom management skills, effective communication skills, and coping skills to manage emotional reactions). The intervention also had the goal of increasing the patients' self-efficacy to improve their level of confidence in dealing with their conditions (Lorig et al., 1999, 2001; Lorig, Ritter, and Jacquez, 2005). Specifically, in a 6-month randomized study over 900 self-selected patients over the age of 40, who had lung disease, heart disease, stroke or arthritis, were asked to provide self-evaluations of their health status, health behaviors, and health care utilization (Lorig et al., 1999). A follow-up study two years later (Lorig et al., 2001) on these patients indicated that even though the patients' disabilities had worsened, their emergency room visits had decreased, and their health behaviors and level of self-efficacy had improved. As stated by Lorig and colleagues (1999), "These results indicate that it is possible to educate patients with different chronic diseases successfully in the same intervention at the same time." (p. 13).

Additionally, many intervention programs educate patients about the effective use of community resources. It is important to note that having patients rely on peers to support and educate them is not as effective, and does not result in changes in health-related behaviors, as having professionals facilitate educational sessions (Lorig et al., 1999). Thus, it is imperative that intervention programs for individuals with chronic diseases have professionals presiding at educational sessions.

To summarize, the key component of many intervention programs for individuals with chronic disease is teaching self-management skills, with a focus on positive changes in health-enhancing behaviors to improve patients' mental and physical status and to maintain those health-enhancing changes. In order for an intervention to be effective, skills, such as cognitive symptom management skills, effective communication skills, and coping skills to manage fear, anger, depression and fatigue, need to be taught (Lorig et al., 1999). Additionally, individuals with chronic diseases need to be taught the skills necessary to manage their conditions on a regular basis (e.g., to take medications as prescribed, to recognize and correctly evaluate the severity of new symptoms, to manage stress levels, etc.).

Although many intervention programs have focused on providing patients with educational sessions, numerous current self-management intervention programs, including Lorig and colleagues' programs (1999; 2001; 2003) are based on Bandura's Social Cognitive Theory (1977), and its key concept of self-efficacy. Self-efficacy is generally defined as a person's belief in his/her ability to display behaviors to successfully achieve goals. Furthermore, a person's self-efficacy beliefs influence whether he or she will initiate behavior changes and researchers have found that individuals' self-efficacy scores predict the outcome of their behavioral changes. Specifically, high self-efficacy levels are related to a greater likelihood that patients will initiate a behavior change and maintain it; lower scores have been found to be associated with a smaller chance of successful behavior change. According to

Bandura (2004) and others (Lorig and Holman, 2003), changing health behaviors requires a person to self-monitor his/her behavior, recognize the social and cognitive conditions under which he/she does self-monitor, set achievable, short term goals, and recognize motivating incentives and social supports that cause him or her to continue to practice health-enhancing behaviors. Self-efficacy scores have not only been found to be a consistent predictor of health outcomes (higher levels of self-efficacy are related to better outcomes), but are also related to better social functioning and psychological functioning (Arnold et al., 2006). Additionally, researchers have found that increased levels of self-efficacy are related to lower utilization of health care services, providing more evidence that health care costs may be impacted by intervention programs that focus on enhancing patients' level of self-efficacy (Holman and Lorig, 2004). Furthermore, researchers (Osborne, Wilson, Lorig, and McColl, 2007) found that "increased self-efficacy was a significant predictor of positive change in health status" (p.112), indicating that increasing self-efficacy is an important step in helping individuals with chronic diseases enjoy a healthier view of themselves.

Another important objective of some health intervention programs is to encourage a patient to create a partnership relationship with their health care providers in order to be active participants in deciding their health and treatment goals. This process involves having professionals propose different treatment options and then having the patient choose one of those options (Rodin, 1986). This process is suitable in that the physician is the expert regarding the various treatments that are appropriate and available for medical conditions, and the patient is empowered by being able to choose the best option. By having the physician provide both information and treatment options, the patient is able to make an informed decision regarding his or her care (Bodenheimer, Lorig, Holman, and Grumbach, 2002). This exercise of personal control by patients may increase their self-efficacy levels. Increasing self-efficacy levels can influence individuals' level of confidence in their ability to produce behaviors that lead to desired outcomes, and motivate them to continue practicing health-enhancing behaviors (Marks, Allegrante, and Lorig, 2005a). Practicing health-enhancing behaviors, in turn, may have a positive effect on performance levels (Perlmutter, Monty and Chan, 1986), lead to a reduction in harmful psychological reactions, such as a reduction in stress levels and in cortico-steroid levels, and slow down disease progression (Rodin, 1986). Cortico-steroid hormones are released in stressful situations to help the body deal with the situation; however, long-term exposure to these hormones is known to wreak havoc on all body systems, especially the immune system (Wiedenfield et al., 1990). Additionally, patients' improvement in health, and reduction in stress, would result in a reduction of health care expenditures (Kaplan, 1991).

There have been many different approaches taken to help individuals who are dealing with one specific chronic disease, and there are a few interventions that have been created for individuals with different chronic conditions. However, over 60 million Americans suffer from more than one chronic disease (Anderson and Horvath, 2004) and there is a serious need for an intervention program that is specifically tailored to their needs. This program needs to coordinate physical and psychosocial health care services for these patients. This program could prevent the unnecessary duplication of medical tests, oversee medication utilization, and could periodically re-evaluate participants' compliance with their treatment plans (Blendon et al., 2003). As Anderson and Horvath (2004) state so well:

We need information systems that allow clinicians to communicate with each other on a timely basis. Finally, and perhaps most importantly, we need to align financial incentives within health care systems and among medical, psychological, and supportive care systems. Ultimately, care coordination for people with multiple chronic conditions must become a standard of quality care, against which health plans and providers are measured. (p. 270)

It is in response to the current health care climate that the designers of the Integrated Health Advocacy Program began to envision an intervention that would significantly change the health care system, a program that would gradually empower individuals to manage their health care, and that would seriously address the fragmentation issues of the current, acute health care system. The designers of IHAP recognized the importance of Bandura's research findings regarding the positive effects of increasing a patient's level of self-efficacy, and recognized the economic situation of many individuals with chronic conditions, whose access to comprehensive health care and medications was limited by their insurance plans and their co-payments (Joyce, Kuhn, Curtin, and Murphy, 2003).

The Intergrated Health Advocacy Program

The Integrated Health Advocacy (IHAP) program is an innovative, theory-driven, multidisciplinary intervention program designed to improve the quality of life, and the health and health care of individuals with multiple, chronic conditions, while decreasing the long-term financial impact of the health care costs of these individuals (Krause et al., 2006). The initial goals were to improve the health and wellbeing of a heterogeneous group of patients with multiple, chronic conditions, to tear down the "departmental-like" walls that patients and providers experience, and to decrease the long-term health care costs associated with these individuals. These goals would be realized through an empowerment process that would invite, encourage, and support participants as they gradually learn to be accountable and responsible for their conditions, health risks, and health care.

This program is a response to a fragmented, acute care system; in this program medical and treatment information is shared among three advocacy team professionals, the participant, and with his or her various health care providers. This advocacy team of professionals includes a primary advocate (nurse, case manager), medical advocate (M.D. or O.D.), and a psychosocial advocate (psychologist, counselor or social worker) (Joyce, Kuhn, Curtin & Murphy, 2003). These advocates do not provide health care services; they work together in collaboration to: a) define problems, b) set priorities, c) establish realistic goals, d) create treatment plans that include traditional and alternative health care options, and e) address problems related to physical and psychosocial issues. The advocacy team was created with the goal to work towards consensus, ignoring the popular hierarchical realities in the health care professions (e.g., the physician being responsible for all clinical decisions) and to set up a procedure to work together with each participant to achieve his or her best possible state of physical and psychological wellbeing.

In this intervention program, the three professionals work together with the participant to determine realistic goals based on the participant's medical issues, psychological issues, his or her current support system, and a comprehensive life review process. Ordinarily, a health team of this configuration would have the medical advocate as the clinical leader of the team;

however, the IHAP advocacy team members use a collaborative process and it is through that process that consensus decisions are made that allow for a clinical depth and detail that is unique. The advocacy team members also provide support and model effective communication skills, review medications on a regular basis, encourage the participant to prepare questions for health care appointments, discuss the participant's understanding of the health care professionals' responses to questions after appointments, work with the participant to establish realistic short-term goals, and meet monthly with the participant to plan and revise treatment goals.

It is important to make sure that the participants understand that short-term goals must be realistic and are considered to be small steps toward a greater goal, that of a healthier lifestyle. Goals that are set too high may result in failure. However, when individuals achieve their goals, they increase their self-efficacy; an increase in self-efficacy also motivates the individuals to sustain health-enhancing behaviors, and to develop other goals (Bandura, 1977).

The IHAP is not a short term intervention that lasts a few weeks to several months. The IHAP program is different in that it is a long-term disease management program that may last for several years. Other differences occur in that monthly meetings are held with each participant and all of the advocates: the primary advocate, the behavioral advocate, and the medical advocate. Also, the advocacy team meets face to face with the participant as it is the most effective method to address the participants' multiple and complex needs. This face-to-face approach is in contrast to other interventions that had quarterly meetings without the patient or physician (Oppenheimer et al., 2003). Another difference is that the primary care physicians and other health care providers, as well as significant partners and formal or informal caregivers, are invited to attend these meetings with the advocacy team and the participant. Furthermore, communication is initiated by the team to all care providers regarding treatment goals, outcomes or medication changes. Finally, primary care physicians and all other health care providers also receive a copy of the comprehensive treatment plan (the transition plan summary). These differences are all important to meet the complex goal of helping these individuals reach their best possible state of health.

The IHAP program is also unique from other intervention programs because it has both an individual and a group format (Schneiderman, Antoni, Saab, and Ironson, 2001). Each participant's program goals are different and tailored to meet his/her unique physical, psychological, financial, spiritual, social, and health care needs given his/her multiple chronic conditions, and the planning process acknowledges and respects his/her unique abilities and limitations, as well as the work and care-giving responsibilities of each participant. Additionally, the participant is empowered to be responsible for his/her health and wellbeing through a gradual process of increasing his/her personal involvement in planning and prioritizing realistic short- and long-term personal health and wellbeing goals. This gradual process is to allow the participant time to increase his/her level of self-efficacy. In addition to the individual format, a group format is utilized in monthly educational sessions (which address topics such as the wise use of the health care system, medication issues, the use of complementary self-care, stress reduction techniques, etc.). These educational sessions provide participants the opportunity to obtain social support from professionals, as well as from other participants in the program. Also, given the research findings that peer educational or support sessions are not as effective as professional sessions (Lorig et al., 1999), group health education sessions are led by either team advocates or by a local professional in collaboration with a team advocate.

Each member of the advocacy team does an extensive, whole-person assessment of each participant which involves reviewing all the obtainable health care records and documents, medical as well as psychological over the individual's lifetime. The assessment process also involves reviewing all previous and current prescribed and over-the-counter medications, herbal supplements, the person's life history and lifestyle, and examining historical and current social, financial, spiritual and vocational issues. The advocacy team members perform a utilization review of all treatment records, and write comprehensive medical, psychological and social reports regarding the history of the individual (Joyce et al., 2003). The assessment process, therefore, involves examining the life pattern of issues for individuals to determine the issues that need to be resolved in order to treat the whole person.

The Primary Advocate

The participant is encouraged to develop a relationship with each of the advocacy team members, the first of which is the primary advocate. The participant is instructed to contact the primary advocate with any concerns that might interfere with his or her ability to work towards the transition plan goals (e.g., financial difficulty regarding obtaining medications, loss of resources such as phone or electricity, unexpected injury or illness, etc.). The primary advocate serves as a resource to the participant regarding the effective utilization of the health care system. The primary advocate directs and facilitates communication with all ancillary health care providers.

The Psychosocial Advocate

Unlike most intervention programs, behavioral health issues are aggressively addressed in this intervention program, and they are tailored to each individual's needs. This process is a crucial part of IHAP as participants frequently identify symptoms consistent with Axis I diagnoses (e.g., depression, stress, anxiety, trauma, addictions, etc.) (American Psychiatric Association, 1994). The psychosocial advocate works within the existing benefit plan to identify and educate psychosocial professionals who have the clinical expertise to work with this unique population. The psychosocial advocate links each participant to a clinician, oversees the utilization of services, performs clinical reviews of progress, and facilitates communication between the providers and the advocacy team.

The Medical Advocate

The medical advocate reviews and analyzes all health care records and conducts a comprehensive physical on the participant, then synthesizes all of the information into a comprehensive report with an extensive biometrics section, a review of body systems, and the identification of all major diagnoses. The medical advocate is a critical resource who provides information regarding available medical procedures and treatments. This advocate also periodically reviews all medical tests, consultation reports, and pharmacy changes to insure the wellbeing of the participant and the wise use of the health care system. Through dialogue and education (e.g., disease prevention guidelines, benefit plan promotion) this advocate serves as a valuable resource to the participants, the participants' health care providers and the advocacy team.

The Advocacy Team

The advocacy team is viewed as a repository of clinical information, but these advocates also serve as role models, or change agents, as the participants go through the program. The advocacy team models and teaches problem-solving skills, cognitive symptom management, and communication skills; these skills are also beneficial in that they increase participants' self-efficacy, which has been shown to result in "higher motivation, greater persistence, more effective performance, and ultimately greater success." (Bandura, 2004, p. 199).

During monthly meetings with each individual participant, casual conversation is exchanged and positive feedback is given to the participant for reaching transition plan goals. This process is to acknowledge the successes of the participant, and to provide encouragement. When appropriate, the advocacy team also asks questions regarding the events or situations that may have interfered with the participant's goals that were agreed upon and set in the individual's transition plan. The participants also report on their compliance with treatment goals by bringing their calendars that contain information regarding their behaviors involved in achieving their treatment goals. The other expectation of each participant is to be an active, productive, and willing participant in all components of the collaborative process, but the expected level of participation is determined by his/her functional level. Participants are also expected to have regular communication with their primary advocate and advocacy team members, and to show a genuine desire to enhance their level of functioning and wellbeing.

The processes of gradually empowering the participant through a self-monitoring process (i.e., use of a calendar), increasing his/her level of self-efficacy, and increasing perceptions of personal control is imperative in the IHAP program. Previously, researchers have found that having patients involved in the management process of their health care improves their health status and decreases health care costs (Kaplan, 1991; Kaplan and Greenfield, 1994; Barry et al, 1994, as cited in Groessl and Cronan, 2003). However, 50% of patients reported that their physicians did not consult with them regarding their treatment options (Blendon et al., 2003). In response to these research findings, the advocacy team encourages participants to become more and more active in the process of setting realistic goals, and this gradual process of empowering participants is made possible through the use of phases. Each person moves through three phases at his or her own rate. Movement is determined by the individual's ability to meet transition plan goals and the individual's level of self-efficacy, including his/her level of confidence in being able to manage his/her health conditions. Participants move through phases that are hierarchically arranged and require the participants to develop self-management and effective communication skills.

After the team completes the whole person review of all available health records, the team develops the first summary transition plan. This plan is then reviewed with the participant and when agreement is reached, Phase I begins. In this phase the goal is to increase self-efficacy through gradually addressing all the areas in the plan, which involves working towards short-term, realistic treatment goals. In phase II the participant is required to be more actively involved in the transition plan process. The participant works with the Primary Advocate to set realistic health-related goals and then presents the new transition plan to the entire advocacy team for discussion and collaborative input. In this phase the participant is expected to be more active in communicating his or her progress with the team by identifying issues that interfered with new or revised transition plan goals, by taking the initiative to self-monitor his/her behaviors, and by demonstrating self-efficacy over health issues. In phase III the participant plans his or her health goals, and then presents the transition plan to the entire advocacy team for feedback. In this phase of self-actualization, the focus for the participant is on maintaining his/her whole person well-being. The individual is asked to anticipate issues, to respond to challenges, to accept ongoing life changes, and to maintain his or her best possible level of wellbeing (Joyce et al., 2003)

At any time in any of these phases, transition plan goals may be modified with the advocacy team at meetings, either when the realistic goals are reached or when the goals are unrealistic for the individual at that point in time. Also, participants may move back into a previous phase, if they become overwhelmed by health or life issues.

The IHAP Participants

Initially, the majority of IHAP participants in this program were hospital employees or their family members. This intervention program was initiated in hospital settings as hospital employees were viewed as a group of individuals who would provide unique feedback on the program design, given their involvement with the health care system. Additionally, most hospitals are self-insured and have flexibility regarding program design in their benefit plan. At this time, however, the program has been utilized at city municipalities, manufacturing companies, small businesses, a school district, a bank and at numerous hospitals in both urban and rural settings, with the number of employees at these hospitals varying from 110 to 35,000.

The procedure used to identify participants was based on previous findings that 20% of individuals account for 80% of health care costs (Parmenter, 2003). Participants who were spending the most health care dollars were identified through claims data (Joyce et al., 2003). Specifically, individuals eligible for this program were identified though a process of examining the utilization history of health care costs. During this process, health care records were reviewed with the purpose of finding individuals who have diagnoses that are frequently consistent with multiple, chronic conditions. The individuals who were identified through this process were sent an invitation to set up a meeting with the primary advocate to obtain information about the program. As a means to encourage voluntary participation, health care benefits were amended to allow increase usage of regular, behavioral and alternative care treatments, treatments not usually covered in health care plans. According to Oppenheimer and colleagues (2003), expanding benefits is an effective way to encourage volunteer participation in intervention programs. It is important to recognize that when an intervention program is effective there is a temptation to require mandatory participation; however, this mandated approach may negatively impact the self-efficacy of the participants, and ultimately impact the outcomes.

Materials

Surveys are used to measure participants' physical and psychological well-being. Each participant completes these surveys every six months that they are participating in the program. The SF-36 Health Survey (Ware, Snow, Kosinski and Gandek, 1993) is used to measure participants' level of physical functioning, actual health, as well as perceived physical health. The Perceptions of Personal Control Questionnaire (Krause and Saarnio, 1996) is utilized to measure participants' level of health, and to measure their personal perceptions of control over numerous domains in their lives (e.g., stress, family relationships, spirituality, physical health, mental health, job, etc.). The Self-efficacy to Manage Disease (Lorig et al., 1996) measures participants' level of self-efficacy in managing their health care, in continuing activities, and in being able to decrease their use of emergency care. The Client Satisfaction Questionnaire (Attkisson and Greenfield, 1999) was modified for this study to determine the participants' level of satisfaction with their health care services in IHAP, in contrast to their services before the intervention process.

DESCRIPTIVE AND STATISTICAL RESULTS

Descriptives

The data have been examined at various times and presentations made at various conferences. At this time, over 500 participants have been through the process, 69% of these participants are females. Sixty-four percent of the participants are married, 13% divorced, and 13% single, the other 10% are either widowed, or have a significant partner after being divorced. Over 70% of the individuals are employed, 10% are disabled, 15% are unemployed (dependents of an employee). The average age of the participants is 52 years, with the most common age (the mode) of 53 years. The average years of education is 14 years, with 13% of the participants reporting between 16 and 23 years of education.

When joining the program the individuals reported in their screening forms an average 4.66 current health problems (10% reported 10 or more current health problems), the average number of current medications as 7 medications (5% reported taking 15 or more medications at the current time). These individuals also reported taking an average 1.7 over-the-counter medications (5% reported 4 or more over-the-counter medications), and an average of 2 vitamin supplements (5% reported taking 5 or more vitamins, with 1% reporting 10 or more vitamins). Fifty percent of these individuals reported having more than 7 previous health conditions (with 10% reporting 13 or more previous health conditions), and 50% reported having had 5 or more hospital stays in their lives (10% reported 12 or more hospital stays). Fifty percent had 4 or more operations (10% reported 9 or more operations).

Twenty four percent of the individuals reported that they did not exercise, not even once a week. Forty percent reported that they slept less than 7 hours a night. Furthermore 5% of the individuals reported that they had more than 8 cups of caffeinated beverages per day. On average, these individuals were employed at their current site for an average of 13 years, with 10% employed at their current site for 30 or more years.

Twenty-five percent of the participants reported that they smoked cigarettes, at least occasionally; 20% of these individuals reported smoking more than 10 cigarettes a week, 10% reported smoking more than 20 cigarettes a week, 1% smoked more than 70 cigarettes a week. One percent of this group reported that they chewed tobacco at least once a day.

Statistical Results

An analysis of participants' physical functioning from the time they entered the program to a year later (on the SF-36 and Perceptions of Personal Control) indicates that the participants perceive an improvement in their overall physical health. Additionally, level of self-efficacy was examined by means of the Self-efficacy to Manage Disease Survey, which presents a series of six questions about the participants' beliefs in being able to manage their conditions. This questionnaire uses a Likert scale of 1(*not at all confident*) to 10 (*totally confident*). Three examples of these questions are: "How confident are you that you can keep the tiredness caused by your health condition(s) from interfering with activities that you want to do?", "How confident are you that you can perform the tasks and activities necessary to control your health condition(s) in order to decrease your use of emergency care?", and "How confident are you that you can keep the emotional distress caused by your health condition(s) from interfering with activities that you want to do?" (Lorig et al., 1996). Participants significantly increased their level of self-efficacy in being able to keep their conditions from interfering with desired activities, being able to manage their conditions, and being able to avoid emergency care in each of the six areas examined from time 1 to time 3, all $ts > 3.060$, $ps < .01$.

Finally, participants rated their level of satisfaction with the IHAP intervention program using a scale of 1(*quite dissatisfied*) to 4 (*very satisfied*). The results indicate that participants rate their health care services with the IHAP program as significantly more effective in helping them deal with their conditions, and they report being more satisfied with their health care services, as compared to their previous health care services, $ts > 2.70$ $ps < .01$.

To summarize the findings, the participants report an improvement in their physical health, an increase in their level of self-efficacy in being able to manage their health issues, they report being more satisfied with their health care services, and also indicate that the IHAP services are more effective in helping them deal with their conditions, as compared to previous health care services.

CONCLUSION

The IHAP program was created in response to the current crisis in our health care system. The number of Americans with chronic conditions is over 125 million, the number of Americans with multiple, chronic conditions is over 60 million, and the number of individuals with multiple chronic conditions is expected to escalate rapidly in the future. The current health care system is not equipped to handle the millions of individuals who have numerous and complex needs. This IHAP program is a response to the issue of fragmentation in U.S. health care; it is a collaborative and comprehensive intervention that attempts to meet the whole person and health needs of individuals with multiple, chronic conditions: their physical, psychological and social needs. The goal of the program is to increase the participants' level of self-efficacy by helping them set realistic, short-term goals regarding their health and well-being, and to set up a system of collaboration with their health care providers. This gradual and empowering process provides the participants with an advocacy team, who act as mentors, who helps the participants learn to communicate effectively and self-manage their health and health care.

The IHAP program provides an effective information system for health care providers and their patients to communicate with each other in a timely fashion. Even through the participants are receiving services that were not covered previously by insurance, the program is effective in controlling health care costs, in that the advocacy team's ongoing utilization review process prevents the duplication of services and unnecessary treatments, and oversees effective medication and treatment compliance. This intervention is innovative in its uncompromising process of integrating medical, psychological, and social care into one comprehensive whole person treatment plan. This whole person approach is required because chronic conditions have negative effects on individuals' psychological and social functioning.

The designers of this program responded to an invitation to create a program that addressed the complex needs of this unique population for it was understood that these individuals were most at risk in the current health care climate. Additionally, this group of individuals has been utilizing the healthcare dollars at an increasing rate. It would be gratifying to the designers, those involved in implementing this program, and the numerous healthcare systems who committed to this whole person, integrated and collaborative process, if this intervention process became "the standard of quality of care, against which health plans and providers are measured" (Anderson and Horvath, 2004, p. 270). This process offers a serious solution to the fragmentation issue in the current American healthcare system.

REFERENCES

American Psychiatric Association. (1994). *Diagnostic and statistical manual of mental disorders* (4th ed.). Washington, DC: Author.

Anderson, G., and Horvath J. (2004). The growing burden of chronic disease in America. *Public Health Reports, 119,* 263-270.

Arnold, R., Ranchor, A., Koëter, G.H., de Jongste, M.J.L., Wempe, J.B., ten Hacken, N.H.T., Otten, V., and Sanderman, R. (2006). Changes in personal control as a predictor of quality of life after pulmonary rehabilitation. *Patient Education and Counseling, 61,* 99-108.

Attkisson, C.C., and Greenfield, T.K. (1999). The UCSF Client Satisfaction Scales: I. The Client Satisfaction Questionnaire-8. In M. Marsh (Ed). *The use of psychological testing for treatment planning and outcomes assessment* (pp 1333-1346). New Jersey: Lawrence Erlbaum Associates.

Bandura A., (1977). Self-efficacy: Toward a unifying theory of behavioral change. *Psychological Review, 84,* 191-215.

Bandura, A. (2004). Health promotion by social cognitive means. Health *Education and Behavior, 31(2),* 143-164.

Blendon, R. J., Schoen, C., DesRoaches, C., Osborn, R. and Zapert, K. (2003). Common concerns amid diverse systems: Health care experiences in five countries. *Health Affairs* *22*(3), 106-122.

Bodenheimer, T., Lorig, K., Holman, H., and Grumbach K. (2002). Patient self-management of chronic disease in primary care. *Journal of the American Medical Association,* *288(19),* 2469-2475.

Center for Disease Control and Prevention. (2005). *Chronic Disease Overview.* Retrieved January 2, 2008, from http://www.cdc.gov/nccdphp/overview.htm.

Center for Prevention and Health Services. (2005). *An employer's guide for behavioral health services: A roadmap and recommendation for evaluating, designing, and implementing behavioral health services.* Washington, DC: National Business Group on Health.

Clark, N.M., Janz, N.K., Becker, M.H., Schork, M.A., Wheeler, J., Liang, J., Dodge, J.A., Keteyian, S., Rhoads, K. L., and Santinga, J. T. (1992). Impact of self-management education on the functional health status of older adults with heart disease. *The Gerontologist, 32(4),* 438-443.

Fitzsimmons, S., and Buettner, L.L. (2003). Health promotion for the mind, body, and spirit: A college course for older adults with dementia. *American Journal of Alzheimer's Disease and Other Dementias, 18(5),* 282-290.

Groessl, E.J. and Cronan, T.A. (2003). A cost analysis of self-management programs for people with chronic illness. *American Journal of Community Psychology 28*(4), 455-480.

Holicky, R. (2008). Rehab today: Better or worse? *New Mobility, 19*(174), 19-23.

Holman, H., and Lorig, K. (2004). Patient self-management: A key to effectiveness and efficiency in care of chronic disease. *Public Health Reports, 119,* 239-243.

Joyce, S.T., Kuhn, M.E.J., Curtin, K., and Murphy, L. (2003). *Integrated advocacy health handbook.* Unpublished manuscript.

Kaplan, R.M. (1991). Health-related quality of life in patient decision making. *Journal of Social Issues, 47*(4), 69-90.

Krause, C.M., and Kuhn, M.E.J. (2007). Help for the caring: The stress, the value, and the perception of informal caregivers. *Annals of the American Psychotherapy Association,* *10,* 32-37.

Krause, C.M., Jones, C.S., Joyce, S., Kuhn, M.E.J., Curtin, K., Murphy, L.P., Krause, C.M.J., Boan, B., and Lucas, D.R. (2006). The impact of a multidisciplinary, integrated approach on improving the health and quality of care for individuals dealing with multiple chronic conditions. *American Journal of Orthopsychiatry, 76*(1), 109-114.

Krause, C.M., and Saarnio, D. (1996). *Personal perceptions of control.* Washington, D.C.: Library of Congress.

Lev, E.L. (2000). Counseling women with breast cancer using principles developed by Albert Bandura. *Perspectives in Psychiatric Care, 36*(4), 131-139.

Lorig, K., and Holman, H. (2003). Self-management education: history, definition, outcomes, and mechanisms. *Annals of Behavioral Medicine, 26(1),* 1-7.

Lorig, K., Ritter, P., and Jacquez, A. (2005). Outcomes of border health Spanish/English chronic disease self-management programs. *The Diabetes Educator, 31*(3), 401-409.

Lorig, K.R., Ritter, P., Stewart, A.L., Sobel, D.S., Brown, B.W., Bandura, A., Gonzales, V.M., Laurent, D.D., and Holman, H.R. (2001). Chronic disease self-management program: 2-year health status and health care utilization outcomes. *Medical Care, 39(11),* 1217-1223.

Lorig, K.R., Sobel, D.S., Stewart, A.L., Brown, B.W., Bandura, A., Ritter, P., Gonzales, V. M., Laurent, D.D., and Holman, H.R. (1999). Evidence suggesting that a chronic disease self-management program can improve health status while reducing hospitalization: A randomized trial. *Medical Care, 37*(1), 5-14.

Lorig, K., Stewart, A., Ritter, P., Gonzalez, V., Laurant, D. and Lynch, J. (1996). *Outcome measures for health education and other health care interventions.* Thousand Oaks, CA: Sage.

Marks, R., Allegrante, J.P., and Lorig, K. (2005a). A review and synthesis of research evidence for self-efficacy-enhancing interventions for reducing chronic disability: Implications for health education practice (Part I). *Health Promotion Practice, 6*(1), 37-43.

Marks, R., Allegrante, J.P., and Lorig, K. (2005b). A review and synthesis of research evidence for self-efficacy-enhancing interventions for reducing chronic disability: Implications for health education practice (Part II). *Health Promotion Practice, 6*(2), 148-156.

Newman, S., Steed, L., and Mulligan, K. (2004). Self-management interventions for chronic illness. *The Lancet, 364*(9444), 1523-1537.

Oppenheimer, C.C., Shapiro, J.R., Beronja, N., Dykstra, D.M., Gaylin, D.S., Held, P.J., and Rubin, R.J. (2003). Evaluation of the ESRD managed care demonstration operations. *Health Care Financing Review, 24*(4) 7-29.

Osborne, H., Wilson, T., Lorig, K.R., and McColl, G.J. (2007). Does self-management lead to sustainable health benefits in people with arthritis? A 2-year transition study of 452 Australians. *The Journal of Rheumatology, 34*(5), 1112-1117.

Ostbye, T., Yarnall, K.S.H., Krause, K.M., Pollak, K.I., Gradison, M., and Michener, J.L. (2005). Is there time for management of patients with chronic diseases in primary care? *Annuals of Family Medicine, 3*(3), 209-214.

Parmenter E.M. (2003, July). Controlling health care cost: Components of a new paradigm. *Journal of Financial Service Professionals*, 59-68.

Perlmutter, L.C., Monty, R.A., and Chan, F. (1986). Choice, control and cognitive functioning. In M.W. Baltes and P.B. Baltes (Eds.), *The psychology of control and aging* (pp.91-118). Hinsdale, NJ: Lawrence Erlbaum Associates.

Rodin, J. (1986). Aging and health: Effects of the sense of control. *Science, 233*(4770), 1271-1276.

Schneiderman, N., Antoni, M.H., Saab, P.G., and Ironson, G. (2001). Health psychology: Psychosocial and biobehavioral aspects of chronic disease management. *Annual Review of Psychology, 52*, 555-580.

Ware, J.E., Snow, K.K., Kosinski, M., and Gandek, B. (1993). *SF-36 health study: Manual and interpretation guide.* Boston: Health Institute, New England Medical Center.

Wiedenfield, S.A., O'Leary, A., Bandura, A., Brown, S., Levine, S., and Raska, K. (1990). Impact of perceived self-efficacy in coping with stressors on components of the immune system. *Journal of Personality and Social Psychology, 59*(5), 1082-1094.

In: Integrated Health Care Delivers
Editor: Leonie A. Klein and Emily L. Neumann

ISBN 978-1-60456-851-6
© 2008 Nova Science Publishers, Inc.

Chapter 2

A COMPARISON OF INTEGRATED DUAL DIAGNOSIS TREATMENT SERVICE DELIVERY MODELS ON FIDELITY AND CLIENT OUTCOMES AT 1- AND 2-YEAR FOLLOW-UPS

Laurel F. Mangrum[*1], *Richard T. Spence*[1] *and Molly Lopez*[2]
[1]Addiction Research Institute, University of Texas, Galveston, Texas, USA
[2]Texas Department of State Health Services, Texas, USA

ABSTRACT

The measurement of treatment fidelity is an important, yet often omitted component in examining the efficacy of various treatment models. Although the measurement of fidelity is often complex, the potential benefits of including fidelity measures in studies of treatment models are numerous. Fidelity measures are useful in evaluation studies as a means of documenting appropriate implementation and adherence to the model under study, as well as confirming treatment differentiation in research designs that include control groups. Further, fidelity measures provide a potential method for determining critical ingredients in treatment models that are most strongly associated with client outcomes. Despite these important benefits, studies of the relation between fidelity and client outcomes are limited. The current study in this chapter compares two integrated dual diagnosis service delivery models on fidelity and 1- and 2-year psychiatric hospitalization and arrest outcomes of clients with severe mental illness and substance use disorders. Two modes of implementation, the integrated treatment (n=3) and adjunct service (n=3) models, were identified through qualitative process evaluation of six pilot sites participating in an integrated dual diagnosis treatment demonstration project. The integrated treatment and adjunct service models were contrasted on the Texas Integrated Treatment Integrity Scale (TITIS) to explore potential differences in implementation of specific components of integrated dual diagnosis treatment. Psychiatric hospitalization and arrest outcomes of 256 clients were compared between the implementation models at 1 and 2 years post treatment entry. On the TITIS subscales, the integrated treatment model achieved higher fidelity scores on the Staffing and Treatment Team Structure scale

* E-mail: lmangrum@mail.utexas.edu

but no differences were found on the Treatment Program Structure and Services, Integrated Treatment Documentation, or Overall Fidelity scales. Although the comparison of hospitalization days 24 months pre- and post-baseline indicated greater reduction in hospitalization for the integrated treatment group, two other models analyzing 12 months pre- and post-baseline and contrasting 12-month baseline, year 1, and year 2 hospitalization days and arrests did not reveal significant differences between the service delivery models. The overall results of this study indicated that the two service delivery models achieved comparable fidelity ratings and outcomes at 1 and 2 years post treatment entry. These findings suggest that mode of service delivery may be a less essential component of the integrated dual diagnosis treatment model relative to other elements of the framework, such as program structure, service array, and documentation. Future studies of this nature are needed to assist in isolating critical components of integrated treatment to inform technology transfer of this evidence-based practice into community settings.

INTRODUCTION

Individuals with severe mental illness and substance use disorders present multifaceted treatment needs that are often difficult to address in single service settings providing either substance abuse or mental heath treatment. Recognition of the complexity inherent in treating clients with co-occurring disorders led to the development of integrated dual diagnosis treatment programs, which are designed to provide coordinated psychiatric and substance abuse interventions and intensive case management to address individualized adjunct service needs. The evolution of integrated treatment and the demonstration of enhanced outcomes for co-occurring disorder clients receiving integrated dual diagnosis treatment are documented in literature reviews (Drake, Mercer-McFadden, Mueser, McHugo, and Bond, 1998; Mueser, Noordsy, Drake, and Fox, 2003) and more recent studies assessing integrated treatment effectiveness (Gonzales and Rosenneck, 2002;Judd, Thomas, Schwartz, Outcalt, and Hough, 2003; Mangrum, Spence, and Lopez, 2006; McCoy, et al. 2003). Few studies, however, have examined fidelity to the integrated dual diagnosis treatment model as a potential factor affecting client outcomes.

The measurement of treatment fidelity is an important, yet often omitted component in examining the efficacy of various treatment models. Although the measurement of fidelity is often complex, the potential benefits of including fidelity measures in studies of treatment models are numerous (Bond, Evans, Salyers, Williams, and Kim, 2000). Fidelity measures are useful in evaluation studies as a means of documenting appropriate implementation and adherence to the model under study, as well as confirming treatment differentiation in research designs that include control groups. The use of standardized fidelity measures may also enhance communication in the field by providing common terminology, model definition, and facilitation of meta-analytic reviews of a body of literature. Further, fidelity measures provide a potential method for determining critical ingredients in treatment models that are most strongly associated with client outcomes. More expanded research is needed to determine the effects of departures from fidelity; as evidence-based practices are diffused in real-life clinical settings, treatment models are often adapted according to local resource constraints and other community and system characteristics. Measurement of the potential effects of these adaptations can inform technology transfer practices by identifying crucial aspects of treatment models associated with client outcomes that are less amenable to change.

Although research is limited, several studies have examined the relation between model fidelity and outcomes in the areas of supported employment and assertive community treatment for clients with severe mental illness. Drake, McHugo, Becker, Anthony, and Clark (1996) conducted a study that contrasted two models of supported employment for clients with severe mental illness, group skills training and individual placement and support programs. The group skills training program constituted a brokered service model in which vocational and mental health services were provided in separate agencies and emphasized pre-employment training. By contrast, the individual placement and support program encompassed an integrated service model in which vocational and mental health services were combined within the same program and did not include pre-employment training. The study sites were located in two New Hampshire cities, a large city and a small city, and each of the two program types was represented in each city. Clients were randomly assigned to the two programs, resulting in group sizes of 69 in the group skills training model and 74 in the individual placement and support model. Overall results at 18-month follow-up indicated the clients who received individual placement and support program services had better outcomes in competitive employment than those participating in the group skills training program. The study also included a process component to examine program fidelity to the models. Results of these process studies indicated that the individual placement and support program was poorly implemented in the smaller city site. Given these differences in implementation, analyses by site were conducted and revealed that competitive employment outcomes were stronger for individual placement services in the larger city relative to group skills training but the outcome difference between the two program types was not significant in the smaller city. These findings suggest that the quality of implementation of the model may have affected client outcomes and that the outcome difference in the larger city, which had enhanced implementation of the individual placement and support model, appeared to be carrying the overall effect in the study.

A second study examined client employment outcomes from a multi-site, randomized clinical trial of intensive psychiatric community care, the Veteran's Administration's model of assertive case management (Resnick, Neale, and Rosenheck, 2003). Clients were randomly assigned to the intensive psychiatric community care model ($n = 271$) or to standard care ($n = 257$). The intensive psychiatric community care program was designed to provide four core elements: 1) intensity, with frequent client contact and low staff to client ratio; 2) provision of services in the community; 3) focus on psychosocial rehabilitation; and 4) continuity of care. The standard care condition consisted of inpatient psychiatric treatment, pharmacotherapy, outpatient psychiatric treatment, and traditional Veteran's Administration rehabilitation services, such as work therapy. Further, the quality of implementation of the intensive psychiatric community care model was measured using an assertive community treatment fidelity scale. Results of this fidelity measurement indicated that five sites demonstrated adequate fidelity and two sites had less than adequate fidelity. Employment results at 1-year follow-up indicated that, after controlling for prior work history and level of public support payments, clients who received intensive psychiatric community care had enhanced employment outcomes relative to the standard care model. In addition, those clients receiving intensive psychiatric community care in well-implemented programs were more likely to be employed than those who had received services in poorly implemented programs.

Studies of the development of assertive community treatment fidelity measures and the effects of implementation quality on client outcomes are more numerous. In an initial study, McGrew, Bond, Deitzen, and Sayers (1994) developed and piloted a fidelity measure of assertive community treatment that assessed critical ingredients of the program in three domains, consisting of program staffing, organization, and services. The fidelity measure was then used to assess 18 assertive community treatment programs for validity analyses. Among these programs, four groups were defined to provide a generational variable to assess potential departures from the original model as the programs were disseminated over time and distance from the original model program. Comparisons of fidelity scale scores across these generations of programs revealed a significant linear decline in scores through the generations, indicating program drift from the original model over time. Fidelity scores were also positively correlated with reduction in days hospitalized, suggesting that departures from fidelity were associated with decreased program effectiveness. Analyses of fidelity scale domain scores revealed that the staffing, organizational, and total scores were correlated with reduction in hospitalization but the services score was not significantly associated with hospitalization outcomes.

Teague, Drake, and Ackerson (1995) created a 13-item fidelity scale to measure an assertive community treatment program model that was adapted to serve clients with severe mental illness and substance use disorders. The fidelity measure was then used to assess the degree of program implementation across seven sites in a demonstration study. In each of these sites, clients with co-occurring disorders were randomly assigned to either continuous treatment teams (the adapted assertive community treatment model) or standard case management programs. Overall assessment of fidelity indicated that the continuous treatment team programs scored significantly higher on the fidelity measure than the standard case management programs. In addition, the fidelity scores of the continuous treatment teams programs revealed substantial variation across sites, with one team scoring below adequate levels of implementation. At this site, the continuous treatment team and standard case management team had nearly identical scores on the fidelity measure, whereas in the remaining six sites the fidelity scores between treatment conditions were significantly different. These results allowed for the identification of a site with poor implementation and lack of critical differentiation between treatment conditions, which provides a potential confound in analyses comparing the overall effectiveness of the two service delivery models.

Building on these earlier studies of the development of assertive community treatment fidelity scales, Teague, Bond, and Drake (1998) refined existing measures and created the Dartmouth Assertive Community Treatment Scale (DACTS). In their psychometric studies, the DACTS was used to evaluate 50 programs in four categories: 1) assertive community treatment research site programs ($n = 14$); 2) VA intensive psychiatric community care programs ($n = 10$); 3) Access to Community Care and Effective Services and Supports (ACCESS) demonstration programs ($n = 15$); and 4) standard case management models as control sites ($n = 11$). The ACCESS and VA intensive psychiatric community care programs are designed to have elements of assertive community treatment but are not intended to fully implement all aspects of the model. Comparisons of fidelity scores among these program types revealed that the assertive community treatment research sites had the highest overall fidelity scores relative to all other programs and the standard case management models achieved the lowest scores. The ACCESS and VA intensive psychiatric community care programs fidelity scores were in the intermediate range and were not significantly different from each other. These findings lend support to the use of the DACTS to differentiate degree of implementation among various programs types. For example, the DACTS was later used by Johnsen, et al. (1999) to assess programs participating in the ACCESS project, a 15-year, 18 site demonstration project designed to enrich services for homeless individuals with severe mental illness. ACCESS programs were encouraged, but not required, to implement the assertive community treatment program in this project. Participating sites self-identified their programs as implementing four different models, including assertive community treatment, modified assertive community treatment, continuous treatment team, and the Strengths Model. DACTS scores were compared across these program types and the assertive community treatment programs group achieved the highest fidelity scores. Comparisons along the DACTS scales also allowed for quantification of similarities and differences in structural program characteristics among the sites to inform the process evaluation.

Two studies have specifically examined the relation between assertive community treatment program fidelity and client outcomes. In the first study, McHugo, Drake, Teague, and Xie (1999) examined fidelity to an assertive community treatment model adapted for clients with co-occurring disorders using the 13-item fidelity measure previously described in this chapter (Teague, Drake, and Ackerson, 1995). The fidelity measure includes 9 items assessing essential components of assertive community treatment and 4 items evaluating dual diagnosis treatment elements. Based on fidelity scores, 4 programs were placed in the high fidelity group and three in the low fidelity group. At 3-year follow-up of 83 clients, clients in high fidelity programs reported significantly fewer days of substance use, were more likely to be in remission, had higher levels of treatment engagement, and had a lower number of hospital admissions during the three years of the study; however, no difference was found in mean number of days spent in the hospital. Further, no differences were found in the domains of psychiatric symptoms, functional status, or client-reported quality of life, which were considered secondary outcomes that are not specifically targeted by assertive community treatment. By contrast, the second study produced differing results regarding the relation between fidelity and client outcomes. Bond and Salyers (2004) examined the correlation between DACT fidelity scores and psychiatric hospitalization outcomes at 1-year follow-up for 317 clients receiving assertive community treatment services. The DACTS scores for 10 assertive community treatment programs indicated that the sites varied in implementation from marginal to high fidelity to the model. Analyses revealed that the correlation between the programs' fidelity scores and reduction in state hospital days for clients was moderately large ($r = .49$) but did not achieve statistical significance.

In summary, the extant literature regarding supported employment and assertive community treatment fidelity highlight the importance of measuring the quality of program implementation, particularly in studies examining the effectiveness of program models. Measurement of fidelity ensures that essential elements of the program under study have been adequately implemented and that sufficient treatment differentiation exists in comparison or control programs when contrasting client outcomes. Although studies are limited, initial research also suggests that fidelity may be associated with enhanced client outcomes and that certain elements of program models may be more strongly linked to outcomes, rendering these features less amenable to local adaptation during implementation.

The current study compares two integrated dual diagnosis treatment service delivery models on fidelity measures and 1- and 2-year outcomes of 256 clients with severe mental illness and substance use disorders. Treatment programs were participating in the Texas Dual

Diagnosis Pilot Project, which was designed to develop integrated treatment programs through coalitions of state-funded substance abuse and mental health treatment providers. Each program was trained on the essential elements of the integrated dual diagnosis treatment model and subsequently designed and implemented a treatment program unique to their local characteristics. It was hypothesized that programs with service delivery models that more closely match the integrated dual diagnosis treatment model would have enhanced outcomes in reduced psychiatric hospitalization days and number of arrests.

METHOD

The Texas Dual Diagnosis Pilot Project consisted of a joint effort by the state-funded mental health and substance abuse treatment agencies to provide integrated dual diagnosis treatment for individuals with co-occurring disorders. To gain entry into the dual diagnosis program, clients were required to: 1) meet criteria for a DSM-IV substance abuse or substance dependence diagnosis; 2) have documented use of a substance or substances during the six months prior to program entry; and 3) meet criteria for inclusion in the state of Texas adult mental health priority population (i.e., be diagnosed with a severe and persistent mental illness, such as schizophrenia, major depression, or bipolar disorder, or other mental disorder resulting in severe and chronic impairment).

The 6 pilot sites included in the current analyses were located in West, Central, and East Texas. A subset of these sites participated in an experimental design comparing integrated dual diagnosis treatment to traditional parallel services and the findings of this study are reported elsewhere (Mangrum, Spence, and Lopez, 2006). In each of these sites, a regional state-funded substance abuse treatment and mental health service provider formed a coalition to develop an integrated treatment program based on the nine core principles of integrated dual diagnosis treatment (Drake, Bartels, Teague, Noordsy, and Clark, 1993). Each program was trained on the essential elements of the integrated dual diagnosis treatment model and directed to design and implement a dual diagnosis treatment program unique to their local characteristics. The core principles of integrated treatment are:

1) Assertiveness to encourage client engagement in treatment, including providing in-vivo services and concrete assistance in a variety of life domains, such as medication management, housing assistance, skills training, facilitation of Medicaid or SSI benefits applications, and working with members of the client's support system, including family members, landlords, and employers;

2) Close monitoring to encourage treatment compliance, including frequent contact with clinicians, supervised living situations, drug testing, payeeships, court commitment, or establishing treatment as a condition of probation or parole;

3) Integration of mental health and substance abuse interventions in a simultaneous and coordinated manner;

4) Comprehensive treatment addressing a broad range of skills, activities, relationships, and supports beyond the immediate manifestations of the dual diagnosis disorder, such as living situation, family and peer support relationships, vocational skills, interpersonal skills;

5) Stabilization of the client's living situation to ensure housing that provides safety, freedom from alcohol and drugs, positive social support, and companionship;

6) Flexibility and specialization among clinicians in acquiring new beliefs, skills, and therapeutic approaches appropriate for treatment of clients with dual disorders;

7) Treatment tailored to the client's stage-wise level of treatment engagement, including engagement, persuasion, active treatment, and relapse prevention;

8) A longitudinal perspective with treatment provided continuously over years rather than episodically or during crises; and

9) Maintenance of optimism regarding treatment outcomes and recognition that client engagement and motivation is likely to increase as treatment progresses.

Fidelity was assessed through two process evaluation site visits conducted in 1998 during the second year of the project, using semi-structured interviews assessing the essential elements of integrated dual diagnosis treatment. The site visits consisted of evaluators spending a half day with the mental health partner and another half-day with the substance abuse partner, during which treatment staff, case managers, and intake personnel were interviewed. The interviews focused on the following central themes: client recruitment, screening, and intake; dual diagnosis treatment services; interagency relationships; support services; crisis protocols; family interventions; training; community resources; and policy issues.

The qualitative process evaluation data identified two general modes of implementation across programs, the integrated treatment model ($n = 3$; see Figure 1) and the adjunct service model ($n = 3$; see Figure 2). Programs in the integrated treatment category were characterized by complete integration of substance abuse and mental health systems, with the mental health and substance abuse experts co-located in the same clinic. Further, the dual diagnosis team was the primary decision-making unit and responsible for coordinating and delivering services. In the adjunct services model, a case manager coordinated a team of specialized service providers and the dual diagnosis team was a separate additional component in the client's service array. Case managers had the opportunity to consult dual diagnosis counselors about other elements of the clients' services at their discretion but functioned as the primary service coordinator. Although 7 sites participated in the pilot project, one site was unable to be classified in either of these two models and was excluded from the current study. Further, anomalies in client outcome data at the excluded site precluded comparative analyses as a third model type.

In addition to the qualitative process evaluation interviews, the Texas Integrated Treatment Integrity Scale (TITIS) was completed for each site using multiple data sources, including interview data, site self-report instruments, client chart review, and service records. The TITIS is a 30-item measure based on the Dartmouth Assertive Community Treatment Scale (DACTS) (Teague, Bond, and Drake, 1998), adapted to capture service system features in Texas. Each TITIS item is scored on a 5-point scale, with higher scores indicating greater fidelity. The TITIS items were conceptually grouped into three scales reflecting Staffing and Treatment Team Structure (13 items), Treatment Program Structure and Services (12 items), and Integrated Treatment Documentation (5 items), similar to the a priori scale groupings on the DACTS. TITIS scale and total scores reflect item averages. Although the DACTS has

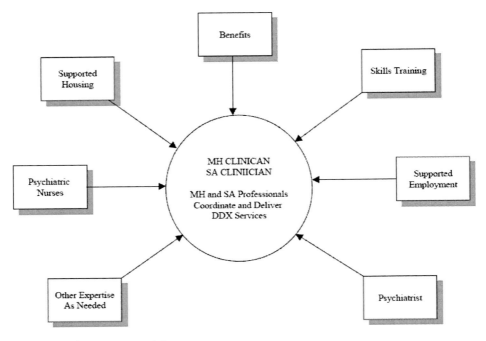

Figure 1. Integrated treatment model.

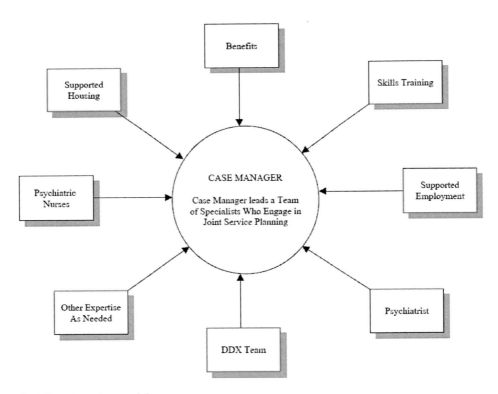

Figure 2. Adjunct service model.

established psychometric properties, the adapted TITIS was developed specifically for this pilot project and has not been tested for reliability or validity.

The client sample consisted of 256 clients receiving integrated dual diagnosis treatment in the integrated treatment ($n = 120$) or adjunct service ($n = 136$) model. These clients were consecutive admissions into the pilot programs during 1997 and 1998, the first two years of the project. Baseline demographic and diagnostic data were collected by the sites at program entry. Outcome data for psychiatric hospitalization and arrest were obtained from state-level data systems for all clients through interagency agreements. Measures of 1- and 2-year follow-ups of psychiatric severity, treatment engagement, and employment were available for a subset of clients; however, the follow-up rates on these measures were too low to be considered representative, precluding the use of these variables in outcome analyses. Data on these measures are missing due to inconsistent use of measures in the treatment programs at the start up of the project, changes in domain measures over the course of the project, or inability to contact clients at the follow-up periods. After a complete description of the study procedures, clients signed written informed consent agreeing to participate in the evaluation of the pilot project services. The original evaluation study was approved by the Texas A and M University Institutional Review Board. Subsequent data analyses and reporting were approved by the Texas Department of State Health Services and the University of Texas Institutional Review Boards.

TITIS ratings of the integrated treatment and adjunct service models were compared using Wilcoxon rank sums tests to explore potential differences in fidelity scores. One- and two-year outcome analyses were conducted contrasting clients who received integrated treatment versus adjunct services on psychiatric hospitalization days and arrests. Baseline comparisons indicated that the integrated treatment group was older, had a higher proportion of schizophrenia-spectrum diagnoses, and had greater levels of psychiatric hospitalization in the year prior to admission (see Table 1). Due to these initial group differences, a propensity analysis (Rosenbaum and Rubin, 1983) using logistic regression was conducted to determine if age, schizophrenia diagnosis, and hospitalization days predicted group membership. Results revealed that the three variables significantly predicted integrated treatment or adjunct services group membership ($X^2(3, N = 256) = 47.57$, $p < .0001$); consequently, propensity score weighting was used to control for group non-equivalency in the outcome analyses. Propensity scores are used in quasi-experimental designs to control for pre-existing conditions between comparison groups. A propensity score is the conditional probability of a client's treatment group membership given observed baseline characteristics; for the current analyses, the propensity score was calculated for each client using the age, schizophrenia diagnosis, and hospitalization days variables. Propensity scores are then used as a variable in the prediction model to adjust for pre-existing group differences, similar to covariate or case-mix adjustment in regression. General linear modeling with generalized estimating equations for repeated measures and Poisson distribution was conducted to compare psychiatric hospitalization days and number of arrests during the 1- and 2-year periods pre- and post-baseline. These same analyses were also conducted for a third statistical model comparing hospitalization and arrests during the year prior to baseline with those occurring between baseline and year 1 and between year 1 and year 2.

Table 1. Baseline Client Characteristics of Treatment Model Groups

	Integrated Treatment (n =120)	Adjunct Service (n =136)	df	X^2/ t-value	P
Male	60%	51%			
Mean Age	39.0 ±10.7	35.2 ± 9.4	254	-2.96	.004
Race/Ethnicity					
Black	15%	14%			
Hispanic	19%	11%			
White	63%	74%			
Other	3%	1%			
Principal Diagnosis					
Schizophrenia Spectrum	43%	13%			
Major Depression	23%	34%			
Bipolar disorder	16%	19%			
Substance Use Disorder	5%	10%			
Other	13%	24%	4	30.44	.001
Mean Hospitalization Days					
12 months Pre-Baseline	10.1 ± 31.5	1.2 ± 5.9	126	-3.04	.003
Mean Number of Arrests					
12 months Pre-Baseline	.13 ± .44	.13 ± .43			

RESULTS

Comparisons on the TITIS fidelity measure indicated a significant difference between the integrated treatment and adjunct services models on the Staffing and Treatment Team Structure scale score but no differences were found on the Treatment Program Structure and Services, Integrated Treatment Documentation, or Overall Fidelity scores (see Table 2). Group contrasts on individual TITIS items revealed that the adjunct services programs scored higher on one item measuring Integrated Progress Notes. The Integrated Progress Notes item measures whether progress notes consistently address both the psychiatric and substance use disorder and the interplay between the two disorders.

Table 2. Mean Fidelity Ratings for Integrated Treatment and Adjunct Service Models

TITUS Scale Items	Integrated Treatment (n = 3)		Adjunct Service (n = 3)	
	M	SD	M	SD
Staffing and Treatment Team Structure				
Caseload Size	4.5	0.7	4.0	1.0
DDX Provider Meeting	4.0	1.0	4.3	0.6
Team Approach	5.0	0.0	2.3	2.3
Attendance at Staffing	4.7	0.6	3.7	2.3
Continuity of Staffing	4.3	1.2	2.0	1.0
Staff Capacity	4.5	0.0	4.0	1.7
Intake Rate	5.0	0.0	5.0	0.0
Substance Abuse Specialist on Staff	5.0	0.0	3.7	2.3
Mental Health Specialist on Staff	5.0	0.0	5.0	0.0
Psychiatrist on Staff	2.0	1.0	3.3	2.1
Dual Diagnosis Training	3.3	1.7	2.0	1.0
Open Communication	4.0	1.7	3.3	2.1
Centralized Treatment	3.7	0.6	3.0	1.7
All Scale Items*	4.2	0.1	3.5	0.7
Treatment Program Structure and Services				
Intensity of Service	2.3	0.6	4.0	0.0
Frequency of Contact	1.3	0.6	1.5	0.7
Dual Disorders Groups	2.7	1.2	4.3	1.2
Adapted Substance Abuse Treatment	3.0	1.0	3.3	0.6
In-Vivo Services	2.3	0.6	1.7	1.2
Work with Support System	2.7	0.6	1.7	0.6
Assertive Outreach	1.3	0.6	3.0	1.4
Assertive Engagement Mechanism	1.0	0.0	1.7	1.2
Housing Services	1.0	0.0	1.0	0.0
Employment Services	1.3	0.6	1.0	0.0
Tailored Intensity	2.7	0.6	2.3	0.6
Assertive Retention	2.7	1.5	1.7	0.6
All Scale Items	2.0	0.5	2.2	0.2
Integrated Treatment Documentation				
Admission Criteria	4.0	1.0	4.0	1.0
Integrated Treatment Plans	4.5	0.7	5.0	0.0
Integrated Progress Notes**	4.0	0.0	5.0	0.0
Involvement in Discharge Planning	2.7	2.1	3.3	2.1
Stage of Treatment	3.3	2.1	4.0	0.0
All Scale Items	3.4	1.3	4.3	0.3
Overall Fidelity Score (All TITUS Items)	3.2	0.6	3.3	0.2

Notes: TITIS = Texas Interated Treatment Intergrity Scale.
$X^2(1) = 3.86, p < .05$; **$X^2(1) = 4.00, p < .05$.

Table 3. Generalized Estimating Equation Results for Client Outcomes by Time, Treatment Model Propensity Score, and Interaction Effects

Outcome	Time			Treatment Model			Propensity Score			Treatment Model by Time		
	Parameter	Z	p	Parameter	Z	p	Parameter	Z	p	Parameter	Z	p
12 Month Pre-Post Outcomes												
Hosptial Days	0.287	0.82		0.428	0.66		4.952	4.32	.001	-1.415	-1.63	
Arrests	0.511	1.35		0.253	0.48		-2.902	-2.98	.01	-0.622	-1.02	
24 Month Pre-Post Outcomes												
Hospital Days	0.583	2.08	0.04	-0.082	-0.13		3.374	3.28	.001	1.874	-2.68	.01
Arrests	0.606	1.73		0.144	0.31		-1.680	-2.09	.04	-0.018	-0.03	
Baseline, Year 1, Year 2 Outcomes												
Hospital Days: Year 1	0.769	1.66		-0.031	-0.03		4.256	4.26	.001	-1.324	-1.12	
Year2	0.488	0.97								0.282	0.24	
Arrests: Year1	1.069	1.43		-1.564	-1.83		-2.596	-2.8	.004	1.223	0.99	
Year2	1.098	1.60								1.845	1.45	

Client outcome analyses for the two models comparing hospital days and arrests in the 12 and 24 month periods pre- and post-baseline are reported in Table 3. Results for the 1-year outcomes indicate that, after controlling for group non-equivalency at baseline, treatment model and time effects were not significant for either hospitalization or arrest. At 2-years, however, the propensity score, time, and the treatment model by time interaction effect were significant for hospital days.

Exploration of the interaction effect revealed that the mean days of hospitalization decreased in the integrated treatment group from 21.5 to 12.0, whereas the mean increased in the adjunct services group from 1.5 to 5.4. Two-year outcomes in reduction of arrests were not significantly different between the two models.

A third analysis compared hospitalization days and arrests in the year prior to baseline with those that occurred during the first and second year periods to provide an alternative means of examining longitudinal trends post treatment entry. When all three time periods were entered into the model, results indicated that, after controlling for group non-equivalency at baseline, treatment model and time effects were not significant for either hospitalization days or arrest.

DISCUSSION

The current study compares two integrated treatment service delivery models on fidelity and client outcomes in the areas of psychiatric hospitalization and arrests. The two models, integrated treatment and adjunct services, were identified through qualitative process evaluation measures indicating differences in methods of service delivery, with one model adhering more closely to the traditional integrated dual diagnosis treatment structure and the other being similar to a case management structure. Contrasts on the TITIS fidelity scores revealed that the adjunct services programs scored significantly lower on the Staffing and Treatment Team Structure scale but did not differ on the Treatment Program Structure and Services, Integrated Treatment Documentation, or Overall Fidelity scores. This finding indicates that the TITIS fidelity measure was sensitive to the structural differences identified through qualitative process evaluation methods. Further, the TITIS results indicate that, although the method of service delivery may have differed, both model types implemented comparable levels of the other essential elements of integrated dual diagnosis treatment.

Comparisons on baseline client characteristics revealed that the integrated treatment group had a greater percentage of schizophrenia spectrum diagnoses and a higher number of psychiatric hospital days in the year prior to treatment entry, suggesting that clients in the integrated treatment group displayed greater psychiatric severity at baseline relative to the adjunct services group. When controlling for these pre-existing group differences, the preponderance of evidence from the current analyses suggests that the type of service delivery model used in this sample had minimal impact on client outcomes. Although the comparison of hospitalization days 24 months pre- and post-baseline did indicate greater reduction in hospitalization for the integrated treatment group, the other two models analyzing 12 months pre- and post-baseline and contrasting 12-month baseline, year 1, and year 2 hospitalization days and arrests did not reveal significant differences between the service delivery models. These results suggest that when outcomes are considered with a baseline that is more proximal to treatment entry, the service delivery models achieved comparable outcomes. Thus, the majority of the results did not support this study's hypothesis that programs with service delivery models more closely matching traditional integrated dual diagnosis treatment would have enhanced client outcomes.

The current results indicating comparable outcomes between different modes of service provision are in line with the findings of a recent study comparing the delivery of integrated services in assertive community treatment versus standard clinical case management models for clients with co-occurring disorders (Essock, et al., 2006). In one of their two study sites, clients displayed more rapid improvement on substance use variables in the assertive community treatment model during the early stages of treatment; however, clients made steady improvement in the standard case management model and outcomes were equivalent between the two models by 3-year follow-up. The current findings also found that a case management model achieved comparable levels of treatment fidelity and produced similar outcomes when compared to a more traditional integrated dual diagnosis service delivery model.

The present study contributes to the growing area of research assessing the effects of service delivery models and fidelity on client outcomes. Strengths of this study include the use of both qualitative and quantitative measures of integrated dual diagnosis treatment fidelity and the availability of both 1 and 2 year hospitalization and arrest data for all clients. The TITIS, however, was created specifically for this project and has not been tested for reliability or validity. In this study, the TITIS scores did reflect the differences in mode of service delivery identified through qualitative measures, lending some support to the validity of the measure. In addition, the study is naturalistic in nature and lacks randomized assignment to treatment models. Also, the study's outcome measures are limited and do not include measures of substance use, which is an essential area of evaluation of integrated treatment. Further, the program sample size in each model was small, limiting both the power of the study and generalizability of the results. Only three treatment programs were in each group, which increases the potential for individual program characteristics, such as staffing and local resources, to provide confounds when measuring client outcomes related to service delivery models.

CONCLUSION

The results of the current study provide converging evidence that consideration of service delivery models and measurement of fidelity are important components in studies assessing the effectiveness of treatment models. Similar to previous results examining integrated dual diagnosis service delivery models, the current study found that a case management model achieved comparable fidelity ratings and outcomes at one and two years post treatment entry. These findings suggest that mode of service delivery may be a less essential component of integrated dual diagnosis treatment model relative to other elements of the framework. Studies of this nature have significant implications for technology transfer of evidence-based practices; as these treatment models are diffused into community treatment programs, elements of the practice are often adapted given local resources and other system constraints. Evidence regarding the program components that are most closely associated to client outcomes can provide guidance regarding the potential effects of local adaptations. Future studies assessing the impact of service delivery models and elements of integrated dual diagnosis treatment fidelity that include more comprehensive outcome measures and larger sample sizes are needed to replicate and expand on these findings.

ACKNOWLEDGMENTS

Laurel F. Mangrum and Richard T. Spence, Addiction Research Institute, University of Texas; Molly Lopez, Texas Department of State Health Services.

The authors would like to acknowledge the leadership and support of the Texas Department of State Health Services (formerly the Texas Commission on Alcohol and Drug Abuse and the Texas Department of Mental Health and Mental Retardation) in designing and implementing this project and assisting in retrieval of archival data for the present analysis. We would also like to acknowledge the Public Policy Research Institute at Texas A and M University for their efforts in collecting process evaluation data for this project. Portions of this manuscript were presented at the annual Addiction Health Services Research Conference in Little Rock, Arkansas, October 23-25, 2006. The findings and conclusions of this article represent the opinions of the authors and do not necessarily reflect the official position of the Texas Department of State Health Services. The authors of this paper have no known conflicts of interest.

REFERENCES

Bond, G. R., Evans, L., Salyers, M. P., Williams, J., and Kim, H. (2000). Measurement of fidelity in psychiatric rehabilitation. *Mental Health Services Research*, *2*, 75-87.

Bond, G. R., and Salyers, M. P. (2004). Prediction of outcome from the Dartmouth assertive community treatment fidelity scale. *CNS Spectrums*, *9*, 937-942.

Drake, R. E., Bartels, S. J., Teague, G. B., Noordsy, D. L., and Clark, R. E. (1993). Treatment of substance abuse in severely mentally ill patients. *Journal of Nervous and Mental Disease*, *181*, 606-611.

Drake, R. E., McHugo, G. J., Becker, D. R., Anthony, W. A., and Clark, R. E. (1996). The New Hampshire study of supported employment for people with severe mental illness. *Journal of Consulting and Clinical Psychology*, *64*, 391- 399.

Drake, R. E., Mercer-McFadden, C., Mueser, K. T., McHugo, G. J., and Bond, G. R. (1998). Review of integrated mental health and substance abuse treatment for patients with dual disorders. *Schizophrenia Bulletin*, *24*, 589-608.

Essock, S. M., Mueser, K. T., Drake, R. E., Covell, N. H., McHugo, G. J., Frisman, L. K., et al. (2006). Comparison of ACT and standard case management for delivering integrated treatment for co-occurring disorders. *Psychiatric Services*, *57*, 185-196.

Gonzalez, G., and Rosenheck, R. A. (2002). Outcomes and service use among homeless persons with serious mental illness and substance abuse. *Psychiatric Services*, *53*, 437-446.

Johnsen, M., Samberg, L., Calsyn, R., Blasinsky, M., Landow, W. and Goldman, H. (1999). Case management models for persons who are homeless and mentally ill: The ACCESS demonstration project. *Community Mental Health Journal, 35*, 325-346.

Judd, P. H., Thomas, N., Schwartz, T., Outcalt, A., and Hough, R. (2003). A dual diagnosis demonstration project: Treatment outcomes and cost analysis. *Journal of Psychoactive Drugs, SARC Supplement 1, May*, 181-192.

Mangrum, L. F., Spence, R. T., and Lopez, M. (2006). Integrated versus parallel treatment of co-occurring psychiatric and substance use disorders. *Journal of Substance Abuse Treatment, 30*, 79-84.

McCoy, M. L., Devitt, T., Clay, R., Davis, K. E., Dincin, J. Pavick, D., et al. (2003). Gaining insight: Who benefits from residential integrated treatment for people with dual diagnoses? *Psychiatric Rehabilitation Journal, 27*, 140-150.

McGrew, J. H., Bond, G. R., Dietzen, L., and Salyers, M. (1994). Measuring fidelity of implementation of a mental health program model. *Journal of Consulting and Clinical Psychology, 62*, 670-678.

McHugo, G. J., Drake, R. E., Teague, G. B., and Xie, H. (1999). Fidelity to assertive community treatment and client outcomes in the New Hampshire dual disorder study. *Psychiatric Services, 50*, 818-824.

Mueser, K. T., Noordsy, D. L., Drake, R. E., and Fox, L. (2003). Research on integrated dual disorder treatment. In D. H. Barlow (Ed.), *Integrated treatment for dual disorders: A guide to effective practice* (pp. 301-305). New York: Guilford Press.

Resnick, S. G., Neale M. S., and Rosenheck, R. A. (2003). Impact of public support payments, intensive psychiatric community care, and program fidelity on employment outcomes for people with severe mental illness. *Journal of Nervous and Mental Disease, 191*, 139-144.

Rosenbaum, P. R., and Rubin, D. B. (1983). The central role of the propensity score in observational studies for causal effects. *Biometrika, 70*, 41-55.

Teague, G. B., Bond, G. R., and Drake, R. E. (1998). Program fidelity in assertive community treatment: Development and use of a measure. *American Journal of Orthopsychiatry, 68*, 216-232.

Teague, G. B., Drake, R. E., and Ackerson, T. H. (1995). Evaluating the use of continuous treatment teams for persons with mental illness and substance abuse. *Psychiatric Services, 46*, 689-695.

In: Integrated Health Care Delivery
Editor: L. A. Klein and E. L. Neumann

ISBN 978-1-60456-851-6
© 2008 Nova Science Publishers, Inc.

Chapter 3

OPERATING ROOM COSTS AND RESOURCE UTILIZATION IN LUMBAR FUSION WITH INSTRUMENTATION PROCEDURES: INTEGRATED DELIVERY SYSTEM IS IMPLICATED

Wei-Ching Chung[1], Herng-Chia Chiu[2] and Dong-Sheng Tzeng[3,4]

[1]Division of Nursing Department, Military General Hospital, Kaohsiung, Taiwan
[2]Graduate Institute of Healthcare Administration, Kaohsiung Medical University, Kaohsiung, Taiwan
[3]Department of Psychiatry, Military Kaohsiung General Hospital, Kaohsiung, Taiwan
[4]Graduate Institute of Occupational Safety and Health, Kaohsiung Medical University, Kaohsiung, Taiwan

ABSTRACT

Very few studies have addressed the magnitude of hospital costs in lumbar fusion with instrumentation in Asian countries. The objectives of the study were to analyze and compare lumbar fusion with instrumentation operating room (OR) costs between two hospitals.

Patients who underwent lumbar fusion with instrumentation in 2004 at one medical center and one public teaching hospital were invited to participate. Patient demographics and clinical information were derived from patient charts. Cost information was obtained from detailing billing charges and the hospital financial accounting divisions. In the linear regression analysis, significant differences in age and severity were observed between the two study hospitals in terms of total costs.

There were significant differences in patient demographics and disease severity at the two hospitals (p=0.000). The case mix in the medical center was 1.76, and in the public teaching hospital, 1.05. The medical center consumed more resources than did the public teaching hospital (NT$106,462 vs. NT$87,643). A difference was found in direct materials costs (p=0.000~0.199), direct professional costs (p=0.000~0.342), and indirect costs in the two study hospitals (p=0.000). Patients who scored higher in the American

* Telephone number: 886-7-749-0056, Fax number: 886-7-749-8706, E-mail: tzengds@seed.net.tw

Society of Anesthesiologists physical status index incurred significantly higher costs and longer hospital stays (p=0.011) than did patients with lower scores (p=0.000).

The knowledge and experience of surgeons and hospital management are equally important to maintain a hospital's competitive position. These results showed the different patient severity referred to different care provider, different resource utilization from different health care delivery system which are critical factors in care management. A vertically integrated health care delivery system would be a suitable model to cover the demands of patients when providers face the cost considerations of National Health Insurance.

Key works: Integrated delivery system, Lumbar fusion with spinal instrumentation, Operating Room Cost.

INTRODUCTION

Lumbar spine fusion is commonly performed for various pathologic diseases, back pain and gross instability. Over the past 20 years, significant technical advances in spinal surgery have made the concept of interbody fusion a reality [1-2]. The literature has reported a wide variation in outcomes for these different techniques. Clinical, economic, functional, and radiographic data were assessed to determine differences in clinical and functional results and biomechanical properties [3-4]. Spinal fusion involving instrumentation-assisted segmental fixation represents a valid procedure in the treatment of spinal instability, such as in spondylolisthesis, lumbar spinal stenosis and degenerative disease, and supplemental lumbar interbody fusion may improve the fusion rate and endurance of the construct [5-8].

The procedure, whether approached anteriorly or posteriorly, or posterolaterally, appears to improve patient satisfaction and radiographic fusion rates [9-10]. The evaluation of spinal fusion surgery as the preferred technique is associated with the short operating time, less blood loss, shorter hospital stay, and lower incidence of complications. The recovery period can offer the accessibility of immediate stability, correction of deformity, and early walking on the postoperative stage. There are few complications requiring repeated and more costly surgery, including infection, blood loss, pain, neurologic deficits, graft collapse, nonunion, dislodged graft, and plating complications. Surgery substantially improved one-year outcomes based on established outcomes of instrumentations in patients with spondylolisthesis and stenosis [11-12]. The procedures result in acceptable rates of clinical fusion outcomes, and a minimal incidence of morbidity when performed by an experienced surgeon. The spinal fusion surgery involved placement of fixation is effective options in patients with indications for lumbar structural defects [13-14]. Most importantly, operating times significantly depend on the surgeon in the team, especially to longer operating times of residents and less-experienced junior consultants when compared with senior consultants on the basis of surgical routine procedures. These higher costs derive from junior consultants performing operations without proper supervision from senior consultants [15].

Under the current National Health Insurance System in Taiwan, lumbar fusion with instrumentation is one of the procedures paid for by case payment. For the entire lumbar fusion with instrumentation procedure, hospitals are reimbursed by a fixed rate of New Taiwan (NT) $29,691(about US$ 928), which includes expenses associated with the OR, professional fees, and hospitalization-related costs. As with the case payment scheme, hospitals have a strong motivation to contain costs and resource utilization to increase profit margins and maintain equivalent quality. Also, OR time has been previously indicated as a major cost component for surgical procedures [16-18]. In a sense, OR costs should be a target for savings. The objectives of this study were two-fold: 1) to analyze the lumbar fusion with instrumentation cost components of two hospitals; 2) to examine the relationships of hospital volume and surgeon volume with lumbar fusion with instrumentation operating costs and resource utilization.

In assessing the relationship of volume-outcome, previous studies indicated the effect of volume on the quality of surgical care [19–22]. A high volume of procedures was associated with lower hospital costs and a shorter length of stay (LOS) [23–24]. Economic evaluation of lumbar fusion with instrumentation mainly focused on avoiding peri-operative and post-operative complications. Very few studies have used true cost, rather than charge data, as data basis for cost analysis [25]. The present study may be the first attempt to disclose pure operating costs based on a two-center study design.

MATERIALS AND METHODS

Sample and Data Sources

The study subjects were derived from two acute tertiary hospitals in southern Taiwan. The first hospital was a 1200-bed university medical center and the second was a 750-bed public teaching hospital. Patients with low back pain and who had a primary procedure for lumbar fusion with instrumentation in 2004 participated in the study. In total, 59 cases received lumbar fusion at the academic medical center; 18 cases of which were handled by surgeon A, 16 cases by surgeon B, 15 cases by surgeon C, 4 cases by surgeon D, and 6 cases by surgeon E. For the public teaching hospital, three surgeons handled 26 cases for surgeon F, 15 cases for surgeon G, and 4 cases for surgeon H. By surgical volume, the academic medical center represented the high-volume hospital, while the public teaching hospital represented the low-volume hospital.

The study design was a retrospective chart review, which summarized the information on patient demographics, resource utilization, and medical outcomes. Secondary cost data provided by the hospital financial accounting departments and detailed billing charges were also used. For certain item costs, the department ratio of cost to charge (RCC) was used.

There were two areas of interest variables included for analysis: patient information and cost data. Patient demographics included age, gender, and the American Society of Anesthesiologists Physical Status (ASA PS) score, (ASA PS 1–3). The ASA PS score was used as a measurement of severity of illness since it is simple and well accepted in the OR [26]. The ASA PS incorporates comorbid conditions and activity levels and excludes the surgical or anesthetic risk. The ASA has been validated as a fine instrument to predict cost [26], surgical outcome [27], and hospital days [28]. The indicators of patient resources utilization and medical outcomes included operating time, anesthesia time, hospitalization days, discharge status, and surgical complications. Surgical complications included wound infections; complications that occurred after discharge, such as failure of the instrumentation and nonunion, were excluded. The complications were categorized as pulmonary, gastrointestinal, wound-related, hematologic, operative, neurologic, cardiac, renal, and miscellaneous. They were further categorized as major or minor. A complication that adversely affected the recovery of the patient was considered a major complication. A complication that was noted in the medical records but did not alter the patient's recovery was considered a minor complication. [29–30].

The cost structure was divided into direct and indirect costs. Direct costs comprised direct material costs and professional costs. *Direct material costs* were those spent on surgical instruments, anesthesia drugs, laboratory, and others. Specifically, surgical instruments, and the instrument costs were calculated by the number of total units multiplied by unit purchasing price. Anesthesia materials costs included all intraoperative drug costs, airway supplies, and internal arterial and venous supplies. For laboratory and blood transfusion, the cost information was derived from the department RCC. The laboratory department ratios in the two hospitals were 0.57 and 0.60, respectively. The blood bank ratios in the two hospitals were 0.68 and 1.00, respectively. The laboratory and transfusion charges were converted into costs by using the ratios.

Direct professional costs covered salaries/wages for clinical professionals involved in surgery. The clinical professionals included surgeons, anesthetists, residents, anesthesia nurses, and operation nurses. For each study hospital, the OR for lumbar fusion surgery was staffed with one each surgeon, anesthetist, surgical resident, anesthesia resident (teaching cost), and anesthesia nurse, and two OR nurses. All professional costs were calculated by their hour cost (rate) multiplied by attendant time. The hour rate was a summation of the total salaries (basic salary, performance-based pay salary, annual bonus, and other benefits) divided by the total working hours (40 hours per week). Since the two study hospitals have been qualified by the Taiwan Joint Commission of Accreditation as teaching hospitals, resident costs were considered as teaching costs.

Indirect costs included indirect labor costs and depreciation for the study, which could not be changed by procedure volume or operation time. Labor costs were measured by the salaries/wages of those involved in OR administration such as the supervisor, clerks, and cleaning and sterilization personnel. Depreciation was estimated for buildings and operating machines. Depreciation of building and OR equipment was generated by the operation hours multiplied by hourly rates. The depreciation criteria were based on the government accounting principal: a seven-year life cycle for machines and 35 years for medical buildings.

Statistical Analysis

SPSS version 13.0 for Windows was used for statistical analysis. An independent t-test and Chi-square test were used to examine continuous and categorical variables, respectively. One-way analysis of variance was used to explore the differences in the utilization of health care resources among the three lumbar fusion surgeons; post-hoc analysis was also performed. The linear regression model was used to examine the volume-cost-utilization relationship while controlling for selected covariates.

RESULTS

Table 1 shows the patient demographics, OR resources utilization, and medical outcome data. The lumbar fusion with instrumentation subjects' mean age at both study hospitals was early 50s and late 20s. By gender, the proportions of male and female subjects at the medical center differed significantly from the public hospital. The medical center had an average ASA score of 2.12 (SD= 0.494) compared with 1.16 (SD=0.367) at the public hospital. In terms of ASA score, the severity of physical status was statistically significantly different between the two hospitals.

Table 1. Patient Characteristics and Operating Room Utilization

Variables	Medical center (n=59)		Public teaching (n=45)		p-value
	n	%	N	%	
Patient Demographics					
Sex					
Male	25	42.37	42	93.3	0.000
Female	34	57.63	3	6.67	
Age (SD)	53.63 ±16.97		26.93 ± 12.74		0.000
Severity of Disease					
ASA PS score	2.12± 0.494		1.16 ± 0.367		0.000
1	4	6.78	38	84.44	0.000
2	44	74.58	7	15.56	
3	11	18.64	0	0	
Recovery room					
yes	52	88.14	45	100	0.017
no	7	11.86	0	0	
Discharge					
OPD follow up	57	96.61	23	76.67	0.403
AAD discharge	2	3.38	0	0	
Utilizations and Clinical Outcome					
Surgical time (hour)	5.41 ± 2.24		4.29 ± 1.27		0.003
Anesthesia time (hour)	6.67±2.43		5.21 ±1.44		0.001
LOS (day)	20.83 ± 22.33		12.09 ± 3.87		0.011
Complication					
Yes	1	1.69	0	0	0.382
No	58	98.31	45	100	

For average operating time, the operating process of the public hospital was significantly shorter than that of the medical center (4.29 vs. 5.41 hours, p =.003). Similarly, the medical center used 6.67 hours (SD=2.43) for anesthesia compared with 5.21 hours (SD=1.44) for the public teaching hospital, which also reached a level of significant difference (p =.001). The LOS for the medical center hospital was 20.83 days (SD=22.33), which was statistically significantly shorter than that of the public teaching hospital at 12.09 days (SD=3.87) (p =.0011). One case with wound infection was found at the medical center, which also did not reach a level of significant difference (p=.382).

Table 2 shows the OR cost components analysis for the two hospitals.

Table 2. Cost Components Analysis by Hospital Volume

Variables	Medical center (n=59)		Public teaching Hospital (n=45)		p-value
	NT $	SD (%)	NT $	SD (%)	
Direct Materials Costs					
Instruments	64370	38745	50870	6271	0.023
Pharmaceutical costs	2856	1231	430	133	0.000
Laboratory	557	286	0	0	0.000
Blood transfusion	59	29	69	47	0.199
Subtotal	67842	(63.7)	51369	(58.6)	
Direct Professional Costs					
Surgeon costs	16196	3605	16449	4810	0.342
Anesthetist	2906	1181	635	3840	0.000
Anesthesia nurse	3344	551	2793	5397	0.000
Operating nurse	6038	1708	4515	3267	0.192
Teaching costs	4133	886	6954	2291	0.000
Subtotal	32617	(30.7)	31346	(35.8)	
Indirect Costs					
Depreciation	3870	1456	3841	1736	0.000
Administration	2133	819	1087	350	0.000
Subtotal	6003	(5.6)	4928	(5.6)	
Total Costs (NT $)	106462	51085	87643	14838	0.016

US$1= NT$32.

The OR total cost was NT$106,462 for the medical center. This cost was significantly lower than that of the pubic teaching hospital at NT$87,643 (p=.016). The medical center consumed many resources in the three domains of cost: direct materials, direct professional costs, and indirect costs. Except for the direct professional costs of the surgeon and operating nurse, each specific item of cost was statistically significantly different at the two hospitals (p=000). Compared with the medical center, the public teaching hospital incurred less costs in instruments, pharmaceuticals, depreciation, laboratory, anesthetists, pathology, and administration. However, the latter incurred more costs in surgeon fees, which also reached a level of significant difference (p<.001).

It should be noted that the proportions of the three cost components were almost the same for the high- and low-volume hospitals. Direct material costs accounted for more than 58.6%

of the total costs for the two hospitals, while direct professional costs reached 30.7% and 35.8%, respectively (as shown in Table 2). Furthermore, Figure 1 demonstrates the structures of the three cost components between the two study hospitals.

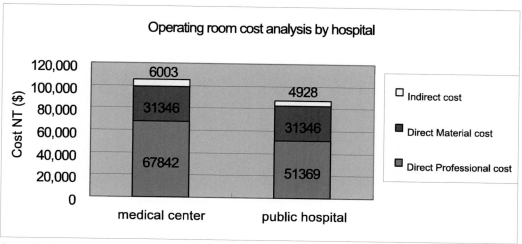

Figure 1. Operating room cost analysis by hospital.

Patient characteristics and resources utilization were analyzed by surgeon volume, as shown in Table 3. Three surgeons were responsible for lumbar fusion with instrumentation at the medical center. Surgeon A accounted for 30.5% (18) of the total cases, surgeon B, for 27.1% (16) and surgeon C, 25.4% (15), whereas the other two surgeons shared 16.9% (10). At the public teaching hospital, all lumbar spinal fusion with instrumentation procedures were performed by surgeon F, with 26 cases (53.1%), surgeon G, with 15 (33.3%), or surgeon H, with 4 (8.9%). The distributions of patient demographics and the patient's severity of physical status were statistically different among the five surgeons. Surgeons A, B and C from the medical center had higher overall costs and longer lengths of hospital stay than surgeon F and G from the public teaching hospital. The average operating time of the three surgeons ranged from 4.35 to 7.12 hours: surgeon A required 4.35 hours to finish a procedure, which was the shortest operating time, and surgeon C spent 7.12 hours for the same procedure. Consequently, surgeon C's patients stayed in the hospital for 24.7 days, which is longer than the LOS of surgeon A's patients at 24.5 days. In comparing surgeons B and C, surgeon B had a shorter operating time and LOS with lower total costs.

Table 4 specifies patient characteristics and resources utilization by severity of disease. Severity of disease was categorized into ASA PS 1, ASA PS 2, and ASA PS 3, to determine differences found in age, gender, surgery hours, anesthesia hours, LOS, surgeon costs, nursing costs, material costs and total costs. The results revealed no significant differences in age, gender, surgery hours, anesthesia hours, nursing costs, material costs and total costs (p< 0.05).

Table 3. Patient Characteristics and Resources Utilization by Surgeon Volume

Type of Hospital	Medical center			Public teaching Hospital		P	Post-hoc Comparison
Surgeon volume	A (n=18)	B(n=16)	C(n=15)	F(n=26)	G (n=15)		
Patient Demographics							
Age (SD)	61.39±9.43	54.75±12.4	45.73±25.3	28.15±15.05	24.13±7.15	0.000	A>C, A,B,C>F A,B,C>G
Sex							
Male	5(5.6%)	8(8.9%)	6(6.7%)	24(26.7%)	14(15.6%)		
Female	13(14.4%)	8(8.9%)	9(10.0%)	2(2.2%)	1(1.1%)		
ASA Score	2.28±0.461	2.06±0.443	1.93±0.594	1.19±0.402	1.07±0.258	0.000	A>C,F,G B>F,G C >F,G
Surgical Time (hour)	4.35±1.27	5.41±1.91	7.12±2.86	4.55±1.43	4.18±0.59	0.000	C>A,B,F,G
Anesthesia time (hour)	5.52±1.48	6.54±1.99	8.59±4.14	5.45±1.67	5.17±0.67	0.000	C>A,B,F,G
LOS (day)	24.5±29.98	15.5±10.95	24.7±25.49	11.46±4.47	12.47±1.73	0.051	A > G C > G
Material Costs	64311±34267	51524±21410	88651±53281	49239±6420	55187±4020	0.001	C>A,B,F,G
Physician Costs	16337±4765	20336±7185	26765±10744	24964±9150	23633±7966	0.003	C>A,B G>A F>A
Nursing Costs	7419±1991	8781±2681	11545±4224	7098±2280	7197±1687	0.000	C>A,B,G,H B>G
Total Costs (NT $)	99068±41528	93845±33137	1428861±68731`	88013±16147	92339±8807	0.000	C>A,B,G,H

Table 4. Patient Characteristics and Resources Utilization by Severity of Disease

ASA Score	ASA 1 (n=42)	ASA2 (n=51)	ASA 3 (n=11)	p	Post-hoc Comparison
Patient Demographics					
Age (SD)	24.4±8.42	52.37±15.99	61.82±18.78	0.000	C>B>A
Sex					
Male	40 (38.5%)	23 (22.1%)	4 (3.9%)		
Female	2 (1.9%)	28 (26.9%)	7 (6.7%)		
Surgical Time (hour)	4.33±1.35	5.37±2.28	5.08±1.79	0.036	B>A
Anesthesia time (hour)	5.26±1.54	6.6±2.46	6.37±2.17	0.010	B>A
LOS (day)	14.29±15.5	17.82±17.47	24.0±23.51	0.238	
Physician Costs (hour)	22550±8133	21483±9648	19074±6710	0.499	
Nursing Costs (hour)	7003±2245	8884±3273	8558±2911	0.007	A>C
Material Physician Costs	52961±21634	59388±31772	75804±43783	0.077	A>C
Total Costs (NT $)	89546±29387	102012±44234	116839±54352	0.097	C>A

Linear regression models (Table 5) were performed to examine the patient characteristics – total cost relationship. After controlling for covariates, the severity of illness (ASA score), age and different hospitals were significantly associated with overall costs.

Table 5. Linear Regression Models by Costs - Patient Characteristics

Independence	Variables	F	p-value	R	R²
		6.926	0.000	0.172	0.147
	age	13.696	0.000		
	ASA score	4.800	0.031		
	Hospital	5.261	0.024		

CONCLUSION

This study found that both the hospital and the surgeons had significant effects on OR resources utilization and associated costs in performing lumbar fusion with instrumentation procedures, after controlling patient demographics and severity of illness. Compared with surgeons and hospital experience (volume) may play a more important role in cost containment and resources conservation.

In comparing the medical center and public teaching hospital, the costs of instruments and pharmaceuticals were significantly different between the two study hospitals, even though the surgeons at both hospitals used the same kinds of instruments. As regards the differences in the specific items of direct materials costs, it should be noted that the direct materials costs accounted for more than 58% of the total OR costs for both study hospitals [16].

Recent studies of surgical costs have found that the proportion of direct materials costs has increased faster than that of personnel costs. Our study found substantial costs for surgical supplies, including not only the normal depreciation of high-cost machines and instruments, but also the increasing use of disposable surgical supplies like sutures, gauze and artificial implants. Furthermore, more than 99% of direct materials costs were instrument costs. The high proportion of instrument costs was mainly due to preferring high-cost implanting instruments to surgical lumbar fusion with instrumentation, which was cost effective and did not cause infection. Under cost containment pressure, hospitals might have to evaluate alternative expensive surgical instruments for lumbar fusion with instrumentation surgery.

The differences in direct material costs further reflect the variations in the practice pattern between the two study hospitals. The practice patterns of the two hospitals also caused differences in lab and transfusion blood costs in the RCC. Further investigation is needed to determine whether the OR lab examination and transfusion blood costs were necessarily in different patient groups.

With respect to the volume-cost-utilization relationship, it may be concluded that the high-volume hospital has more bargaining power for acquiring needed materials at relatively lower prices compared with the low-volume hospital. In addition, the ownership of hospital may also influence the price of purchased materials. Moreover, it should be noted that the patients at the medical center were a middle-aged group, and the patients at the public hospital were a younger group. The one-way ANOVA models indicated that surgeon-specific volume did affect lumbar fusion with instrumentation costs and resources utilization. In the model of the total costs and operating time and anesthesia time, the three surgeons (surgeons A, B and C) from the medical center C incurred significantly expensive costs, longer operating time and lengths of stay. It should be noted that surgeons F and G from the public hospital but had his own high volume of practice as compared with surgeon F. However, the lower total costs and shorter lengths of stay associated with surgeon F may be a benefit of efficient hospital management. From the perspective of overall hospital management, a high surgeon volume needs the support of excellent OR management to minimize total costs and to maximize medical outcomes.

In the greater analysis of direct costs, however, surgeon volume was the most significant determinant of professional costs. The surgeon from the medical center with an individually high volume of practice (surgeon A) demonstrated lower professional costs (physician and nursing costs) compared with the surgeon with a low volume of practice (surgeon C). Also in the public hospital, the surgeon with a high volume of practice (surgeon F) demonstrated lower professional costs (material, nursing and total costs) compared with the surgeon with a low volume of practice (surgeon G). It may be concluded that surgeon volume or experience does matter in terms of OR cost savings. These results confirm that surgeon volume and hospital management are equally important in OR cost savings and resources, which are also translated to the volume-cost-utilization relationship indicated in other studies [19-21]. As mentioned earlier, lumbar fusion with instrumentation is included in the list of fixed case payment procedures. Hospitals need to design more surgical training programs to standardize the skills of surgeons; consequently, direct professional costs could be reduced [14-15].

In addition to the effect of physician volume consistently playing an important role in predicting OR total costs, direct-professional costs, and LOS, the greater complexity of the lumbar fusion procedure does not mean that ASA PS scores increase costs. These topics are worthy of further investigation, to define and understand clearly the impact of lumbar fusion severity of disease on cost, which, in turn, would benefit hospital management and operation. The present findings do not confirm the appropriateness of using the ASA PS as the measure of severity of illness in predicting hospital costs and utilization [32–34]. For elective surgeries such as lumbar spine fusion, under a prospective payment system, severity of illness should be considered when adjusting reimbursement; otherwise, hospital managers or physicians may resist providing care for more seriously ill patients.

One should be more cautious in interpreting the findings to specify the volume-cost-utilization relationship. Nonetheless, the cost information for each specific utilization item is valuable and important for uncovering the real picture of lumbar spine fusion OR costs in the two hospitals. Yet, the present study only focused on the costs incurred within the operating room; the costs involved pre- and post-operatively were not analyzed. In addition, the study only focused on the costs of lumbar fusion with instrumentation surgery in the two hospitals, and did not consider overall hospitalization costs, including the ward stay and post-op care, to produce an overall cost per admission, and to compare this with the Bureau of National Health Insurance's diagnosis-related group reimbursement in the current system. Also, only those patients receiving lumbar fusion with instrumentation during one year were considered as study subjects, and so, to overcome this limitation, all the lumbar fusion with instrumentation cases from 2004 at both study hospitals were reviewed; the result was that there was no significant difference in the distribution of patient volume for that year.

The global budget was run for eight years to the reason of financial stress in National Health Insurance in Taiwan. The dumping situation was complained not only by the patient, family and society, but also the health care workers of emergency services. From the point of policy maker, the component management by outcome measurements and disease management by DRG (diagnosis related group), standardized clinical protocol can not overcome the difficulty in comorbid and complicated cases exactly. The integrated delivery system may provide commitment between different region, different level and different volume providers to collaborative, coordinative and continue care [35]. In this study, the two different culture hospitals may cooperate in health care system such as the transfer by the characteristics of severity of disease, age, geographic factors in patients; facility and efficiency factors in hospitals. Compensate the weakness of two hospitals by vertical integration [35].

The present study supports the saying that practice makes perfect [14-15]. Both the hospital and surgeon volumes play an important role in cost/resource saving and in providing better clinical outcomes. It should be noted that high-volume hospitals also have more purchasing power to reduce direct material costs, and high-volume surgeons still need the support of efficient hospital management for cost saving and better resource utilization. In conclusion, the knowledge and experience of surgeons and hospital management are equally important to maintain a hospital's competitive position in the market, especially under the case payment system for lumbar fusion with instrumentation in Taiwan.

REFERENCES

[1] Subach, BR; Haid ,RW; Rodts, GE Jr and Mclaughlin, MR.(2001). Do current outcomes data support the technique of lumbar interbody fusion? *Clinical Neurosurgery* ; 48:204-18.

[2] Ghogawala, Z ; Benzel, EC ; Amin-Hanjani, S ; Barker, FG 2nd ; Harrington, JF ; Magge, SN ; Strugar, J ; Coumans, JV and Borges, LF .(2004). Prospective outcomes evaluation after decompression with or without instrumented fusion for lumbar stenosis and degenerative Grade   spondylolithesis. *Journal of Neurosurgery* ; 1:267-72.

[3] Bono, CM ; Lee, CK .(2004). Critical analysis of trends in fusion for degenerative disc disease over the past 20 years: influence of technique on fusion rate and clinical outcome. *Spine* ; 29:455-63.

[4] Freeman, BJ ; Licina, P and Mehdian, SH.(2000) Posterior lumbar interbody fusion combined with instrumented postero-lateral fusion:5-year results in 60 patients. *European Spine Journal* ;9:42-6.

[5] Tajima, N; Chosa, E and Watanabe, S.(2004) Posterolateral Lumbar fusion. *Journal of Orthopaedic Science ;9*:327-33.

[6] Turner, JA; Ersek, M ; Herron, L; Haselkorn, J ; kent, D; Ciol, MA and Deyo, R.(1992) Patient outcomes after lumbar spinal fusion. *JAMA* ; 268:907-11.

[7] Park, YK ; Chung, HS.(1999) Instrumented facet fusion for the degenerative lumbar disorders. *Acta Neurochirurgica* ;141:915-20.

[8] Glassman, SD ; Pugh, K ; Johnson, JR and Dimar, JR 2nd.(2002) Sugical management of adjacent level degeneration following lumbar spine fusion.*Orthopedics* ; 25:1051-5.

[9] La Rosa, G ; Conti, A ; Cacciola, F: Cardali, S ; La Torre, D ; Gambadauro, NM and Tomasello, F.(2003) pedicle screw fixation for isthmic spondylolisthesis: does posterior lumbar interbody fusion improve outcome over posterolateral fusion? *Journal of Neurosurgery* ; 99:143-50.

[10] Madan, S ; Boeree, NR .(2002) Outcome of posterior lumbar interbody fusion versus posterolateral fusion for spondylolytic spondylolisthesis. *Spine* ; 27:1536-42.

[11] Humphreys, SC; Hodges, SD; Patwardhan, AG ; Eck, JC ; Murphy, RB and Covington, LA.(2001) Comparison of posterior and transforaminal approaches to lumbar interbody fusion. *Spine* ; 26: 567-71.

[12] Rosenberg, WS ; Mummaneni, PV.(2001) Transforaminal lumbar interbody fusion: technique, complication, and early results. *Neurosurgery* ;48:569-74.

[13] Sweet, FA ; Lenke, LG ; Bridwell, KH ; Blanke, KM and Whorton, J.(2001) Prospective radiographic and clinical outcomes and complications of single solid rod instrumented anterior spinal fusion in adolescent idiopathic scoliosis. *Spine* ; 26:1956-65.

[14] Rivet, DJ ; Jeck, D ; Brennan, J ; Epstein, A and Lauryssen, C (2004) Clinical outcomes and complications associated with pedicle screw fixation-augmented lumbar interbody fusion. *Journal of Neurosurgery Spine* ;1:261-6.

[15] Koperna.(2004) How long do we need teaching in the operating room? The true costs of achieving surgical routine. *Langenbecks Archives of Surgery* ; 389:204-8.

[16] Fu, L ; Hsu, N ; Chen, C ; Yao, L and Chung, WJ.(1995) The related factors of operation costs and charges for operating rooms. *VGH Nursing* ; 12: 305–314.

[17] Lin, HC ; Yang, CH ; Chen, CC.(2003) Hospital ownership and its effect on medical cost from case payment using data from cesarean section patients. *Tzu Chi Univerity Department of Medicine* ; 25:55-61.

[18] Whitecloud, TS 3rd; Roesch, WW and Ricciardi, JE.(2001) Transforaminal interbody fusion versus anterior-posterior interbody fusion of the lumbar spine: a financial analysis. *Journal of Spinal Disorders* ; 14:100-3.

[19] Luft, HS; Bunker, JP and Enthoven, AC.(1979) Should operations be regionalized? The empirical relation between surgical volume and mortality. *New England Journal of Medicine* ; 301: 1364–1369.

[20] Phillips KA ; Luft, HS and Ritchie, JL.(1995) The association of hospital volumes of percutaneous transluminal coronary angioplasty with adverse outcomes, length of stay, and charges in California. *Medicine Care* ;33:502–514.

[21] Hannan, EL ; O'Donnell, JF; Kilburn, H Jr; Bernard, HR and Yazici, A.(1989) Investigation of the relationship between volume and mortality for surgical procedures performed in New York State hospitals. *JAMA* ; 262: 503–510.

[22] Katz, JN; Phillips, CB and Baron, JA.(2003) Hospital and surgeon volume of total hip replacement with functional status and satisfaction three years following surgery. *Arthritis Rheum* ; 48: 560–568.

[23] Arndt, M ; Bradbury, RC ; Golec, JH and Steen, PM.(1998) A comparison of hospital utilization by Medicaid and privately insured patients. *Medicine Care Research and Review* ; 55: 32–53.

[24] Strum, DP; Sampson, AR ; May, JH and Vagas, LG.(2000) Surgeon and type of anesthesia predict variability in surgical procedure times. *Anesthesiology* ; 92: 1454–1466.

[25] Traverso, LW; Hargrave, K.(1995) A prospective ct analysis of laparoscopic cholecystectomy. *American Journal Surgery* ;169:503-6.

[26] Macario, A ; Vitez, TS ; Dunn, B ; McDonald, T and Brown, B.(1997) Hospital costs and severity of illness in three types of elective surgery. *Anesthesiology* ; 86:92–100.

[27] Forrest, JB; Rehder, K ; Cahalan, MK and Goldsmith, CH.(1992) Multicenter study of general anesthesia. III. Predictors of severe perioperative adverse outcomes. *Anesthesiology* ; 76: 3–15.

[28] Carreon, LY; Puno, RM ; Dimar, JR 2nd; Glassman, SD and Johnson, JR.(2003) Perioperative complications of posterior lumbar decompression and arthrodesis in older adults. *Journal of Bone and Joint Surgery - American Volume* ; 85:2089-92.

[29] Duggl, N ;Mendiondo, I ; Pares, HR ;Jhawar, S ;Das, K ; Kenny, KJ; Dickman, CA.(2004)Anterior lumbar interbody fusion for treatment of failed back surgery syndrome: an outcome analysis. *Neurosurgery* ; 54:636-43.

[30] Turner, JA ; Ersek, M; Herron, L; Haselkorn, J; Kent, D; Ciol, MA and Deyo, R.(1992) Patient outcomes after lumbar spinal fusion. *JAMA* ; 268:907-11.

[31] Pfeiffer, M ; Hildebrand, R ; Grande, M and Griss, P.(2003) Evaluation of indication-based use of transpedicular instrumentations with different rigidity for lumbar spinal fusion: a prospective pilot study with 3 years of follow-up. *European Spine Journal*; 12:369-77.

[32] Reindl, R ; Steffen, T; Cohen, L and Aebi, M. (2003) Elective lumbar spinal decompression in the elderly: is it a high-risk operation? *Canadian Journal of Surgery* ; 46:43-6.

[33] Cullen, DJ; Nemeskal, AR ; Cooper, JB and Zaslavsky, A.(1992) Dwyer MJ. Effect of pulse oximetry, age, and ASA physical status on the frequency of patients admitted unexpectedly to a postoperative intensive care unit and the severity of their anesthesia-related complications. *Anesthesia and Analgesia* ;74: 181–188.

[34] Hee, HT; Castro, FP Jr ; Majd, ME ; Holt, RT and Myers, L.(2001) Anterior/posterior lumbar fusion versus transforaminal lumbar interbody fusion: analysis of complications and predictive factors. *Journal of Spine Disorders* ;6:533-40.

[35] Tzeng, DS; Lian, LC; Chang, CU; Yang, CY; Lee, GT; Pan, Peter and Lung, FW.(2007) Healthcare in schizophrenia: effectiveness and progress of a redesigned care network. *BMC Health Service Research*, 7:129.

In: Integrated Health Care Delivery
Editor: L. A. Klein and E. L. Neumann

ISBN 978-1-60456-851-6
© 2008 Nova Science Publishers, Inc.

Chapter 4

SOCIAL CAPITAL AND PARTNERSHIP OPPORTUNITIES: MANAGEMENT IMPLICATION IN INTEGRATED HEALTHCARE NETWORKS

Blossom Y. J. Lin[1] and Thomas T. H. Wan[2]
[1]Department of Health Service Administration,
China Medical University, Taichung, Taiwan, ROC
[2]Public Affairs, Health Services Administration, and Medical Education,
College of Health and Public Affairs,
University of Central Florida, Orlando, Florida, USA

ABSTRACT

Social capital as a multidimensional construct measurable from a spirit of trust, cooperation, and commitment could be considered integral to understanding how health care organizations may enhance their survival and growth potential in networks. The organization and dynamics of Taiwan's primary community care network (PCCN) could serve as a good example to illustrate the role of social capital in establishing partnership opportunities. This chapter employs integrated health networks as a framework to identify the importance of social capital and to explicate managerial issues related to health care network management. Analytical issues pertaining to social capital were raised and relevant arguments were reviewed. Finally, using Taiwan's primary community care network (PCCN) as a thinking model, we propose several indicators to study the nature of social capital from three domains: structural, relational, and cognitive. The principles of social capital applicable to network management in the health care sector were discussed.

INTEGRATED HEALTH NETWORKS

The term integrated health network has been pervaded practically for the past decade in the healthcare sector. The concept of integrated health networks can be traced back to the Lord Dawson Report (1920), which called for the regionalization and greater integration of health care delivery in England. The same call was applied in the United States by the Committee on the Cost of Medical Care, in 1932. Subsequently, the Commission on Hospital Care in 1956, the Regional Medical Program in 1966, American Hospital Association's Ameriplan proposal in 1970, and the Health Resources Planning and Development Act of 1974 also emphasized the concept of integration (Brown and McCool, 1986; Pointer, Alexander, and Zuckerman, 1995).

In an integrated health network, various types of organizations are connected along a continuum of care through horizontal and vertical integration (Coddington, Moore, and Fischer, 1994; Johnson, 1993; Longest, 1998; SMG Market Group, 1998). Integrated health network has several interchangeable terms such as integrated health system, integrated delivery system (network), integrated care system (network), organized delivery system, community care network, integrated health care organization, integrated service network, population-based integrated delivery system, and so on, which all emphasize as a multi-organization form characterized by serving a defined population across multi-disciplines, including professionals, units, or service-lines of primary care, acute care and long term care.

The word *integrated,* or *integration,* is commonly viewed as a catch-all term for " a point on a continuum of the various levels and types of interrelationship in any service integrated initiative" (Konrad, 1996, p. 9). In this context, integration refers to "the blending or merging of the separate components of a health care organization to form a cohesive and seamless interoperating whole" (Friedman, 1998). Using this general definition, the meanings of "integration" can be applied on two levels: horizontal and vertical. Horizontal integration means " a group of programs within similar service domains that, regardless of administrative entity, might join together", whereas vertical integration delineates "the extent that various levels of government, the community, and the private sector within appropriate program areas join together" (Konrad, 1996, p. 12). In business, horizontal integration can be viewed as a strategy to "lump together several locations of the same production stages," and vertical integration can be a form to "integrate different stages of production" (Katz, Mitchell, and Markezin, 1982, p. 4).

As has occurred in agriculture, manufacturing, and the retail sector, the healthcare sector has been trying to use vertical integration to secure and retain customers for the traditional and original business (Fox, 1989). For example, hospitals have integrated with ambulatory surgery and post-discharge services such as subacute cares, nursing homes, and home care facilities, to capture any specialized referrals or inpatient business (Conrad and Dowling, 1990; James, 1998; Robinson, 1994). Also, in response to the pervasive capitation payment methods, hospitals have sought to acquire medical groups and individual physician practices, to develop integrated medical service systems (Shortell, Gillies, and Anderson, 1994). On the other hand, horizontal integration is used to improve efficiency by increasing the economies of scale, preventing and eliminating duplicated facilities and improving the use of capability (Robinson, 1996). For example, the medical providers such as hospitals, nursing homes, physician practices, and even health maintenance organizations make their own organizational expansions to improve efficiency and expand market coverage (Herzlinger, 1998; Robinson, 1996). Finally, an integrated health network represents the structural combination of vertical and horizontal integration and is presumed to gain benefits such as accessibility and efficiency (Caplan, Lefkowitz, and Spector, 1992).

MANAGERIAL ISSUES FOR HEALTH CARE NETWORK MANAGEMENT

Contingency theorists (for example, Galbraith, 1973; Lawrence, and Lorsch, 1967) argue that the effectiveness of an organization lies in the fit between organizational internal structure and external environments. On the other hand, rather than embracing rational system assumption that administrators are highly constrained by the external environment, strategic contingency theorists (for example, Child, 1972) assert that administrators have the power to choose the best way for an organization to prevail. Medical providers are attracted to the presumed benefits of integrated healthcare organizations. Several health care studies have drawn on economic and organizational theories to discuss the potential benefits of an integrated system (Conrad, 1992; Conrad and Shortell, 1996). Clinical and administrative efficiency, profitability, increased market power, and environmental acceptance are the benefits commonly cited and described. For example, Conrad and Dowling (1990), Findlay (1993), Johnson (1993), Peters (1991), and Wirth (1993) pointed out that vertical integration can increase an organization's negotiating power to compete for external resources such as suppliers and managed care business. Brown and McCool (1986) and Ackerman (1992) viewed integration as a way to enlarge the economies of scale. The benefit most frequently mentioned is that an integrated organization has the potential to reduce costs and eliminate unneeded services — so-called organizational efficiencies (Ackerman, 1992; Brown and McCool, 1986; Conrad and Dowling, 1990; Findlay, 1993; Johnson, 1993; Peters, 1991; Shortell, Gillies, and Anderson, 1994). Because of these presumed benefits from the integrated health networks, their formation has been considered necessary to adapt to the present ever-increasing health care costs, aging demographics, rapid advances in technology, limited human resources, and shifts of responsibility (Ackerman, 1992; Fox, 1989).

However, there have been only limited studies of the "efficacy" of an integrated organization. For example, from the research evidences of multihospital systems and hospital mergers, which are viewed as multidivisional organizations or as horizontally integrated organizations, it was found that not all multidivisional organizations achieve the expected benefits. To be sure, some researchers have shown that the integration of organizations (or entities) provides a solution to the problems of constraining costs. For example, comparing cost structure between hospitals in multihospital systems and independent hospitals, Menke (1997) showed that hospitals in the multihospital systems have lower costs than independently owned hospitals do. Lynch and McCue (1990) found that for-profit multihospital systems can improve the financial and operating conditions of acquired facilities, such as their access to long-term debt, improvement of plant and equipment, increased profitability, and efficiency. Exploring the factors correlated with the risk of closings in rural hospitals, Mullner, Rydman, Whiteis, and Rich (1989) found that accreditation by JCAHO, the number of facilities and services, and membership in a multihospital system are negatively associated with risk of closing. Burda (1993) and Greene (1994) pointed out that merged hospitals have lower costs, less acute service utilization, and higher profits. On the other hand, the statistical data showed that in the U.S., as the number of mergers and acquisitions increased, the performance of the resulting organizations fell below the industry average more often than not (Ashkenas, DeMonaco, and Francis, 1998). For example, in examining the effects of multihospital system affiliation on hospitals' survival, it was found that system affiliation with investor-owned systems significantly reduces the survival chances of rural hospitals; however, there was no significant relationship between rural hospitals' affiliation with not-for-profit systems or contract management, and their survival (Halpern, Alexander, and Fennell, 1992). The research on the performance of multihospital systems has shown that little economic value is generated by affiliation (Shortell, 1988; Zuckerman, 1979), and little evidence of efficiency has been achieved (Erman and Gabe, 1984). Furthermore, Dranove and Shanley (1995) found no evidence of cost reduction in multi-hospital systems. Lin and Wan (1999) revealed that no evidence supports that the development of integrated structural designs such as governance, clinical, marketing, financial, and information integrated designs, may benefit an IHN's performance in terms of clinical efficiency and financial viability, using the integrated health network as unit of analysis. Friedman and Goes (2001) based on the field reports and available evidences argued that misalignment of cultures and incentives, problems associated with trust building among/between stakeholders, inadequate time and attention paid to manage employee response to changes, problematic leadership, uncertain vision of the desired outcome, lack of overall organizational commitment and understanding, and poor or inadequate communication, were the major contributing factors for the failure of integrated health networks, from functional and process perspective. Clearly, we need to further explore the benefits of forming integrated health networks.

Huerta, Casebeer, and Vander Plaat (2006) identified the roles and future of health service delivery networks and included to: 1) foster cross-disciplinary approaches to problem solving that would lead to better health outcomes; 2) encourage cultures of trusts and mutual respect among members; 3) require a new conceptual framework for evaluating values; 4) profile evolutionarily for better understanding the needs; 5) compare and understand the differences from top-down and bottom-up outcomes; and 6) re-examine the problems for which the use of the network forms are not inappropriate.

WHAT WE FOCUS ON ARE SOCIAL CAPITALS: THE ROLE OF SOCIAL CAPITAL IN THE MANAGEMENT OF INTEGRATED HEALTH NETWORKS

Using the humanized words, social capital is the useful interpersonal ties with friends, relatives, neighbors, and workmates when the people could not get helps from governments, charities or buy and trade for it (Tindall and Wellman, 2002). Social capital is defined as identifying the nature and extent of the impact of social relationships (Szreter, and Woolcock, 2004). Burt (2001, 2005), a network researcher, referred social capital as resources flow (i.e., ideas, information, money, services, and favors) through networks including information, supports and social control.

Social capitals in networks are further categorized into three kinds, including bonding social capital networks, bridging social capital networks, and linking social capital networks (Granovetter, 1973; Gittell and Vidal, 1998; Woolcock, 2001). Bonding social capital networks tie the people akin to others in the similar situations and it could refer to trust and cooperative relations between the members of a network who see themselves as being similar; bridging social capital networks tie people to others who are somewhat different, and it could refer to respect and mutuality between people who know they are not alike; and linking social capital networks refers to vertical ties with people who are unlike themselves and in dissimilar situations, institutions or in positions of authority, and it could refer to norms of respect and networks of trusting relationships between people who are interacting across explicit, formal, and institutional authority or power (Putnam, 2001; Woolcock, 2001; Szreter, and Woolcock, 2004; Szreter, and Woolcock, 2004). On the other hands, Nahapient and Ghoshal (1998) studied social capital from a multidimensional perspective that includes structural, relational, and cognitive domains. Structural domain refers to a network structure's overall patterns of connections; relational domain refers to personal relationships developed; and cognitive domain refers to shared representations, interpretations, and system meaning among actors (De Carolis and Saparito, 2006). Flora (1998) and Woolcock (1998) agreed these classifications and described that social capital can provide both solidarity (i.e., social norms and bonds) and expansive linkages (ties to different groups and individuals), which are called on bonding and bridging social capital in Putnam (2000).

Social capital could be analyzed in a number of ways and applied to a wide range of social processes at various levels of analyses. For example, the issues of social capital have influenced in the field of compensation of chief executive officers (Belliveau, et al., 1996), individual occupational attainment (Lin and Dumin, 1986), economic performance of firms (Baker, 1990), the development of human capital (Coleman, 1988), industry creation (Aldrich and Fiol, 1994), organization growth (Ostgaard and Birley, 1994), and how the organizations form and manage their network and what their outcomes are (Florin, et al, 2003; Larson and Starr, 1993; Aldrich and Zimmer, 1986; Liao and Welsch, 2005) in the social fields.

Cohen and Prusak (2001) argued that social capital could be one of the key factor to determine organizational effectiveness for employees' ability to having access to relevant information to effectively solve problem at workplaces (Scott and Hofmeyer, 2007). The loss of social capital would have a negative impact on organizational performance (Bamford, Bruton, and Hinson, 2006). And Cooke (2007) examined the effect of social capital on small and medium-sized enterprise performance in the UK and revealed that high performance firms were most intensive users of social capital. Greene (1998) pointed out the importance for an integrated health network of strategies to fit one's internal and external conditions. Johnson (1993) pointed out that the lack of the ability to resolve cultural conflicts and established communication channels is one of the major reasons for the failure of an integrated health system, in the case of Chicago's Northwest Network. A significant point is that from the patient's perspective, Sherer (1998) found no added value or benefits for "customers", although an integrated health system is designed to reduce costs and to leverage an organization in the managed care markets. Gilchrist (2006) argued that networks operate best when they share the relationship of trusts and mutual respects, which involves interpersonal interaction and investment of emotional labors. Healthcare delivery networks require organizational representatives to see the mission of their own organizations and engage as multi-organizational participants. And the network-supporting behaviors have to become embedded in the organizational routine works (Clarke and Rollo, 2001) as job responsibilities. Huerta, Casebeer and VanderPlaat (2006) postulated that health care delivery networks, encouraging cultures of trusts and mutual respects among members, would lead to improved rates of knowledge transfers, sharing not only the best practices but also the organizational failures. It also includes people empowerment, learn from each others, working more operatively, equitable distribution of power and resources among network members, all would lead to a network's continuing effectiveness such as better functioning and collaboration (Gilchrist, 2006).

The application of social capital in the healthcare sector is not without any difficulties. For example, Lee et al., (2007) documented a human capital model to improve population health and reduce health inequity through an effective primary care system. They viewed social capital as glue which could hold the communities together and informally as a social network. Through the investments in social development so that citizens would have equitable access to basic resources for good health. In public health, several studies have examined the relationships of social capital (such as trust, reciprocity, mutual helps, and civic engagement) to mortality (Kawachi et al., 1997; Lochner et al., 2002), to violent crime (Kennedy et al., 1998; Sampsom, et al., 1997), to teen birth rate (Gold, 2002), to self-rated health status (Kawachi et al, 1999; Veenstra, 2000; Wan and Lin,2003), to binge drinking (Weitzman and Kawachi, 2000), to lower drug-related risks at the community level (Friedman et al., 2007), to enhance both negative and positive health-related behaviors in an investigation of illegal anabolic steroid networks (Maycock and Howat, 2007), to lower adjusted neighborhood death rates (Lochner et al., 2003) and improve health and well-being in the rural areas (Yip, et al., 2007), and to better access to care and reduce socioeconomic disparities in health (Kawachi, 1999; Hendryx et al., 2002; Sterk, Elifson, and Theall, 2007).

EXAMPLE OF TAIWAN'S PRIMARY COMMUNITY CARE NETWORK (PCCN) DEMONSTRATION PROJECT: CONCEPTUALIZATION AND MEASURES OF SOCIAL CAPITAL

Unique Characteristics in Taiwan's Healthcare Industry

Taiwan's National Health Insurance (NHI), under the control of the Bureau of National Health Insurance (BNHI), was launched in March 1995 to replace its social insurance system that covered 59% of its population: government employees, laborers, farmers and servicemen (Bureau of National Health Insurance in Taiwan). By June 2003 the number of people insured had reached 21,956,729 (99%). There were 17,259 medical providers (92%), including 575 hospitals and 16,684 clinics contracted with the BNHI for serving the enrolled population. The unique phenomenon, characterized in Taiwan's healthcare industry different from those in the western countries, is the freedom of patients to choose their healthcare providers they want, irrespective of their disease severity. Furthermore, Taiwan's people favor the use of larger facilities. This fallacy leads to the phenomenon of shopping for a big hospital for care. For example, people will choose the medical centers with the greatest reputation in medical practice when they only suffer from a common cold.

Backgrounds of the Health Reform for PCCNs in Taiwan

Although the collaboration of health care providers for integrated health networks/systems used to have their volunteerism, dynamics, and autonomy. However, in some instance, the government could influence the network formation and processes to foster the achievement of integrated care. One special case, driven by governmental authority, was the health reform launched and named as the "Primary Community Care Network (PCCN) demonstration project", a nationwide healthcare financing program funded by the Bureau of National Health Insurance (BNHI) in March 2003.

"Primary Community Care Network (PCCN) demonstration project" was established to respond to the SARS epidemic in the spring of 2003. The people's freedom to choose medical providers caused the national health authority to barely control and traced the flow of epidemic. The Primary Community Care Network (PCCN) demonstration project, a nationwide health care financing program, was funded by the Bureau of National Health Insurance (BNHI) in March 2003 as a new model for the Taiwan government to redefine the role of family physicians in the healthcare delivery system. A PCCN in Taiwan consists of a group of clinic physicians whose medical practices are viewed as family care and at least one hospital for secondary or tertiary care. The idea of member component design in PCCNs was aimed to lead the Taiwan citizens to choose one clinic physician as their personal family physician for health maintenance and this family physician also would have the responsibility of referring the patients to specialty care if it is necessary. From a national health authority perspective, they expected the people to put an end to their fallacy that "bigger is better" for healthcare organizations and to establish the idea of "human health", starting with prevention and primary care, followed by secondary or tertiary care, emphasizing health promotion and maintenance instead of disease curing. Furthermore, it could decrease the inappropriateness of medical service use, i.e., over-uses of secondary and tertiary medical services in the high-tech hospitals. In addition, the national health authority was expected to drive the traditional fragmented heath care providers into coordinated medical multidisciplinary teams and to share the limited medical resources through the PCCN demonstration project. The PCCN demonstration project was aimed to: 1) change the traditional patients' customs of freely choosing health care organizations and establish referral channels along the continuum of care, and 2) establish partnerships among the primary care clinics and hospitals to provide a continuum of health care services. It was also expected to establish the primary care system of family physicians, provide holistic health care and improve care quality (Bureau of National Health Insurance in Taiwan).

Structures and Responsibilities for PCCNs in Taiwan

Partnership structures in the PCCNs represent the virtual vertical (i.e., between the member clinics and hospitals) and virtual horizontal (i.e., among the member clinics) aspects of organizing, which designate the formal relationships between individuals and the total network and include organizational design to ensure effective communication, coordination, and integration across the total network. Each PCCN consists of five to ten clinics: half of them should offer the services of general medicine, internal medicine, surgery, obstetrics and gynecology, pediatric, or family medicine. And each PCCN has a central headquarters, usually in one of the clinic facilities, to coordinate and integrate the network. All the clinic physicians in a PCCN are assigned the roles of "family physicians" or "gatekeeper" who recruit people from the local community, keep background and medical files on them, certify family physician education training programs, and hold office hours in the member hospital, where they serve as joint faculty members for further medical consultations or medical utilizations of labs and tests, if necessary. In addition, the hospital member is asked to help clinic physicians in their network to set up a medical information system, share hospital resources (medical equipment and library literature) with the clinic physicians in their network and establish referral channels among the network members. Furthermore, this new demonstration model tries to minimize the barriers to patient access by setting up 24-hour a day, 7-day a week medical consultation telephone lines for providing urgent services onsite and for taking care of the patients whose family physicians' practices are closed to assure seamless care channels. The BNHI funded these extra demonstration actions, at around one hundred thousand US dollars (i.e., NT$3,500,000) for each PCCN under the current fee-for-service payment system (Bureau of National Health Insurance in Taiwan).

There have been 268 PCCNs formed in the period of 2003 to 2005 around Taiwan with the geographical distributions of PCCNs shown in Figure 1. Figure 2 describes the organizational structure of individual PCCNs introduced in the demonstration project in Taiwan. Analyzing all 1,557 participating clinic members in the demonstration project in terms of medical specialties, they cover general medicine, internal medicine, surgeries, obstetrics and gynecology, pediatrics, family medicines, otolaryngology, ophthalmology, rehabilitation medicine, dermatology, and psychiatry, with 237 clinics providing more than two specialties. On the other hand, each PCCN recruits at least one district or regional accredited hospital for acute care demands (required for network members) and a medical center for tertiary care support (not required for network members). There are 6 medical centers, 52 regional hospitals, and 71 district hospitals joining in the demonstration project.

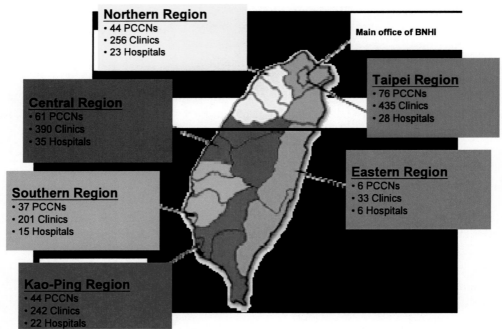

Note: The regions were described based on the authority regions of Bereau of national Health Insurance.

Figure 1. Geographic distributions of the PCCNs in Taiwan.

Medical specialty of clinic members identified in Figure 1		
General medicine	407	(clinics)
Internal medicine	230	
Surgery	109	
Obstetrics and gynecology	181	
Pediatric	279	
Family medicine	323	
Otolaryngology	155	
Ophthalmology	68	
Rehabilitation medicine	25	
Dermatology	27	
Psychiatry	9	

Classification of hospital members identified in Figure 1		
Medical centers	6	(hospitals)
Regional hospitals	52	
District hospitals	71	

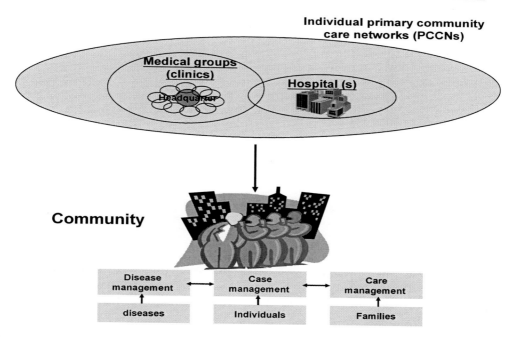

Figure 2. Models and inter-organizational structures in Taiwan PCCN Demonstration Project.

Conceptualization and Measures of Social Capital: Partner Relationships among PCCN Members

The health and health care services need co-production among patients and providers (Alford, 1993; Cahn, 1997) and co-operation among health care providers (Gilson, 2003). The successful therapeutic effectiveness lies one not only the supply of healthcare providers, but also how patients behaves as healthy beings and how the patients interact with the healthcare providers. Charns (1997) argued that reciprocal interdependence of the integrated health networks, including physicians, hospitals, and community systems, may address a system's effectiveness. Social capital in the healthcare sector has been viewed as the nature and extent of ones' social relationships and relevant norms of reciprocity, which can be connected to health outcomes (Forbes, 2001; Eckersley, Dixon, Douglas, 2001; Kawachi, 1999). And the broader concepts include social cohesion (Kaqachi and Nerkman, 2000), social support (Berkman, 2000; Cooper, Arber, et al., 1999; Gorski, 2000; Lennartsson, 1999), social integration (Berkman and Glass, 2000), which could be viewed as relationship levels (Szreter, and Woolcock, 2004). Social capitals also refer to the degree to which an organization has relationships to collaborate and cooperate among organization members and also to the external parties including suppliers, customers, or regulators (Bamford, Bruton, and Hinson, 2006). Knowledge and learning (Meijboom et al., 2004), and trusts (Mechanic, 1998), viewed as the relevant concepts of social capitals, play critical roles in the therapeutic outcomes. Partnership, collaboration, interdisciplinary teams and networks have all represented the relational strategies, different from the traditional practices, to improve health services and to enhance knowledge exchange between professionals in the healthcare systems (Scott and Hofmeyer, 2007). The social relationship built among multiple partners is usually referred to as social capital that can motivate key stakeholders, facilitate resource exchanges, enhance opportunities for changes, and serve as outside motivators (Scott and Hofmeyer, 2007).

Social capital flows through the Taiwan PCCN demonstration projects could be described from multiple perspectives, such as administrators, health professionals (i.e., physicians, nurses, pharmacists, et al.) within a clinic or hospital, and healthcare providers (i.e., clinic-clinic relationships and clinic-hospital relationships). In addition, social capital has been generated through the established relationships of the national authority to health care providers and people (the public/patients), and of healthcare providers to people (the public/patients).

In a proposed study, we employed a multidimensional model of social capitals of clinic-to-clinic and clinic-to-hospital relationships. The measurements of social capital were validated empirically by the Taiwan's PCCN members' social relationships and by the PCCN pioneers and hospital providers that have partnerships with other healthcare organizations (i.e., hospitals, clinics, long-term care facilities).

Structural capitals. The basic concept of structural capital in the networks is that connection between actors provides access to resources and information through the forms of access, timing, and referrals (Burt, 1992). Structural capitals concern the impersonal infrastructure of leakages between units or people (Salvatore, 2006). Governance or administrative integration infrastructure in establishing network partnerships refers to administrative structures (or responsibilities) created to facilitate communication, clear lines of authority, accountability, and responsibility for patient care services; to negotiate budgets and financial trade-offs; and to present a cohesive, consistent message in interactions with external agencies and the community (Evashwick , 1993; Alexander, Weiner, Succi, 2000; Toomey, 2000; Lozon and Vernon, 2002). Most importantly, it is for members with contractual agreements to manage participation (Conrad and Dowling, 1990), which could be viewed as the tool of structuring capitals of integrated networks. It could include the tasks of engaging and maintaining organizational members' interest in a shared vision and mission, providing appropriate structures and coordination mechanisms for the specified strategies, promoting constructive conflicts and managing destructive conflicts, implementing information systems to monitor the dynamics, adjusting the leadership in the overall membership, and so on (Lin, 2007). The possible indicators which could be proposed for the measures of structural social capitals among network members (partners) within a network, includes:

- Adhere to the rules established by the network
- Control the network plans and monitor goal achievements
- Design and employ network performance indicators
- Provide timely performance feedbacks for network members
- Regulate the availability of patient data
- Determine the principals of distributing gains
- Determine cooperation policy and principals
- Determine disintegration policy and principals
- Determine conflict resolution models
- Communicate business strategies among network members
- Establish fair coordination mechanisms
- Establish communication models and channels
- Understand the roles of network members
- Take care of all members' benefits on strategic planning
- Foster unified principals for individual members' development
- Understand the members' goals and strategies
- Develop compatible goals and strategies for network members
- Invest sufficient resources for the network development
- Establish coordination mechanisms for the entire network and for each individual member's development.

Relational capital. The relational domain of social capital is built upon the emotional relationships among the actors. It includes respect, trust, trustfulness, and friendliness (Granovetter, 1992; Salvatore, 2006), which were viewed as channels for the actors to access to the information, resources and supports. Meijboom et al. (2004) also mentioned that independent healthcare organizations seek cooperation through networks and develop relationships with each other in which trust plays an important role. And trust-based cooperation could enhance dependability and quality across the supply chains. The possible indicators which could be proposed for the measures of relational social capitals among network members (partners) within a network, includes:

- Offer assistance when partners have problems
- Share the risks when partners have problems
- Do not care about how much efforts are required when partners are experiencing problems
- Adjust contract contents to adapt to the environmental uncertainty in order to maintain reciprocal benefits
- Adjust contract contents to share the risks in order to maintain reciprocal benefits
- Offer beneficial information to the partners

- Provide the information in persons to partners
- Provide sufficient partnership cooperation documents to partners
- Share beneficial information with partners
- Share the information limited to the contract contents with partners
- Provide sufficient partnership cooperation information to partners
- Believe in partners that would comply with the contract policies
- Believe in the accuracy of information provided by partners
- Believe in that partners would provide the best assistance when needed
- Believe in that partners would care about your interests
- Believe in partners as honest partners
- Believe in that partners would have the commitments to you
- Update the information and distribute it to partners
- Inform any possible threats to partners
- Emphasize the information sharing among partner communication
- Emphasize the goal commitments among partner communication
- Share and communicate information very frequently with partners

Cognitive capital. The cognitive domain of social capital refers to the resources which share representations, interpretations and system meaning, which could refer as the norms, values and beliefs (Coleman, 1990; Salvatore, 2006). Organizational culture has been viewed as the factor for an organization to create the competency and adaptation in the competitive and changing environment (Cameron and Quinn, 1999). It guides an organization's employees to think, behave and react, reflecting the values and beliefs that shape employees' behavior. The possible indicators, which could be proposed for the measures of cognitive social capitals among network members (partners) within a network, include:

- Share the norms and values among members
- Share the common goals among members
- Understand the strategies among members
- Keep commitments when the demonstration project is terminated
- Exhibit high loyalties to members
- Select and identify priorities for existing members when the future cooperation is needed

IMPLICATION AND FUTURE

Not all network members possess the same amount of social capital among the network members. Gilson (2003) argued that funding arrangement, network member relationships, and inter-network dynamics within the health system would influence trusts between patients and providers (Meijboom et al., 2004). Mur-Veeman, van Raak, and Paulus (1999) argued that the government could play an important role on collaborative networks using the experience of Dutch government (Mur-Veeman, van Raak, and Paulus, 1999), through considering four contextual factors including financial arrangements and stimuli, innovation tradition (i.e., the extent the parties involved has internalized innovative values and behavior derived from the previous collaborative practices), network structure (i.e., the clear arrangement of the task divisions, responsibility, and accountability), and local situation (i.e., the structure, culture, and power-relations of network member and their direct environments).

We propose a multidimensional model of social capital and attempt to validate these domains empirically with the Taiwan's PCCN members. This research will guide us to identify possible opportunities among the network members and to understand the extent and nature of social relationships established by network members. We will empirically validate the conceptual domains of social capital from the structure, relational and cognitive perspectives and further verify their effects on patient care outcomes and organizational effectiveness. Ultimately, our research will yield fruitful results to enrich the body of knowledge on the determinants and consequences of social capitals at both individual and organizational levels.

REFERENCES

Ackerman, F. K. (1992). The movement toward vertically integrated regional health systems. *Health Care Manage Review, 17*(3), 81-88.

Aldrich H. E., and Zimmer, C. (1986). Entrepreneurship through social networks. In *The Art and Science of Entrepreneurship*. Edited by D. L. Sexton, and R. W. Smilor. Cambridge, MA: Ballinger Publishing, 3-23.

Aldrich, H. E., and Fiol, C. M. (1994). Fools rush in? The institutional context of industry creation. *Academy of Management Review, 19*, 645-670.

Alexander, J. A., Weiner, B. J., and Succi, M: (2000). Community accountability among hospitals affiliated with health care systems. *Milbank Q, 78*(2), 157-84, 149.

Alford, J. (1993). Toward a new public management model: beyond managerialism and its critics. *American Journal of Public Administration, 52*(2), 135-148.

Ashkenas, R. N., DeMonaco, L. J., and Francis, S. C. (1998). Making the deal real: how GE Capital integrates acquisitions. *Harvard Business Review, 76*(1), 165-170.

Baker, W. (1990). Market networks and corporate behavior. *American Journal of Sociology, 96*, 589-625.

Bamford, C. E., Bruton, G. D., and Hinson, Y. L. (2006). Founder/chief executive officer exit: a social capital perspective of new ventures. *Journal of Small Business Management, 44*(2), 207.

Belliveau, M. A., O'Reilly, C. A., and Wade, J. B. (1996). Social capital at the top: effects of social similarity and status on CEO compensation. *Academy of Management Journal, 39*(6), 1568-1593.

Berkman, L., and Glass, T. (2000). Social integration, social networks, social support and health. In L. Berkman, and I. Kawachi (eds). *Social Epidemiology*. New York: Oxford University Press. 137-173.

Berkman, L. F., and Kawachi, I. (2000). *Social Epidemiology*. London: Oxford University Press.

Brown, M., and McCool, B. P. (1986). Vertical integration: exploration of a popular strategic concept. *Health Care Manage Review, 11*(4), 7-19.

Burda, D. (1993). Study -- merger cut costs, services, increase profits. *Modern Healthcare,* *23*(46), 4.

Bureau of National Health Insurance in Taiwan [http://www.nhi.gov.tw/].

Burt, R. (2001). Structural holes versus network closure as social capital. In *Social Capital:* *Theory and Research.* Edited by N. Lin, K. S. Cook, R. Burt, N. Y. Hawthrone, and A. de Gruyter. 31-56.

Burt, R. S. (1992). *Structural holes.* Cambridge, MA: Harvard Business Press.

Burt, R. S. (2005). *Brokerage and closure: an introduction to social capital.* Oxford University Press.

Cahn, E. (1997). The co-production imperative. *Social Policy, 27*(3), 62-67.

Cameron, K. S., and Quinn, R. E. (2005). *Diagnosing and Changing Organizational Culture:* *Based on the Competing Values Framework.* The Jossey-Bass Business and Management Series.

Caplan, P. A., Lefkowitz, B., and Spector, L. (1992). Health care consortia: a mechanism for increasing access for the medically indigent. *Henry Ford Hospital Medical Journal,* *40*(1-2), 50-55.

Charns, M. P. (1997). Organization design of integrated delivery systems. *Hospital and* *Health Service Administration, 42*(3), 411-32.

Child, J. (1972). Organizational structure, environment and performance: The role of strategic choice. *Sociology, 6*(1), 1-22.

Clarke, S., and Rollo, M. (2001). Corporate initiatives in knowledge management. *Education* *and Training, 43*(4/5), 206.

Coddington, D. C., Moore, K. D., and Fischer, E. A. (1994). Costs and benefits of integrated healthcare systems. *Healthcare Financial Management, 48*(3), 20-24, 26, 28-29.

Cohen, D., and Prusak, L. (2001). In good company. In *How social capital makes* *organizations work.* Boston: Harvard Business School Press.

Coleman, J. S. (1988). Social capital in the creation of human capital. *American Journal of* *Sociology, 94,* S95-S120.

Coleman, J. S. (1990). *Foundations of Social Theory.* Cambridge, MA: Harvard Business Press.

Conrad, D. A, and Dowling, W. A. (1990). Vertical integration in health services: theory and management implications. *Health Care Management Review, 15*(4), 15-22.

Conrad, D. A. (1992). Vertical integration. In W. J. Duncan, P. Ginter, and L. Swayne (eds.) *Strategic Issues in Health Care: Point and Counterpoint.* Boston: PWS Kent.

Conrad, D. A., and Dowling, W. A. (1990). Vertical integration in health services: theory and management implications. *Health Care Management Review, 15*(4), 15-22.

Conrad, D. A., and Shortell, S. M. (1996). Integrated health systems: promise and performance. *Frontiers of Health Service Management, 13*(1), 3-40.

Cooke, P. (2007). Social capital, embedded ness, and market interactions: an analysis of firm performance in UK regions. *Review of Social Economy, 65*(1), 79.

Cooper, H., and Arber, S. et al. (1999). *The influence of social support and social capital on* *Health.* London: Health Education Authority.

De Carolis, D. M., and Saparito, P. (2006). Social capital, cognition, and entrepreneurial opportunities: a theoretical framework. *Entrepreneurship: Theory and Practice, 30*(1), 41.

Dranove, D. and Shanley, S. (1995). Cost reductions or reputation enhancement as motive for mergers: the logic of multihospital systems. *Strategic Management Journal, 16*(1), 55-74.

Eckersley, R., Dixon, J., and Douglas, R. (2001). *The Social Origins of Health and Well-being*. Cambridge: Cambridge University Press.

Ermann, D., and Gabel, J. (1984). Multi-hospital systems: issues and empirical findings. *Health Affairs, 3*(1), 51-64.

Evashwick, C. J. (1993). The continuum of long-term care. In *Introduction to Health Services*. Edited by Williams S J, Torrens PR. 4th edition. Chapter 7. Delmar Publishers Inc; 1993.

Findlay, S. (1993). How new alliances are changing health care? *Business and Health, 11*(12), 28-33.

Flora, J. (1998). Social capital and communities of place. *Rural Sociology, 63*, 481-506.

Florin, J., Lubatkin, M., and Schulze, W. (2003). A social capital model of high growth ventures. *Academy of Management Journal, 46*(3), 374-384.

Forbes, A., Wainwright, S. P. (2001). On the methodological, theoretical and philosophical context of health inequalities research: a critique. *Social Science Medicine, 53*, 801-816.

Fox, W. L. (1989). Vertical integration strategies: more promising than diversification. *Heath Care Manage Review, 14*(3), 49-56.

Friedman, L, and Goes, J. (2001). Why integrated health networks have failed? *Frontiers of Health Services Management, 17*(4), 3-28.

Friedman, B. A. (1998). Integrating laboratory processes into clinical processes, web-based laboratory reporting, and emergence of the virtual clinical laboratory. *Clinical Laboratory Management Review, 12*(5), 333-338.

Friedman, S. R., Mateu-Gelabert, P., Curtis, R., Maslow, C., Bolyard, M., Sandoval, M., and Flom, P. L. (2007). Social capital or networks, negotiations, and norms? A neighborhood case study. *Am. J. Prev. Med., 32*(6 Suppl), S160-70.

Galbraith, J. (1973). *Designing Complex Organizations*. Reading, MA: Addison-Wesley.

Gilchrist, A. (2006). Maintaining relationships is critical in network's success. *HealthcarePaper, 7*(2), 28-31.

Gilson, L. (2003). Trust and the development of health care as a social institution. *Social Science Medicine, 56*(7), 1453-68.

Gittell, R. A., and Vidal, A. (1998). *Community Organizing: Building Social Capital as a Developmental Strategy*. Thousand Oaks, CA: Sage.

Gold, R., Kennedy, B., Connell, F., and Kawachi, I. (2002). Teen births, income inequality, and social capital: developing an understanding of causal pathway. *Health and Place, 8*, 7-83.

Golden, B. R., Dukerich, J. M., and Fabian, F. H. (2000). The interpretation and resolution of resource allocation issues in professional organizations: a critical examination of the professional-manager dichotomy. *Journal of Management Studies, 37*(8), 1157-87.

Gorski, P. A. (2000). Caring relationships: an investment in health? *Public Health Rep, 115*, 144-150.

Granovetter, M. (1973). The strength of weak ties. *American Journal of Sociology, 78*, 1360-1380.

Granovetter, M. S. (1992). Problems of explanation in economic sociology. In *Networks and Organizations: Structure, Form, and Action*. Edited by N. Nohria, and R. Eccles. Boston: Harvard Business School Press, 29-56.

Greene, J. (1994). Merger monopolies. *Modern Healthcare, 24*(49), 38-48.

Greene, J. (1998) Coaching the entire team. Do you have what it takes to manage an integrated delivery system? *Healthcare Executive, 13*(1),16-19.

Halpern, M. T., Alexander, J. A., and Fennell, M. L. (1992). Multihospital system affiliation as a survival strategy for rural hospitals under the prospective payment system. *Journal of Rural Health, 8*(2), 93-105.

Hendryx, M. S., Ahern, M. M., Lovrich, N. P., and McCurdy, A. H. (2002). Access to health care and community social capital. *Health Services Research 37*(1), 87-103.

Herzlinger, R. E. (1998). The managerial revolution in the U.S. health care sector: lessons from the U.S. economy. *Health Care Management Review, 23*(3), 19-29.

Huerta, T. R., Casebeer, A., and VanderPlaat, M. (2006). Using networks to enhance health services delivery: perspectives, paradoxes and propositions. *HealthcarePapers, 7*(2), 10-26.

James, D. M. (1998). An integrated model for inner-city health-care delivery: the Deaconess Center. *Journal of the National Medical Association, 90*(1), 35-39.

Johnson, D. E. L. (1993). Integrated systems face major hurdles, regulations. *Health Care Strategic Management, 11*(10) 2-3.

Katz, G., Mitchell, A., and Markezin, E. (1982). *Ambulatory Care and Regionalization in Multi-Institutional Health Systems.* Chapter 1. p3-8, Aspen Systems Corporation.

Kawachi, I. (1999). Social capital and community effects on population and individual health. *Ann N Y Acad Sci, 896*, 120-30.

Kawachi, I., and Berkman, L. (2000). Social cohesion, social capital, and health. In L.F. Berkman, and I. Kawachi (eds.). *Social Epidemiology.* New York: Oxford University Press.

Kawachi, I., Kennedy, B. P., Lochner, K., and Prothro-Stith, D. (1997). Social capital, income equity, and mortality. *American Journal of Public Health 87*(9), 1491-1498.

Kennedy, B.P., Kawachi, I., Prothrow-Stith, D., Lochner, K., and Gupta, V. (1998). Social capital, income inequality, and firearm violent crime. *Social Science and Medicine 47*, 7-17.

Konrad, E. L. (1996). A multidimensional framework for conceptualizing human services integration initiatives. In J. M. Marquart and E. L. Konrad (1st Ed.). *Evaluating Initiatives to Integrate Human Services.* Jossey-Bass Inc.

Larson, A., and Starr, J. (1993). A network model of organization formation. *Entrepreneurship Theory and Practice, 17*, 5-15.

Lawrence, P. R., and Lorsch, J. W. (1967). *Organization and Environment.* Richard D. Irwin, Inc.

Lee, A., Kiyu, A., Milman, H. M., and Jimenez, J. (2007). Improving health and building human capital through an effective primary care system. *J. Urban. Health, 84*(3 Suppl), i75-85.

Lennartsson, C. (1999). Social ties and health among the very old in Sweden. *Res. Ageing, 21*, 657-681.

Liao, J., and Welsch, H. (2005). Roles pf social capital in venture creation: key dimensions and research implications. *Journal of Small Business Management, 43*(4), 345.

Lin, B.Y.J. (2007). Integration in primary community care networks (PCCNs): examination of governance, clinical, marketing, financial, and information infrastructures in a national demonstration project in Taiwan. *BMC Health Services Research, 7*, 90.

Lin, B.Y.J., and Wan, T.T.H. (1999). Integrated healthcare networks' performance: a contingency-strategy management perspective. *Journal of Medical Systems, 23*(6), 477-495.

Lin, N., and Dumin, M. (1986). Access to occupations through social ties. *Social Networks, 8,* 365-385.

Lochner, K. A., Kawachi, I., Brennan, R. T., and Buka, S. L. (2003). Social capital and neighborhood mortality rates in Chicago. *Social Science Medicine, 56*(8), 1797-805.

Longest, B. B. Jr (1998). Managerial competence at senior levels of integrated delivery systems. *Journal of Healthcare Management, 43*(2), 115-135.

Lozon, J. C., and Vernon, S. E. (2002). Governance as an instrument of successful organizational integration. *Hospital Quarterly, 6*(1), 68-71.

Lynch, J. R., and Mccue, M. J. (1990). The effects of for-profit multihospital system ownership on hospital financial and operating performance. *Health Services Management Research, 3*(3), 182-192.

Maycock, B. R., and Howat, P. (2007). Social capital: implications from an investigation of illegal anabolic steroid networks. *Health Educ. Res., 22*(6), 854-63.

Mechanic, D. (1998). Public trust and initiatives for new health care partnerships. *The Milbank Quarterly, 76*(2), 281-302.

Meijboom, B., de Haan, J., and Verheyen, P. (2004). Networks for integrated care provision: an economic approach based on opportunism and trust. *Health Policy, 69*(1), 33-43.

Menke, T. J. (1997). The effect of chain membership on hospital costs. *Health Services Research, 32*(2), 177-196.

Mullner, R. M., Rydman, R, J., Whiteis, D. G., and Rich, R. F. (1989). Rural community hospitals and factors correlated with their risk of closing. *Public Health Reports, 104*(4), 315-325.

Mur-Veeman, I., van Raak, A., and Paulus, A. Integrated care: the impact of governmental behaviour on collaborative networks. *Health Policy, 49*(3), 149-59.

Nahapient, J., and Ghoshal, S. (1998). Social capital, intellectual capital and the organizational advantage. *Academy of Management Review, 23,* 242-266.

Ostgaard, T. A., and Birley, S. (1994). Personal networks and firm competitive strategy: a strategic or coincidental match? *Journal of Business Venturing, 9,* 281-305.

Peters, G. (1991). Integrated delivery can ally physician and hospital planning. *Healthcare Financial Management, 45*(12), 21-28.

Pointer, D. D., Alexander, J. A., and Zuckerman, H. S. (1995). Loosing the Gordian Knot of governance in integrated healthcare delivery systems. *Frontiers of Health Services Management, 11*(3), 3-37.

Putnam, R. D. (2001). *Bowling Alone: the Collapse and Revival of American Community.* New York: Simon and Schuster.

Robinson, J. C. (1994). The changing boundaries of the American hospital. *The Milbank Quarterly, 72*(2), 259-275.

Robinson, J. C. (1996). The dynamics and limits of corporate growth in health care. *Health Affairs, 15*(2), 155-169.

Salvatore, D. (2006). Physician social capital: its sources, configuration, and usefulness. *Health Care Management Review, 31*(3), 213-222.

Sampsom, R. J., Raudenbush, S. W., et al. (1997). Neighborhoods and violent crime: a multilevel study of collective efficacy. *Science, 277*(5328), 918-924.

Scott, C., and Hofmeyer, A. (2007). Networks and social capital: a relational approach to primary healthcare reform. *Health Res. Policy Syst., 25*(5), 9.

Sherer, J. L. (1998). Are you marketing your integrated delivery system? *Health Executive, 13*(1), 10-15.

Shortell, S. M. (1988). The evolution of hospital systems: unfulfilled promises and self-fulfilling prophesies. *Medical Care Review, 45*(2), 177-214.

Shortell, S. M., Gillies, R. R., and Anderson, D. A. (1994). The new world of managed care: creating organized delivery system. *Health Affairs, 38*(4), 46-64.

SMG Market Group, Inc. (1998) *IHN (Integrated Healthcare Network) Top 100 Directory.* Chicago, IL.

Sterk, C. E., Elifson, K. W., and Theall, K. P. (2007). Individual action and community context: the Health Intervention Project. *Am. J. Prev. Med., 32*(6 Suppl), S177-81.

Szreter, S., and Woolcock, M. (2004). Health by association? Social capital, social theory, and the political economy of public health. *Int. J. Epidemiol., 33*(4), 650-67.

Tindall, D. B., and Wellman, B. (2002). Canada as social structure: social network analysis and Canadian sociology. *Canadian Journal of Sociology, 26*(3), 265.

Toomey, R. E: (2000). Integrated health care systems governance: prevention of illness and care for the sick and injured. *Health Care Management Review, 25*(1), 59-64.

Veenstra, G. (2002). Social capital and health. *Social Science and Medicine, 54*(6), 849-868.

Wan, T.T.H., and Lin, B.Y.J. (2003). Social Capital, Health Status, and Health Services Use among Older Women in Almaty, Kazakhstan. *Research in the Sociology of Health Care, 21,* 163-180.

Weitzman, E.R., and Kawachi, I. (2000). Giving means receiving: the protective effect of social capital on binge drinking on college campuses. *American Journal of Public Health, 90*(12), 1936-1939.

Woolcock, M. (1998). Social capital and economic development: toward a theoretical synthesis and policy framework. *Theory and Society, 27,* 151-208.

Woolcock, M. (2001). The place of social capital in understanding social and economic outcomes. *ISUMA, Canadian Journal of Policy Research, 2,* 11-17.

Yip W, Subramanian SV, Mitchell AD, Lee DT, Wang J, Kawachi I. (2007). Does social capital enhance health and well-being? Evidence from rural China. *Social Science Medicine, 64*(1), 35-49.

Zuckerman, H. (1979). Multi-institutional systems: their promise and performance. *Chicago: Hospital Research and Educational Trust.*

In: Integrated Health Care Delivers
Editor: Leonie A. Klein and Emily L. Neumann

ISBN 978-1-60456-851-6
© 2008 Nova Science Publishers, Inc.

Chapter 5

INTEGRATED CARE FOR PATIENTS WITH CHRONIC DISEASES

Mariëlle M. M. T. J. Ouwens[1], Rosella R. P. Hermens[1], Marlies M. E. Hulscher[1], Henri A. M. Marres[2], Richard P.[1] and Hub J. Wollersheim[1,3]

[1]Centre for Quality of Care Research,
Radboud University Nijmegen Medical Centre, The Netherlands
[2]Department of Otorhinolaryngology, Head and Neck Surgery,
Radboud University Nijmegen Medical Centre, The Netherlands
[3]Department of General Internal Medicine,
Radboud University Nijmegen Medical Centre, The Netherlands

ABSTRACT

Chronic diseases such as cancer, heart disease, stroke, arthritis, diabetes mellitus, mental illness and obstructive pulmonary diseases are now the leading causes of illness, disability and death. Meeting the complex needs of a growing group of patients with chronic diseases is one of the greatest challenges that health care faces today. New models of health care delivery are needed and integrated care programmes or disease management programmes have begun to receive greater support as approaches to improve quality of care for these groups of patients. This chapter shows that the aim of these programmes are usually very similar, namely to reduce fragmentation and improve continuity and coordination, but that the focus and content of the programmes differ widely. Based on these findings it is concluded that integrated care is based on five principles: patient-centredness, multidisciplinary care, coordination of care, evidence-based medicine and continuous quality improvement. The first three principles are considered as being the main principles of integrated care, the other two are general principles for delivering high quality of care. Interventions mentioned that sustain these principles focus on health care providers and/or the organization of care, while patient education had often been added. To improve integrated care, actual care should be measured and successful integrated care interventions should be implemented. In the presented examples on measuring and improving integrated care for patients with head and neck cancer and patients with lung cancer it is demonstrated that there is much room for improvement and that a multi-component programme can lead to relevant improvements.

INTRODUCTION

It is becoming increasingly complex to provide optimal health care. Fast-growing medical scientific knowledge is leading to more diagnostic procedures and treatment modalities. Furthermore, ageing of the population means larger proportions of people that have illnesses with high impact and a chronic course [1]. As a result, patient care has changed from individual consultation to multiprofessional teamwork and this usually involves many health care providers. Consequently, optimal collaboration and coordination between professionals in the delivery of integrated care have become essential requirements for the provision of high-quality care [2].

Health care improvement programmes at hospitals usually focus on isolated interventions, such as medication supply or multidisciplinary cooperation, rather than on the total care process of the patient [3]. These programmes offer only partial solutions for improving the continuity and coordination of the total care process. Integrated care programmes have begun to receive greater support as approaches to reduce fragmentation and to achieve improved results for patients at acceptable costs [4, 5]. These programmes may appear effective, but it is less evident which components or interventions should be included and how such programmes can be implemented successfully.

This chapter starts with a description of the integrated care concept followed by a paragraph on the development and evaluation of instruments to measure the principles of integrated care. When actual care is measured and it is known where there is room for improvement, care can be improved with an integrated care programme. A description is given of the implementation and evaluation of an integrated care programme to improve care for patients with head and neck cancer. The past paragraph concludes with some key-messages, a description of a so-called 'Tandem-Model for Integrated Care' and some implications for practice and research.

1. INTEGRATED CARE

The growing complexity of care should be supported by new ways of health care delivery that are patient-centred and not disease- or provider-centred. In the Netherlands [6-8] and in other countries [9-12] there are many examples of these new models of health care delivery called "coordinated care", "transmural care", "disease management" or "integrated care". This literature emphasizes the importance of organizing care around the needs and preferences, patients involving patients in their own care, and the importance of multidisciplinary care cooperation. There are several systematic reviews on effects of integrated care or disease management programmes for different groups of patients: patients with heart failure [13-17], patients with diabetes mellitus [18; 19], patients with rheumatoid arthritis, patients with cardiovascular disease [20], stroke patients [21], patients with chronic obstructive pulmonary diseases [22], patients with cancer [23] and patients with chronic illnesses in general [24, 25]. However, there is no clear picture of underlying principles of integrated health care delivery. We analyse the reviews mentioned above on principles, components and effectiveness of integrated care [26].

1.1. Principles of Integrated Care

There are three main principles of integrated care: patient-centredness, multidisciplinary care and coordination of care. These principles are clear and logical and should be combined with the important general principles for good quality of care namely ''evidence-based medicine'' and ''continuous quality improvement''. Evidence-based medicine is conscientious, explicit and judicious use of current best evidence in making decisions about the care of individual patients [27]. Continuous quality improvement means continuously assessing and improving care by collecting data on indicators and improving care where necessary [28]. Therefore, it is assumed that integrated care is based on five principles: patient-centredness, multidisciplinary care, coordination of care, evidence based medicine and continuous quality improvement, with the first three being the main principles of integrated care (Table 1).

These principles are also seen in theories on integrated care. The best known theory for the management of patients with chronic diseases is the chronic care model of Wagner and others [29-31]. The chronic care model (CCM) is a guide to higher-quality chronic illness management within primary care. The model is based on 6 interrelated components: self-management support, clinical information systems, delivery system redesign, decision support, health care organization, and community resources. Improvements within these components can produce a health care system in which informed, activated patients interact with prepared, proactive practice teams.

Table 1. Principles of integrated care

Patient-centredness:	Organizing the care around the preferences and needs of the patients and actively involve patients in their care
Multidisciplinary care:	Optimal collaboration of all professionals involved in the care for the patients
Coordinated care:	Reducing fragmentation by optimal organization of the total care process of patients
Evidence-based medicine:	Delivering care according the best available evidence in making decisions about the care of individual patients
Continuous quality improvement:	Continuously assessing and improving care by collecting data on indicators and improving care where necessary

Improvements to the CCM have been provided by the World Health Organization through the development of the Innovative Care for Chronic Conditions (ICCC) framework.(ref) Another theory is of the Disease Management Association of America (DMAA). (ref) They consider six components in a "full service" disease management programme, including 1) population identification processes, 2) evidence based practice guidelines or performance standards of care, 3) collaborative practice models to include physicians and support service providers, 4) patient self-management education, 5) process and outcome measurement and 6) routine reporting and/or feed-back. Another theory on improving quality and safety of care is on Clinical Microsystems. Mohr and Batalden state that an effective microsystem has eight characteristics: 1) integration of information, 2) measurement, 3) interdependence of the care team, 4) supportiveness of the larger system, 5) constancy of purpose, 6) connection to the community, 7) investment in improvement and 9) alignment of role and training [32]. These theories can be of use for high quality of integrated care for patients but show no clear picture how the principles of integrated care can be measured and improved in practice.

1.2. Components of Integrated Care Programmes

The term used most frequently to describe the management of patients with a chronic illness is disease management. Other terms are care management, case management, or the management of, for example, patients with diabetes [33]. Although the aims of the programmes are often very similar, namely to reduce fragmentation and improve continuity and coordination, the focus and content of the programmes differ widely. Components of the integrated care programmes focus on health care providers and/or the organization of care, while patient education is often added. Six components were explicitly mentioned in the form of definitions or as core components of the programmes [33] (Table 2). The most commonly mentioned component is self-management support and patient education. This intervention is often combined with structured clinical follow-up and case management by, for example, a specialized nurse. Other components often mentioned are a multidisciplinary patient care team and a systematic, evidence-based approach to care, for example, by using multidisciplinary clinical pathways. Feedback, reminders, and education that provide health care professionals with information regarding appropriate care for patients is also an important component. In addition to the six components mentioned above, several requirements or operational needs can be important for the successful implementation of integrated care programmes, namely: a supportive clinical information system; specialized clinics or centres; a shared mission on integrated care between the professionals involved; leaders with a clear vision of the importance of integrated care; finances for implementation and maintenance; management commitment and support; patients capable of and motivated for self-management; and a culture of quality improvement.

1.3. Effectiveness of Integrated Care Programmes

Reviews show that integrated care programmes can have positive effects on hospitalization rate, quality of life and process outcomes, as compliance and adherence to guidelines [33, 34]. However, these effects hardly reach significance. Effects on mortality remain unclear, and few systematic analyses are performed on the cost-effectiveness of integrated care programmes (Table 3).

Table 3 shows that functional health status is the most frequently reported effect outcome of the programmes. There is a positive trend, but only one of two studies that had performed meta-analyses showed a significant positive effect on this outcome. Seven of the 13 reviews mention effects on hospitalization.

Table 2. Description of components of integrated care programmes

Component	Description
Self-management support and patient education	Self-management support involves collaboratively helping patients and their families acquire the skills and knowledge to manage their own illness, providing self-management tools and routinely assessing problems and accomplishments. Education is giving the patients information (materials and/or instructions) regarding their condition and possible management.
Clinical follow-up	Follow-up is monitoring the patient after or during treatment on a close regular base. This is often done by a nurse case manager who uses a phone, mailings, or visits. Clinical follow-up can be seen as part of self-management support.
Case management	Case management is explicit allocation of coordination tasks to an appointed individual (a case manager) or a small team who may or may not be responsible for the direct provision of care. The case manager or team takes responsibility for guiding the patient through the complex care process in the most efficient, effective, and acceptable way.
Multidisciplinary patient-care team	A multidisciplinary patient-care team is composed of a group of professionals who communicate with each other regularly about the care of a defined group of patients and participate in that care.
Multidisciplinary clinical pathway	Clinical pathways or integrated care pathways are structured multidisciplinary care plans which detail essential steps in the care of patients with a specific clinical problem and describe the patient's expected clinical course. Clinical pathways should be derived from evidence-based guidelines translated into practice.
Feedback, reminders, and education for professionals	The aim of feedback, reminders, and education is to provide health care providers with information regarding appropriate care for patients. This information can come from clinical pathways, medical records, computerized databases, patients, or audits by colleagues. Feedback is given after the consultation; education is given before consultation; reminders are given before or during consultation.
Additional requirements	(i) Supportive clinical information system; (ii) specialized clinics or centres; (iii) shared mission on integrated care; (iv) leaders with a clear vision on integrated care; (v) finances for implementation and maintenance; (vi) management commitment and support; (vii) patients capable and motivated for self-management; (viii) culture of quality improvement.

They all show a decreasing trend in hospital readmission or length of stay, but this was only significant in three reviews. Effects on mortality had been assessed in six reviews, four times in a meta-analysis, but effects remained unclear. The only positive significant pooled effect on mortality is found in organized in-patient care for stroke: significant positive effects on death and dependency had been recorded at final follow-up and during institutionalized care. The only significant effect on process outcomes, such as provider monitoring, compliance, and adherence to guidelines, is found by Weingarten et al.

Table 3. Overview of trends in important outcomes of integrated care programmes

	Hospitali-zation	Mortality	Process outcomes[1]	Functional status and health outcomes	Patient satis-faction	Quality of life	Costs
Studies with only Descriptive analyses							
Ferguson, 1998 [24]				+	+	+	?
Moser, 2000 [14]	-			+	+		-
Norris, 2002 [35]			+	+			
Philbin, 1999 [15]	-			+	+	+	?
Renders, 2002 [19]			+	+			
Rich, 1999 [16]	-*	?	+	+	+	+	-
Windham, 2003 [17]	-	?	+	+		+	?
Studies with also *Meta analyses*							
Badamgarav, 2003 [36]				?			
McAlister, 2001 [13]	-*	?		+		+	-
McAlister, 2001 [20]	-*	?					-
Sin, 2003 [22]	?	?					
SUTC, 2001 [21]		-*					
Weingarten, 2002 [25]			+*	+*			

[1] Process outcomes as provider monitoring, compliance and adherence to guidelines
? = effect remains unclear
- = trend shows decrease (in more than half of the included studies)
+ = trend shows increase (in more than half of the included studies)
* = trend is significant

This is supported by all four descriptive reviews that also report on process outcomes. Patient satisfaction and quality of life is mentioned in, respectively, three and six reviews: the trend is positive but no significant effects are stated. In four of the seven reviews that performed economic analyses, there are suggestions of financial benefit, but these conclusions are based on a small number of studies included in the review and had not been based on a meta-analysis.

Appropriate measures

There are positive trends in effects of integrated care programmes [33, 34]. The most successful interventions were interventions that had the aim to improve information supply to patients and interventions regarding revision of tasks and responsibilities (follow-up and case management). Reported effects were mainly on outcomes regarding the process of integrated care and self-report measures as patient satisfaction and quality of life. Objective health outcome measures as mortality or morbidity are often not used and if used, there are hardly any positive effects. Mortality, and some other objective health outcomes, are probably not the appropriate measures to evaluate main effects of integrated care interventions. There are studies that show relations between better processes of care and mortality or tumour growth [37, 38]. However, better organization of care and a better-informed patient does not automatically lead to life extension for patients or a better quality of life. To evaluate integrated care interventions it is better to use outcomes closer to the care process. For example, giving patients an audiotape of their consultation has the intention to improve their recall of information. In all studies using the audiotape for patients, the outcome "recall of information" improved significantly after the intervention. For integrated care programmes it might be useful to evaluate expected improvements in the performance of important process measures as for example "recall of information".

2. How to Measure Integrated Care?

Literature indicates that there is a lack of information about how major illnesses are treated, a lack of systematic outcome assessment and persisting variations among providers in care for similar patients [39, 40]. For most diseases, potential quality problems and their prevalence and incidence are unknown in many countries [41]. To improve the quality of integrated care for patients, the current performance needs to be reliably assessed and effective approaches to improve and change practice performance need to be identified [42] .Measuring integrated care should not be just one step in improving care. Continuous monitoring with review criteria or quality indicators, is required for lasting quality improvements.

2.1. Indicators: Typology, Development and Practice Test Typology

Assessing the quality of integrated care is not straightforward, and selecting appropriate indicators to assess integrated care is difficult. Quality indicators are "measurable elements of practice performance for which there is evidence or consensus that they can be used to assess the quality of care" [43]. Evidence-based guidelines and literature on effective integrated care interventions both provide recommendations for good-quality integrated care. When scientific evidence is lacking, the recommendations can come from an expert panel of health professionals in a consensus process based on their experience. To measure the quality of integrated care, these recommendations need to be translated into quality indicators. Indicators can be related to structure, process or outcome of health care [44]. Structural indicators focus on organizational aspects of service provision.

Table 4. Examples of indicators

Structure indicators	Availability of a multidisciplinary team Number of pulmonologists per 1000 patients
Process indicators	Waiting times Guideline adherence Referral rates
Outcome indicators	Hospital re-admission rates Heath related quality of life Mortality

Process indicators focus on the actual care delivered to and negotiated with the patients as well as communication with the patient. Outcome indicators specify the ultimate goal of the care given and can relate either to health status or patient evaluations of care (Table 4).

Development

Practical examples of indicator development procedures are scarce. There are some initiatives for the development of cancer quality indicators [45-47] but valid sets of indicators to measure the quality of integrated care in general and for patients with head and neck cancer and lung cancer in particular are lacking.

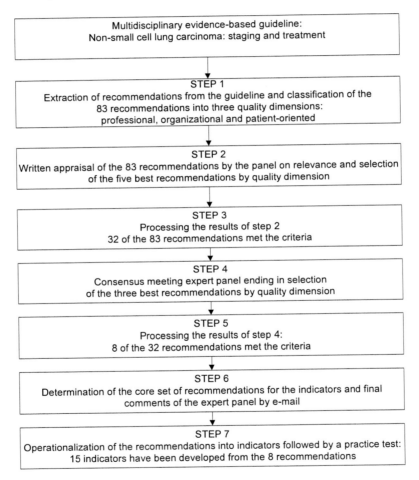

Figure 1. Example of the process of indicator development.

We performed two studies on indicator development for patients with cancer, to assess the quality of integrated care: one study on patient with head and neck cancer [48] and one on patients with lung cancer [49]. These studies showed that a systematic development and testing procedure is needed. The procedures in both studies were roughly the same including the following steps: extraction of the recommendations from evidence-based guidelines and structure indicators for integrated care from literature; written appraisal of the recommendations on health benefit, continuity of care and patient-centredness, by an expert panel; feedback and formal consensus in a face-to-face panel meeting; translation of the recommendations into indicators followed by a practice test (see Figure 1). In both studies we experimented with methods for involving patients and patient representatives in the process of indicator development. This is extremely important to guarantee patient-centredness of care because literature shows that professionals and patient have different opinions about good quality of care [50].

Practice Test

Before use it is important to subject a set of indicators to a practice test in which is measurable if the data needed to fill the indicator can be collected by searching medical records or by means of a patient survey. Indicators must be capable of detecting changes in the quality of care. If indicator performance is already high, there is little room for improvement. When the range between the lowest and highest hospital scores is broad, an indicator has discriminating potential. An indicator is more successful for quality improvement if it is applicable to a large proportion of patients; we refer to this as "feasibility". The most successful indicators for quality improvement are indicators that are measurable, have potential for improvement, have a broad range between practices, and are applicable to a large part of the population.

Table 5. Indicators for NSCLC and some clinimetric characteristics

	Quality Indicator	Adherence (range)	Improvement potentional	Applicablity
	Professional Quality (n= 276)			
1	Number of patients with surgery that had beforehand a FDG-PET before mediastinoscopy (58) Total number of patients with surgery (66)	88% (83-100%)	12%	24%
2	Number of patients that had a cervical mediastinoscopy according the criteria in the guideline (219) Total number of patients (260)	84% (68-100%)	16%	94%
3	Number of patients that had a cervical mediastinoscopy and biopsies of at least 4 of the 6 accessible lymph node stations (24) Total number of patients with cervical mediastinoscopy (48)	50% (0-71%)	50%	17%
4	Number of patient with clinical stage III NSCLC that had a skeletal scinitigraphy and a CT or MRI of the brain before the start of the combination therapy (1) Total number of patients with clinical stage III NSCLC that had combination therapy (29)	3% (0-20%)	97%	11%
5	Number of patients with locally advanced NSCLC and WHO performance status 0 or 1 that is treated with combination therapy Total number of patients with locally advanced NSCLC and WHO performance 0 or 1	NOT MEASURABLE		
	Organisational Quality (n=276)			
1	Number of patients that went through the diagnostic trajectory within 21 calendar days as from the first visist to the pulmonologist (chest CTscan, bronchoscopy, FDG-PET) (189) Total number of patients that had diagnostic procedures (239)	79% (71-84%)	21%	87%

Table 5. (Continued)

	Quality Indicator	Adherence (range)	Improvement potentional	Applicablity
2	Number of patients that started therapy within 35 calendar days as from the first visit to the pulmonolgist (80) Total number of patients that started therapy (157)	51% (38-66%)	49%	57%
3	Number of patients with lungcancer discussed in mulltidisciplinary consultation (156)[d] Total number of patients with lungcancer (276)	57% (26-91%)	43%	100%
	Patient oriented Quality (n=100)			
1	Number of patients with NSCLC that say that attention has been paid to physical symptoms as pain, suffocation, nausea, fatigue, weight loss and insomnia (52) Total number of patients with NSCLC (89)	58% (25-78%)	42%	89%
2	Number of patients with NSCLC that say to be asked for pscychosocial stress factors and psychological symptoms (28) Total number of patients with NSCLC (83)	34% (18-60%)	66%	83%
3	Number of patients with NSCLC that say to be asked for problems in living conditions as psychosocial problems in family and problems at work (31) Total number of patients with NSCLC (85)	36% (23-60%)	64%	85%
4	Number of patients with NSCLC that had need for psychosocial care from trained providers and received that care (11) Total number of patients with NSCLC that had need on psychosocial care from trained providers (28)	39% (0-100%)	61%	28%
5	Number of patients with NSCLC that say to be treated adequately (97) Total number of patients with NSCLC (99)	98% (96-100%)	2%	99%
6	Number of patients with NSCLC that say to be informed on the existence of a (lung) oncology nurse (49) Total number of patients with NSCLC (93)	53% (33-86%)	47%	93%
7	Number of patients with NSCLC that say to be informed adequately on all 10 aspects (18) Total number of patients with NSCLC (95)	19% (17-57%)	81%	95%

Table 5 shows some pyschometric characteristics of the set of 15 indicators for patients with lung cancer. One indicator proved to be not measurable namely "number of patients with locally advanced NSCLC and performance status 0 or 1 who were treated with combination therapy". Professionals wrote down the performance status (WHO or Karnofsky) in only 9% of the cases. All but one indicator has an improvement potential of more than 10%; eleven indicators have a range of 20% or more in scores on the quality indicator and nine indicators are applicable on 75% of the study population. Seven of the 15 indicators fulfil all four psychometric criteria (Table 5 in bold) and are therefore the most suitable for quality improvement.

Process Versus Outcome Indicators

By following the development and test procedures for indicators as described above, a final set of indicators will include many so-called "structure indicators" (e.g. the availability of a multiprofessional team) and indicators regarding the "process of care" (e.g. number of biopsies taken). This phenomenon has also been identified in similar selection procedures for indicators in family practices and gynaecological practices in the Netherlands [53]. Outcome indicators do not originate from study procedures based on guideles, so adding a set of outcome indicators, such as mortality, morbidity, quality of life or patient satisfaction could be considered.

Insurers, policy makers and consumers are usually more interested in outcome measures. However, outcome measures have main disadvantages: they usually have low incidence or prevalence, are often delayed, are difficult to control (e.g. also influenced by lifestyle choices of patients, compliance, health status) or are heavily confounded by for example disease stage [54]. To take mortality as an outcome measure for the effectiveness of the integrated care programmes would be difficult. In contrast with health outcomes, process measures tend to be frequent, immediate, controllable and less likely to be confounded by other factors [43, 55]. That is the reason why process indicators are generally more useful for quality improvement research. A commonly raised criticism of the measurement of process indicators is related to the assumption that a difference in the process represents an important difference in health outcomes. For the reasons mentioned, it is difficult for researchers of quality improvement at organizational level to prove this link between process and outcome at the patient level.

"Living" Indicators

Low scores on an indicator do not automatically mean that there is a problem in the quality of care. Low scores are signals to further explore the situation. For example the study presented in table 5 shows lower scores than to be expected on the indicator "cervical mediastinoscopy according the guideline criteria". A further analysis of the cases that deviated from the guideline criteria showed that the main reason not to perform a mediastinoscopy was the use of alternative forms for staging of the mediastinum (TBNA or EUS-FNA). However, because of their very recent appearance, these techniques have not yet been incorporated into the guidelines on which the indicators were based. The score on the indicator "mediastinocopy according guideline criteria" is a good example of the fact that indicators as well as guidelines should be periodically updated. They should become "living indicators" which are ideally continuously being updated as soon as new evidence demands a change of recommendations.

2.2. Measuring Principles of Integrated

The heart of delivering high-quality integrated care is a prepared, well-functioning multidisciplinary team interacting with a pro-active patient [56]. To measure these principles of patient-centredness and multidisciplinary cooperation, specific indicators or instruments are needed.

2.2.1. Patient-Centredness

Patient-centredness means that care is organized around the physical, social, and emotional needs and preferences of patients (patient perspective style), and that patients are actively involved in their own care (patient activation style) [57, 58]. Important patient outcomes, such as satisfaction, physical health and well-being, and quality of life are related to the patient-centred approach [58, 59]. The 'patient perspective' style is associated with improved patient satisfaction and the 'patient activation' style is more closely associated with better physical health outcomes [57, 58].

Patient-Centred Cancer Care

The first step in improving the quality of patient-centredness of cancer care is to reliably assess current practice [42]. Most evidence-based guidelines on cancer care provide some recommendations for good quality of patient-centredness. The available recommendations from these guidelines should be combined with opinions of the patients themselves to assess additional aspects for which evidence alone is insufficient or absent. To measure patient-centredness, "patient-centred"- recommendations in these guidelines and recommendations from patients need to be translated into quality indicators.

In one of our studies we developed a set of 56 indicators divided into eight dimensions of care to measure patient-centredness and tested these in a group of 132 patients with lung cancer [60]. There were eight domains of patient-centredness: "access", "follow-up", "communication and respect", "patient and family involvement", "information", "coordination", "physical support", and "emotional and psychosocial support" (Table 6).

Table 6. Scores on patient-centredness of care for patients with lung cancer

Domains of patient-centred cancer care (total n = 100)	Mean Score
1. ACCESS (4 indicators)	68%
2. FOLLOW-UP (9 indicators)	81%
3. COMMUNICATION AND RESPECT (7 indicators)	95%
4. PATIENT AND FAMILY INVOLVEMENT (8 indicators)	84%
5. INFORMATION (5 indicators)	68%
6. COORDINATION (13 indicators) specialists specialized nurse(s) paramedics	87% 55% 70%
7. PHYSICAL SUPPORT (3 indicators)	58%
8. EMOTIONAL AND PSYCHOSOCIAL SUPPORT (7 indicators)	46%

The highest score was found within the domains "communication and respect" (mean score of 95%), followed by the domain "patient and family involvement" (mean score of 84%). Most room for improvement was found within the domains "physical support", "emotional and psychosocial support", and "information".

Patient-Centredness and Evidence-Based Medicine

Two principles of integrated care, patient-centredness and evidence-based medicine, might conflict. Evidence-based medicine combines individual clinical expertise and external scientific evidence, offering clinicians the best available evidence about the most adequate treatment for their patients [27]. However, evidence-based medicine is disease-oriented, and not patient-oriented; the best performance in concrete conditions is presented for "all patients". The recommendations are mostly based on randomized controlled trials (RCTs). RCTs are performed under experimental (read artificial) conditions, while the results should also be applicable to "real-life-patients" who may not fulfil the inclusion criteria for participation in the study. Clinical evidence is derived from scientific research on populations and mostly not from patient's unique knowledge and experiences, neither from patients' individual needs and preferences [61]. It is argued that evidence-based medicine is essentially a doctor-centred approach, as it focuses on the doctor's interpretation of evidence and ignores the importance of human relationships and the role of the patient. Sweeney made a plea for a third dimension in clinical decision making; beyond the statistical significance based on randomized clinical trials and clinical relevance that relies on doctor's intuition and experience, he added personal significance from the individual patient as the third complementary source of useful information [62].

To solve the paradox between the principles of evidence-based medicine and patient-centredness, more recommendations regarding patient-centredness should be included in the guidelines, patients should be involved in the process of the development of guidelines and indicators, and professionals should make evidence-based medicine patient-centred by combining best evidence with their individual clinical expertise and the needs and preferences of patients.

2.2.2. Multidisciplinary care

Multidisciplinary cooperation and team functioning are important for delivering high-quality integrated care [63]. Care is given by various physicians, nurses and other health care professionals. Most have a different background of knowledge and skills and they often work in different departments or organizations. Team functioning is not only determined by structural determinants such as workload, team size, or team composition, but also by team processes [64, 65]. Literature shows that a climate in which team members are encouraged to develop and implement new ideas can lead to better health care and health outcomes [66, 67].

Team Climate Inventory

The most studied model for team climate is the model of West [68]. This theoretical model led to the development of a questionnaire to measure team climate, the Team Climate Inventory (TCI) [69]. The 44-item TCI includes four scales, "vision", "participative safety", "task orientation", and "support for innovation" and 13 subscales (Figure 2). The questionnaire includes a fifth scale that was designed to detect socially desirable answers. The TCI has been translated into several languages including Norwegian [70], Swedish [71], Finnish [72], Italian [73], and German [74], and it has been tested on many different teams (e.g. management, social services, psychiatric, oil company, industrial, and primary care teams).

Given this utilization of the TCI-tool in multiple countries and industries, it may become a helpful vehicle in the translation of learning among countries and industries. However, none of these studies tested the questionnaire specifically for hospital teams. We translated the TCI in Dutch and tested the validity, reliability and discriminating capacity in a sample of 36 hospital teams (22 nursing teams and 14 multidisciplinary quality improvement teams) [75]. Our study showed that the TCI is a valid, reliable and discriminating self-report measure of team climate in hospital teams.

Scales
(Factors)

Sub-scales

Items
(questions and their number)

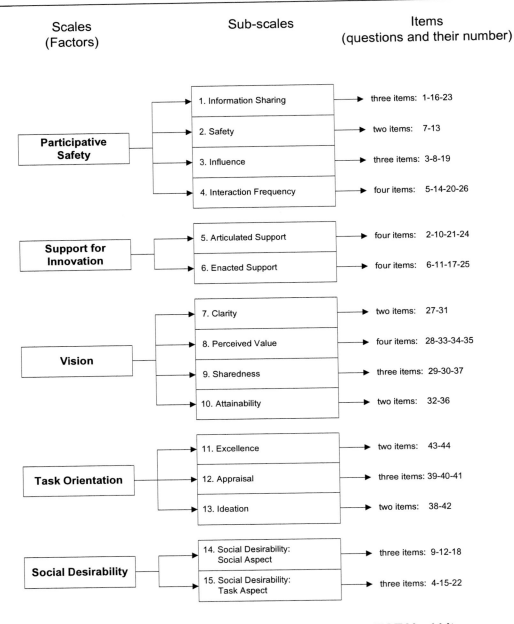

Figure 2. The Original Structure of the 44-item Team Climate Inventory.

Use of the TCI

The TCI has been used as an improvement tool for assessing team function to identify areas that could be improved. In addition, it has been used in research as an outcome measure of quality-improvement strategies or to predict the success or failure of such a strategy.

Example 1

Improving multidisciplinary team working in care for patients with head and neck cancer [76].

The management of care for patients with head and neck cancer is very complex. This type of cancer has a very significant impact on patients because of the location of the tumour, and needs to be managed by different disciplines in a multimodal treatment. The multidisciplinary team (MDT) plays a crucial role in delivering high-quality of care for this group of patients. The assessment of the team climate of the MDT using the TCI, showed overall high scores (74%) but also room for improvement regarding "information sharing", "safety of team members", and "task orientation". After some improvements, e.g. "adding extra experts to the team" and "redefining tasks and goals", the TCI scores improved with 11%.

Example 2

Evaluating the effect of three forms of multidisciplinary team (MDT) care in stroke rehabilitation [77].

The TCI was used in this study to evaluate the effect of three forms of MDT care: a standard weekly MDT meeting using a standard form for documentation; a standard weekly MDT meeting using a newly devised form to enhance the documentation of patients' needs, their goals and their involvement with their rehabilitation; a weekly MDT ward round including the doctor and patients' relatives. The TCI was applied to find out whether the different forms of MDT care resulted in improved team working. The MDT ward rounds not only resulted in significantly better consideration of patients' needs and greater patient involvement. It was also shown that this form of MDT care resulted in improved team working (measured using the TCI) compared to MDT meetings alone.

3. HOW TO IMPROVE INTEGRATED CARE?

Integrated care can be improved for patients with chronic illnesses in general and for patients with cancer in particular [78-80]. To improve integrated care for patients both, interventions are needed that sustain the main principles of integrated care (patient-centredness, multidisciplinary care and coordination of care) and a systematic approach for implementation of these interventions. According to Grol and others [42, 81] the following steps should be taken for implementation of change in clinical practice: get insight into actual care by developing indicators and measuring care with them; analyze barriers and facilitators (what are the problems in care provision and what factors are stimulating or hampering the process of improvement); develop and implement an improvement programme and finally, continuously monitor care on basis of indicators.

3.1. Multi-component Improvement Programme

Integrated care for patients with head and neck cancer was implemented based on literature about effective integrated care interventions, the actual care measurement in one centre for patients with head and neck cancer and the barriers to perform integrated care in this centre. The multi-component improvement programme to implement integrated care for patients with head and neck cancer consisted of interventions covering all principles of integrated care and targeting at patients, professionals and the organization of care and some requirements for integrated care.

Head and Neck Cancer

The management of care for patients with head and neck cancer is very complex because this cancer affects patients significantly because of the location of the tumour and patients often have problems with speech, eating and physical appearance due to treatment effects. Besides, as head and neck cancers are heterogeneous and occur at various sites, they need to be managed via various disciplines in multimodal treatment. The care for head and neck cancer varies widely, and many hospitals cannot guarantee high quality in all three quality dimensions of care, namely patient-oriented quality, organizational quality, and medical-technical quality [82]. Implementation of integrated care is crucial for optimizing care and outcomes. Integrated care is implemented in a clinic for head and neck oncology at the Radboud University Nijmegen Medical Centre (RUNMC) in the Netherlands. The care before and after implementation of the integrated care programme is assessed with a set of 20 indicators that were developed in a previous study [83].

Integrated Care Programme

The integrated care programme for improving the care for patients with head and neck cancer at the RUNMC is based on the actual care as assessed with a validated set of indicators [84], national measurements of barriers during diagnoses and treatment in all head and neck reference clinics, interviews about barriers and facilitators for improving the care with all the professionals involved in the RUNMC, and two systematic reviews on effective integrated care interventions [23, 85]. These assessments showed that waiting times for diagnostic procedures and for the start of treatment, information supply and lifestyle support for patients, and support from allied health professionals could all be improved. Some requirements for the delivery of integrated care were not, or not adequately available such as integrated care pathways, head and neck specialist nurses for case management tasks, and a clinical leader with specific tasks regarding the management of the group of patients with head and neck cancer. On basis of the information mentioned above, developed an integrated care programme is developed that consisted of interventions covering the three quality dimensions of care: patient-oriented quality, organizational quality, and medical-technical quality. Some requirements for integrated care were added to the programme. Table 7 shows an overview of the components of the integrated care programme.

Improvements

The implementation of the integrated care programme for patients with head and neck cancer showed relevant improvements. The study showed positive results on offering support for patients with alcohol (+21% improvement) and smoking problems (+37%), availability and support of case managers (+37%), diagnostic procedures within 10 days (+37%), starting therapy within 30 days (+25%), nutrition support (+44%) and functioning of the multidisciplinary team (+11%). The implementation of integrated care for patients with head and neck cancer showed that a multi-component integrated care programme can improve several aspects of the management of patients with head and neck cancer.

Table 7. The components of the integrated care programme

Quality dimensions	Components
Patient-oriented quality	Patient information record with information about relevant issues
	Specialty nurses who gave extra support for stopping smoking and reducing alcohol consumption
Organizational quality	Optimalization of the diagnostic process (intake day, arrangements about numbers of procedures needed) recorded in a clinical pathway and a checklist
Medical–technical quality	Monitoring of weight change and nutrition by a dietician
	Meetings for physicians, nurses, and allied health professionals about specific topics in the care for patients with head and neck cancer
	Extra radiologists specializing in head and neck cancer
Integrated care requirements	Multidisciplinary patient care team
	Specialist nurses acting as casemanagers
	Integrated care pathways
	Clinical leader

3.2. The tandem-model for integrated care

Based on literature studies and own practice research on assessing and improving care for patients with cancer, we suggest a comprehensive model for integrated care, the so-called "Tandem-Model for Integrated Care" (Figure 3).

The model is based on the five principles of integrated care (see table 1):

- *Patient-centredness* relates to the *Patient*
- *Multidisciplinary care* relates to *Professionals and Processes*
- *Evidence-based medicine* relates to *Professionals*
- *Coordination of care* relates to *Processes*
- *Continuous quality improvement* relates to *Assessing and Improving care*

Patients

Integrated care is based on the needs and preferences of the patient. The key to successful doctor-patient partnerships is recognizing that patients are experts too. Emphasis lays on shared information, shared evaluation, shared decision-making and shared responsibilities [67]. Patients have different preferences for involvement and not all are able or willing to play an active role. Health professionals should be sensitive to individual patients' preferences to provide better patient-centred care [68].

Professionals

Integrated care is multidisciplinary organized. Most clinical professionals have specific expertise in a small field of science. To deliver optimal care, health care professionals should broaden their focus to optimal multidisciplinary cooperation with all professionals involved in the care for patients [69].

Professionals should make evidence-based medicine patient-centred by combining best evidence with their individual clinical expertise and the needs and preferences of patients.

Processes

Integrated care is based on an optimal organization of care processes in which fragmentation of care is minimalized. Care processes of patients are based on evidence-based guidelines and written down in integrated care pathways [70,71].

Assessing and Improving care

To improve patient care a process is needed of continuous assessment of actual care with a balanced set of indicators on three dimensions of quality of care (patient-oriented quality, professional or medical-technical quality and organizational quality). Indicators should be systematically developed and tested and based on evidence or expert opinions of professionals and patients.

Figure 3. The Tandem-model for Integrated Care.

Insight in determinants of variation in actual care is needed to target the improvement strategy. Integrated care can be improved with a multi-component improvement programme that consists of interventions targeting at patients, professionals and the organization of care.

High-quality integrated care can be reached if the patient and the professionals work in tandem with each other. Together on a tandem they reach more than on single bikes. Processes should be optimally organized to support the patient and the professionals. Integrated care is the necessary connection between the patient, the professionals and the processes to obtain the best possible care by continuously assessing and improving actual performance.

4. CONCLUSION

The focus of this chapter was to describe studies in which principles of integrated patient care were explored, and in which was searched for instruments and interventions to measure and improve integrated care, particularly for patients with cancer. The studies led to some key messages.

4.1. Key Messages

Principles of Integrated Care

- Basic principles of integrated care are: care is organized around the needs and preferences of patients, and patients are actively involved in their care (patient-centredness); care is given in optimal collaboration of all professionals involved (multidisciplinary care); and care is seamless and continuous, by optimal coordination of the total care process of the patients (coordinated care).
- Integrated care for patients with chronic diseases can be maintained by a number of interventions: patient self-management support and information, arrangements about clinical follow-up, case management, introduction of a multidisciplinary patient-care team and a systematic evidence-based approach to change processes of care, for example by using clinical pathways. Additional requirements are: a supportive clinical information system, a shared mission on integrated care and leaders who express a clear vision on integrated care.
- The most promising interventions to improve integrated care for patients with cancer are: "audiotaped consultation for patients", "information to patients", "decision aids for patients", "follow-up by nurses or general practitioner", "case management" and "one-stop clinics". These promising interventions should be part of integrated care programmes and should be evaluated using rigorous methods and unequivocal outcome measures linked to the intervention.

Assessing and Improving the Quality of Integrated Care for Patients with Cancer

- Using clinical indicators for assessment of the quality of care is important for delivering high-quality integrated care, as this is the basis for continuous improvement of care. Clinical indicators must be developed and tested with scientific rigour in a transparent process. To get a balanced set of indicators, three dimensions of quality of care should be addressed: patient-oriented quality (support and information for the patient), professional or medical-technical quality (right diagnosis and treatment for effective and safe care) and organizational quality (continuity and coordination of care to enable efficient care).
- Professionals and patients sometimes have different opinions about good quality of care. Including the opinions of patients in the development process for indicators can

make a difference, especially for items like lifestyle support, information supply and the wish for 1-day screening.

- Indicators play an important role in the process of quality improvement. A low score on an indicator does not automatically mean that there is a problem in the quality of care, but is a signal to further explore the situation. Low scores can be signals that care should be improved, but also that there is new evidence that demands changed recommendations. Indicators as well as guidelines should be periodically updated to have "living" indicators, which are ideally continuously being updated as soon as new evidence is available.
- There is much room for improving the quality of care for patients with cancer, on all quality dimensions (patient-oriented quality, professional or medical-technical quality and organizational quality), and regarding additional requirements for integrated care (e.g. multidisciplinary team, case managers, clinical pathways, clinical leader and clinical information system).
- Integrated care for patients with head and neck cancer can be improved with a multi-component improvement programme. This programme should consist of interventions targeting at patients, professionals and the organization of care.

4.2. Implications for Practice and Research

A variety of recommendations can be derived from the different studies described in this chapter. The recommendations are classified into three themes: requirements for integrated care, assessing integrated care, improving integrated care. This paragraph ends with some recommendations specific for further research.

Requirements for Integrated Care
- Professionals need each other to provide optimal multidisciplinary care and they are thus compelled to establish collaborative relationships, beyond the boundaries of their own department or health care system and in spite of the financial, structural barriers and the stimulated competition between health care providers. To promote integrated care governments should take consistent policy measures (financial stimuli and legislative measures) to create facilitating forces for collaboration.
- Case managers may play an important role in delivering high-quality integrated care especially concerning the coordination of care and psychosocial and lifestyle support. The use of case managers should be (financially) supported and the background, tasks and responsibilities of case managers should be further investigated.
- The barrier for good team functioning mentioned most by professionals in our studies was not getting enough or the right information from colleagues. Information and communication technology should facilitate multidisciplinary discussion meetings, patient follow-up, and continuous quality improvement. Data should easily be retrieved across systems or sites of care for example by means of an electronic patient file.
- A more patient-centred approach is positively related to patient outcomes such as satisfaction, physical health and well-being. We strongly recommend that specific

domains for patient-centredness that should always be addressed in clinical guidelines for the management of patients with cancer. If evidence is insufficient or absent, these recommendations should be based on the expert opinions of patients and professionals.

Assessing Integrated Care

- Professionals, represented in professional societies, should take the lead in assuring appropriate assessment of the quality of care by taking care of the development of valid and reliable indicators.
- To facilitate the process of indicator development we suggest that the guideline developers also go through the process of indicator development, and that a set of indicators is a fixed part of clinical guidelines.
- Low scores on an indicator do not automatically mean that there is a problem in the quality of care. Low scores are signals to further explore the situation.
- Indicators, just as guidelines, should be periodically updated.

Improving Integrated Care

- Integrated care for patients with cancer can be improved especially regarding patient-centredness. The impact of cancer and its symptoms on the patient's psychological, social, and physical state should be identified early, and patients should be referred to the appropriate specialist for further assessment, if needed.
- From the patient's point of view, long waiting times for diagnosis and treatment are unacceptable. Our study showed that an integrated care programme focussed on reducing waiting times could be successful. So effort should be made to implement this programme for all patients with cancer.

Implications for Further Research

- Research has shown the efficacy of some interventions of integrated care programmes; more research should be performed to evaluate the efficacy of multi-component integrated care programmes that consist of interventions covering all principles of integrated care: patient-centredness, organization of care, multidisciplinary cooperation, evidence based medicine and continuous quality improvement. A cluster-randomized trial would be an appropriate approach.
- Research on the cost-effectiveness of integrated care interventions is very limited and further research should be done in this area.
- The optimal procedure for the development of clinical indicators needs to be explored further. Questions to be answered are related to composition and size of the expert panel and methods for including patient's opinions.

REFERENCES

[1]   I.o.M.Committee on Quality of Health Care in America, Crossing the Quality Chasm: *A New Health System for the 21st Century*, National Academy Press, Washington, 2001.

[2]   S.Glouberman, H.Mintzberg, Managing the care of health and the cure of disease--Part II: *Integration Health Care Manage. Rev.* 26, (2001) 70-84.

[3]   R.Grol, Between evidence-based practice and total quality management: the implementation of cost-effective care. *Int. J. Qual. Health Care* 12, (2000) 297-304.

[4]   K.Kesteloot, Disease management. A new technology in need of critical assessment. *Int. J. Technol. Assess. Health Care* 15, (1999) 506-519.

[5]   V.Villagra, Strategies to control costs and quality - A focus on outcomes research for disease management. *Medical Care* 42, (2004) 24-30.

[6]   H.Rosendal, W.T.van Beekum, P.Nijhof, L.P.de Witte, A.J.Schrijvers, Can shared care deliver better outcomes for patients undergoing total hip replacement? A prospective assessment of patient outcomes and associated service use. *Int. J. Integr. Care* 1, (2000) e10.

[7]   H.Rosendal, C.A.Wolters, G.H.Beusmans, L.P.de Witte, J.Boiten, H.F.Crebolder, Stroke service in The Netherlands: an exploratory study on effectiveness, patient satisfaction and utilisation of healthcare. *Int. J. Integr. Care* 2, (2002) e17.

[8]   L.Steuten, v.G.Merode, Participation of general practitioiners in disease management: experiences from the Netherlands International Journal of Integrated Care 2, (2002) 1-8.

[9]   T.Bodenheimer, Disease management--promises and pitfalls 7. *N. Engl. J. Med.* 340, (1999) 1202-1205.

[10]   D.J.Hunter, G.Fairfield, Disease management 3. *BMJ* 315, (1997) 50-53.

[11]   I. Mur-Veeman, B.Hardy, M.Steenbergen, G.Wistow, Development of integrated care in England and the Netherlands: managing across public-private boundaries. *Health Policy* 65, (2003) 227-241.

[12]   T.Richards, Disease management in Europe 7. *BMJ* 317, (1998) 426-427.

[13]   F.A.McAlister, F.M.Lawson, K.K.Teo, P.W.Armstrong, A systematic review of randomized trials of disease management programs in heart failure. *Am. J. Med.* 110, (2001) 378-384.

[14]   D.K.Moser, Heart failure management: optimal health care delivery programs *Annu. Rev. Nurs. Res.* 18, (2000) 91-126.

[15]   E.F.Philbin, Comprehensive multidisciplinary programs for the management of patients with congestive heart failure. *J. Gen. Intern. Med.* 14, (1999) 130-135.

[16]   M.W.Rich, Heart failure disease management: a critical review. *J. Card Fail.* 5, (1999) 64-75.

[17]   B.G.Windham, R.G.Bennett, S.Gottlieb, Care management interventions for older patients with congestive heart failure. *Am. J. Manag. Care* 9, (2003) 447-459.

[18]   S.L.Norris, M.M.Engelgau, K.M.Narayan, Effectiveness of self-management training in type 2 diabetes: a systematic review of randomized controlled trials .*Diabetes Care* 24, (2001) 561-587.

[19]   C.M.Renders, E.H.Wagner, Interventions to improve the management of diabetes mellitus in primary care, outpatient and community settings. *Cochrane Library*(2002).

[20]   F.A.McAlister, F.M.Lawson, K.K.Teo, P.W.Armstrong, Randomised trials of secondary prevention programmes in coronary heart disease: systematic review. *BMJ* 323, (2001) 957-962.

[21]   Stroke Unit Trialists' Collaboration, Organised inpatient (stroke unit) care for stroke Cochrane Library(2001).

[22] D.D.Sin, F.A.McAlister, S.F.Man, N.R.Anthonisen, Contemporary management of chronic obstructive pulmonary disease: scientific review. *JAMA* 290, (2003) 2301-2312.

[23] M.Ouwens, M.Hulscher, R.Hermens, M.Faber, H.Marres, H.Wollersheim, R.Grol, *Implementation of integrated care for patients with cancer: a systematic review of interventions and effects submitted*(2008).

[24] J.A.Ferguson, M.Weinberger, Case management programs in primary care *J. Gen. Intern. Med.* 13, (1998) 123-126.

[25] S.R.Weingarten, J.M.Henning, E.Badamgarav, K.Knight, V.Hasselblad, A.Gano, J.J.Ofman, Interventions used in disease management programmes for patients with chronic illness -which ones work? Metaanalysis of published reports. *BMJ* 325, (2002) 925.

[26] M.Ouwens, H.Wollersheim, R.Hermens, M.Hulscher, R.Grol, Integrated care programmes for chronically ill patients: a review of systematic reviews. *Int. J. Qual. Health Care* 17, (2005) 141-146.

[27] D.L.Sackett, W.M.Rosenberg, J.A.Gray, R.B.Haynes, W.S.Richardson, Evidence based medicine: what it is and what it isn't *BMJ* 312, (1996) 71-72.

[28] Anonymous, www.ahrq.gov internet(2007).

[29] T.Bodenheimer, E.H.Wagner, K.Grumbach, Improving primary care for patients with chronic illness: the chronic care model, Part 2. *JAMA* 288, (2002) 1909-1914.

[30] T.Bodenheimer, E.H.Wagner, K.Grumbach, Improving primary care for patients with chronic illness *JAMA* 288, (2002) 1775-1779.

[31] E.H.Wagner, Care for chronic diseases. *BMJ* 325, (2002) 913-914.

[32] J.J.Mohr, P.B.Batalden, Improving safety on the front lines: the role of clinical Microsystems. *Qual. Saf. Health Care* 11, (2002) 45-50.

[33] M.Ouwens, H.Wollersheim, R.Hermens, M.Hulscher, R.Grol, Integrated care programmes for chronically ill patients: a review of systematic reviews. *Int. J. Qual. Health Care* 17, (2005) 141-146.

[34] M.M.T.J.Ouwens, M.E.J.L.Hulscher, R.P.M.G.Hermens, M.J.Faber, H.A.M.Marres, H.C.H.Wollersheim, R.P.T.M.Grol, *Implementation of integrated care for patients with cancer: a systematic review of interventions and effects submitted*(2007).

[35] S.L.Norris, P.J.Nichols, C.J.Caspersen, R.E.Glasgow, M.M.Engelgau, L.Jack, G.Isham, S.R.Snyder, V.G.Carande-Kulis, S.Garfield, P.Briss, D.McCulloch, The effectiveness of disease and case management for people with diabetes. A systematic review. *Am. J. Prev. Med.* 22, (2002) 15-38.

[36] E.Badamgarav, J.D.Croft, Jr., A.Hohlbauch, J.S.Louie, J.O'Dell, J.J.Ofman, M.E.Suarez-Almazor, A.Weaver, P.White, P.Katz, Effects of disease management programs on functional status of patients with rheumatoid arthritis. *Arthritis. Rheum.* 49, (2003) 377-387.

[37] M.Birchall, A.Richardson, L.Lee, Eliciting views of patients with head and neck cancer and carers on professionally derived standards for care. *BMJ* 324, (2002) 516-519.

[38] N.O'Rourke, R.Edwards, Lung cancer treatment waiting times and tumour growth. *Clin. Oncol.* (R.Coll.Radiol.) 12, (2000) 141-144.

[39] R.Grol, Personal paper. Beliefs and evidence in changing clinical practice. *BMJ* 315, (1997) 418-421.

[40] R.Grol, J.Grimshaw, From best evidence to best practice: effective implementation of change in patients' care. *Lancet* 362, (2003) 1225-1230.

[41] M.R.Chassin, R.W.Galvin, The urgent need to improve health care quality. Institute of Medicine National Roundtable on Health Care Quality. *JAMA* 280, (1998) 1000-1005.

[42] R.Grol, M.Wensing, M.Eccles, *Improving Patient Care; the implementation of change in clinical practice,* Elsevier, Butterworth, Heinemann, 2005.

[43] S.M.Campbell, J.Braspenning, A.Hutchinson, M.N.Marshall, Research methods used in developing and applying quality indicators in primary care. *BMJ* 326, (2003) 816-819.

[44] A. Donabedian, The quality of care. How can it be assessed? *JAMA* 260, (1988) 1743-1748.

[45] J.L.Malin, E.C.Schneider, A.M.Epstein, J.Adams, E.J.Emanuel, K.L.Kahn, Results of the National Initiative for Cancer Care Quality: how can we improve the quality of cancer care in the United States? *J. Clin. Oncol.* 24, (2006) 626-634.

[46] M.N.Neuss, C.E.Desch, K.K.McNiff, P.D.Eisenberg, D.H.Gesme, J.O.Jacobson, M.Jahanzeb, J.J.Padberg, J.M.Rainey, J.J.Guo, J.V.Simone, A process for measuring the quality of cancer care: the Quality Oncology Practice Initiative. *J. Clin. Oncol.* 23, (2005) 6233-6239.

[47] E.C.Schneider, A.M.Epstein, J.L.Malin, K.L.Kahn, E.J.Emanuel, Developing a system to assess the quality of cancer care: ASCO's national initiative on cancer care quality 2. *J. Clin. Oncol.* 22, (2004) 2985-2991.

[48] M.M.Ouwens, H.A.Marres, R.R.Hermens, M.M.Hulscher, F.J.van den Hoogen, R.P.Grol, H.C.Wollersheim, Quality of integrated care for patients with head and neck cancer: Development and measurement of clinical indicators. *Head Neck* 29, (2007) 378-386.

[49] R.P.Hermens, M.M.Ouwens, S.Y.Vonk-Okhuijsen, W.Y.van der, V.C.Tjan-Heijnen, L.D.van den Broek, V.K.Ho, M.L.Janssen-Heijnen, H.J.Groen, R.P.Grol, H.C.Wollersheim, Development of quality indicators for diagnosis and treatment of patients with non-small cell lung cancer: a first step toward implementing a multidisciplinary, evidence-based guideline. *Lung Cancer* 54, (2006) 117-124.

[50] P.Durieux, A.Bissery, Comparison of health care professionals' self-assessments of standards of care and patients' opinions on the care they received in hospital: observational study. *Qual. Health Care* 13, (2004) 198-202.

[51] S.M.Campbell, J.Braspenning, A.Hutchinson, M.Marshall, Research methods used in developing and applying quality indicators in primary care. *Qual. Saf. Health Care* 11, (2002) 358-364.

[52] H.Wollersheim, R.Hermens, M.Hulscher, J.Braspenning, M.Ouwens, J.Schouten, H.Marres, R.Dijkstra, R.Grol, Clinical indicators: development and applications. *Neth. J. Med.* 65, (2007) 15-22.

[53] J.S.Burgers, R.P.Grol, J.O.Zaat, T.H.Spies, A.K.van der Bij, H.G.Mokkink, Characteristics of effective clinical guidelines for general practice. *Br. J. Gen. Pract.* 53, (2003) 15-19.

[54] D.M.Eddy, Performance measurement: problems and solutions. *Health Aff.*(Millwood.) 17, (1998) 7-25.

[55] R.Grol, R.Baker, F.Moss, Quality improvement research: understanding the science of change in health care. *Qual. Saf. Health Care* 11, (2002) 110-111.

[56] E.H.Wagner, Meeting the needs of chronically ill people. *BMJ* 323, (2001) 945-946.

[57] S.A.Lewin, M.Zwarenstein, Interventions for providers to promote a patient-centred approach in clinical consultations. *Cochrane Library* 2001, (2001).

[58] S.Michie, J.Miles, J.Weinman, Patient-centredness in chronic illness: what is it and does it matter? *Patient. Educ. Couns.* 51, (2003) 197-206.

[59] D.R.Lauver, S.E.Ward, S.M.Heidrich, M.L.Keller, B.J.Bowers, P.F.Brennan, K.T.Kirchhoff, T.J.Wells, Patient-centered interventions. *Res. Nurs. Health* 25, (2002) 246-255.

[60] M.Ouwens, R.Hermens, S.Y.Vonk-Okhuijsen, V.C.Tjan-Heijnen, H.Marres, H.Wollersheim, R.Grol, *Development of indicators for patient-centred cancer care submitted*(2008).

[61] J.Bensing, Bridging the gap. The separate worlds of evidence-based medicine and patient-centered medicine. *Patient. Educ. Couns.* 39, (2000) 17-25.

[62] K.G.Sweeney, D.MacAuley, D.P.Gray, Personal significance: the third dimension *Lancet* 351, (1998) 134-136.

[63] E.H.Wagner, The role of patient care teams in chronic disease management. *BMJ* 320, (2000) 569-572.

[64] P.Bower, S.Campbell, C.Bojke, B.Sibbald, Team structure, team climate and the quality of care in primary care: an observational study. *Qual. Saf. Health Care* 12, (2003) 273-279.

[65] L.Curral, R.Forrester, J.Dawson, M.West, It's what you do and the way that you do it: Team task, team size, and innovation-related group processes. *European Journal of Work and Organizational Psychology* 10, (2001) 187-204.

[66] S.M.Shortell, J.Schmittdiel, M.C.Wang, R.Li, R.R.Gillies, L.P.Casalino, T.Bodenheimer, T.G.Rundall, An empirical assessment of high-performing medical groups: results from a national study. *Med. Care Res. Rev.* 62, (2005) 407-434.

[67] M.West, The social psychology of innovation in groups, Chichester, 1990.

[68] M.A.West, N.Anderson, Innovation, Cultural-Values, and the Management of Change in *British Hospitals Work and Stress* 6, (1992) 293-310.

[69] N.R.Anderson, M.A.West, Measuring climate for work group innovation: development and validation of the team climate inventory. *Journal of Organizational Behavior* 19, (1998) 235-258.

[70] G.E.Mathisen, S.Einarsen, K.Jorstad, K.S.Bronnick, Climate for work group creativity and innovation: Norwegian validation of the team climate inventory (TCI) *Scand. J. Psychol.* 45, (2004) 383-392.

[71] A. Agrell, R.Gustafson, The Team Climate Inventory (Tci) and Group Innovation - A Psychometric Test on A Swedish Sample of Work Groups 1. *Journal of Occupational and Organizational Psychology* 67, (1994) 143-151.

[72] M.Kivimaki, G.Kuk, M.Elovainio, L.Thomson, T.Kalliomaki-Levanto, A.Heikkila, The team climate inventory (TCI) - four or five factors? Testing the structure of TCI in samples of low and high complexity jobs. *Journal of Occupational and Organizational Psychology* 70, (1997) 375-389.

[73] P.Ragazzoni, P.Baiardi, A.M.Zotti, N.Anderson, M.West, Italian validation of the team climate inventory: A measure of team climate for innovation. *Journal of Managerial Psychology* 17, (2002) 325-336.

[74] F.C.Brodbeck, G.W.Maier, The Team Climate Inventory (TCI) for innovation: A psychometric test on a German sample of work groups Zeitschrift fur Arbeits-und *Organisationspsychologie* 45, (2001) 59-73.

[75] M.Ouwens, M.Hulscher, R.Akkermans, R.Hermens, R.Grol, H.Wollersheim, The Team Climate Inventory: application in hospital teams and methodological considerations in press for Quality and Safety in Health Care(2008).

[76] M.M.Ouwens, H.A.Marres, R.R.Hermens, M.M.Hulscher, F.J.van den Hoogen, R.P.Grol, H.C.Wollersheim, Quality of integrated care for patients with head and neck cancer: Development and measurement of clinical indicators. *Head Neck*(2006).

[77] J.Monaghan, K.Channell, D.McDowell, A.K.Sharma, Improving patient and carer communication, multidisciplinary team working and goal-setting in stroke rehabilitation. *Clin. Rehabil.* 19, (2005) 194-199.

[78] K.M.Kash, R.Mago, E.J.Kunkel, Psychosocial oncology: supportive care for the cancer patient. *Semin. Oncol.* 32, (2005) 211-218.

[79] G.Oskay-Ozcelik, W.Lehmacher, D.Konsgen, H.Christ, M.Kaufmann, W.Lichtenegger, M.Bamberg, D.Wallwiener, F.Overkamp, K.Diedrich, M.G.von, K.Hoffken, S.Seeber, R.Mirz, J.Sehouli, Breast cancer patients' expectations in respect of the physician-patient relationship and treatment management results of a survey of 617 patients. *Ann. Oncol.*(2007).

[80] V.Shilling, V.Jenkins, L.Fallowfield, Factors affecting patient and clinician satisfaction with the clinical consultation: can communication skills training for clinicians improve satisfaction? *Psychooncology.* 12, (2003) 599-611.

[81] D.Kerr, H.Bevan, B.Gowland, J.Penny, D.Berwick, Redesigning cancer care *BMJ* 324, (2002) 164-166.

[82] M.Birchall, P.M.Brown, J.Browne, The organisation of head and neck oncology services in the UK: The Royal College of Surgeons of England and British Association of Head and Neck Oncologists' preliminary multidisciplinary head and neck oncology audit. *Ann. R. Coll. Surg. Engl.* 85, (2003) 154-157.

[83] M.M.Ouwens, H.A.Marres, R.R.Hermens, M.M.Hulscher, F.J.van den Hoogen, R.P.Grol, H.C.Wollersheim, Quality of integrated care for patients with head and neck cancer: Development and measurement of clinical indicators. *Head Neck* 29, (2007) 378-386.

[84] M.M.Ouwens, H.A.Marres, R.R.Hermens, M.M.Hulscher, F.J.van den Hoogen, R.P.Grol, H.C.Wollersheim, Quality of integrated care for patients with head and neck cancer: Development and measurement of clinical indicators. *Head Neck* 29, (2007) 378-386.

[85] M.Ouwens, H.Wollersheim, R.Hermens, M.Hulscher, R.Grol, Integrated care programmes for chronically ill patients: a review of systematic reviews. *Int. J. Qual. Health Care* 17, (2005) 141-146.

In: Integrated Health Care Delivers
Editor: Leonie A. Klein and Emily L. Neumann

ISBN 978-1-60456-851-6
© 2008 Nova Science Publishers, Inc.

Chapter 6

A Case Manager Model for Integrative Healthcare Delivery: Orchestrating Delivery with an Information Management System

Curtis H. Jones

Northern New Mexico College
Espanola, New Mexico, USA

Abstract

This chapter makes the case that the delivery of integrative healthcare would be well served by developing an information management system operated by a Case Manager to reduce the amount of preliminary information about patients the practitioners need to gather. Integrative healthcare (IHc) has been defined in a variety of ways [1]. In this chapter integrative healthcare is understood as "combining of CAM therapies, at times with conventional medicine, and having patient-centeredness as one of its goals."

A Case Manager model would require: 1) an overview of all possible therapies, CAM and conventional, based on a comprehensive organizing principle, see Table I; 2) a Case Manager that facilitates the process of IHc delivery, while not supplying treatments; and, 3) expansion of the definition of 'patient-centeredness' toward increasing patient-input into the treatment selection process, with the goal of inducing the patient's healing response.

The Case Manager (CM) model described here is a delivery system that will deeply honor patient-centeredness, make treatment selections from a broad range of options, account for research on CAM efficacy, and create efficiency in clinical decision-making and practitioner communications. The CM model is an information management system that assists practitioner decision-making in IHc by managing information flow and maintaining the patient-centeredness in the clinical decision-making process. Also, the CM model is scalable, meaning it can be reproduced widely independent of practitioner expertise, which is necessary for the broad dissemination of integrative healthcare.

The Case Manager model is an adaptation of the consultations I conduct with private clients who wish to use integrative healthcare. Kindly respond with your reactions or suggestions, or a clinical setting in which we might apply and refine this model.

I. Background – The Case Manager, Complexity, and New Aspects to the Integrative Healthcare Paradigm

The Case for the Case Manager

As musical instruments and composition developed in complexity through the 17th and 18th centuries it became necessary for a person *not* playing an instrument, the conductor, to manage the orchestra. As the number of musicians playing together grew to a full size of nearly one-hundred, an additional person was needed to *manage the process* of a symphony by guiding the musicians in beat, tempo, and the dynamics of the music.

Integrative healthcare is a remarkable development in which healthcare professionals find themselves in a similar situation. Just as the growing number of instruments required the role of the conductor, it may be the growing complexity of the process of delivering integrative healthcare calls for an individual *not* involved in providing treatment to *manage the processes* of patient education, patient involvement in selection of treatments, and oversight of the process of delivering treatments. This person would be the Case Manager (CM) or Clinical Care Coordinator, titles taken from geriatric care and the mental health professions, in which medical, social, and family factors need to be blended into a seamless whole.

The complexity of IHc arises from the disparate nature of the numerous healthcare paradigms being combined (Table I.) and the inherent complexity of the subject – a person seeking health care, who is defined by numerous personal variables. As IHc begins to incorporate Energy Medicine, Mind-Body Medicine, and a host of non-conventional biochemical approaches (Botanical Medicine, Biological Medicine, etc.) and biomechanical approaches (Applied Kinesiology, Reflexology, etc.), it may be advantageous for a new professional position to develop, the Case Manager, in order to facilitate the process of delivering integrated care.

Appropriate Realistic Care - Complying with Patient Needs, Wants, and Abilities

IHc can be seen, at its heart, as a quest to deal with three fundamental parameters associated with each patient - the patient's facts, the patient's wants, and the patient's abilities. The patient's *facts* are the medical information (diagnosis, research regarding effective treatments, and information on treatment options). The patient's *wants* are indicated by his health care world-view; that is, his feelings and thoughts on the nature of health, illness, and healing and the types of treatment that are consistent with these beliefs. Selecting treatments with a patient's healthcare world-view in mind is related to inducing the healing

Table I. Periodic Table of Healthcare Systems and Practices: The Six Categories of Therapeutic Influence in Healthcare

BIOCHEMICAL	BIOMECHANICAL	ENERGY	MIND-BODY	PSYCHOLOGICAL	NON-LOCAL
SYNTHETIC Pharmaceuticals Some Dietary Supplements Some Vitamins NATURAL Some Dietary Supplements and Vitamins Biological Medicine Ortho-Molecular Med. Western Herbal Med. Nutrition Pancha Karma (Ayur.) Colonics Ozone Therapy INJECTION Neural Therapy Chelation Therapy Reconstructive Therapy Oxygen Therapy Cell Therapy INGESTION Enzyme Therapy Internal Cleansing Products SYSTEMS Allopathic Medicine (CWM) Naturopathic Med.* Herbal Medicine Functional Medicine Biological Medicine	INVASIVE METHODS Surgery Dentistry NON-INVASIVE/ MANIPULATION Massage Osteopathy Chiropractic Medicine Occupational Therapy Rolfing Applied Kinesiology Cranial Sacral Therapy Reflexology PERSONAL ACTIVITY Hatha Yoga Exercise PHYSICAL/ PSYCHOLOGICAL Metamorphic Technique Pancha Karma (Ayur.) Biodynamic Therapy Hellerwork Alexander Technique Pilates SYSTEMS Allopathic Medicine Naturopathic Med.* Osteopathy Chiropractic Med. Naprapathic Medicine	BIO-ENERGY Acupuncture Healing Touch Reiki Polarity Therapy Neuro Modulation Technique Acupressure Tai Chi Qi Gong NATURAL FIELD (other than human) Homeopathy Chinese Herbs Cymatics Radionics EMITTED ENERGY Radiation Laser Therapy Ultra Sound Light Therapy Magnets Sound Therapy Acutonics CONDUCTION and CONVECTION Hydrotherapy Sauna Warm/Cold Objects Hypothermia SYSTEMS CTM Homeopathy Ayurvedic Med.Energy Medicine	MIND-BODY Behavioral Medicine Biofeedback Training Psychoneuro-immunology Autogenic Training Quantum Healing Rebirthing Holographic-Repatterning Meditation Visualization Placebo BODY-MIND Aromatherapy Flower Remedies Emotional Kinesiology Art Therapies (Dance, Pottery) SYSTEMS Mind-Body Medicine	INDIVIDUAL Psychotherapy Neurolinguistic Programming Hypnotherapy Counseling Grief Work Art Therapies (Drawing, Painting, Drama, Music) Ritual GROUP Support Groups (Alcoholics Anonymous) Family Therapy Ritual SYSTEMS Psychotherapy Systems (Freudian, Jungian, Humanistic, Buddhist, etc.)	RELIGIOUS Prayer Faith Practices Distance Healing (Christian Science, intercessory prayer, etc.) EXTRA-RELIGIOUS Distance Healing (Healing Touch, Quantum Healing, Qigong Energy, Reiki, etc.) Positive Intention Practices Shamanic (soul retrieval, power animals, etc.) SYSTEMS Religious and non-religious Healing Traditions

Ayur. = Ayurvedic Medicine. CWM = Conventional Western Medicine CTM = Chinese Traditional Medicine *Naturopaths use numerous Modes of Therapeutic Action response - more on this below. Finally, the patient's *abilities*, which include the set of personal parameters indicating what is possible in selecting treatments (financial considerations, family situation, personal support system, and abilities to change life patterns). When *facts, wants, and abilities* are carefully considered it becomes possible to create a realistic and appropriate treatment plan. The Case Manager model is designed to account for all of these parameters.

The intersection that defines this new field of integrative healthcare is the intersection of the myriad possibilities of care found in complementary-alternative medicine (CAM) *and* patient-centered care, as defined by the facts, wants, and abilities of the patient.

In the following pages a Case Manager model will first be described to suggest a way to manage the complexity of this intersection. This is followed by discussion of some major issues in IHc, including: patient-centeredness, literature review, scalability, inducing the patient's healing response, and financial sustainability of an integrative clinic.

The Growing Complexity of Integrative Healthcare: First - Comprehensively Mapping Treatment Options

Readers of this book are probably aware of the difficulties practitioners face as our populations begin to use complementary and alternative medicine. In the past two decades we have seen an increase in treatment options that is historically unparalleled. One of the dilemmas now facing all practitioners, as well as users of integrative healthcare, is understanding the great variety of treatments that can be combined with conventional healthcare. Numerous ways to organize CAM have developed to manage this plethora of new information [2] [3] [4].

To address this situation the author developed the Periodic Table of Healthcare, Table I [5]. The table creates order in the seemingly numberless treatment possibilities that are available for integration. In the table, all possible treatments are organized in six categories, each category indicating a general type of therapeutic influence to which humans are susceptible. Thus, Table I. is based on *the nature of human being*, and lists CAM *and* conventional treatments. This is relevant to IHc because one of the tenets of this new field is that healthcare is no longer concerned only with the body-machine, it is concerned with the human being and personhood. Table I. makes this absolutely clear because it is a 'mapping' of all the ways we can be influenced, from the most tangible to the most subtle.

The categories are not meant to suggest these six therapeutic influences can be isolated from one another in any strict sense. They are to be used for creating a general direction in selecting treatments and keeping track of a patient's options and progress as treatment develops. This table allows the Case Manager to rapidly orient patients to possible treatments, quickly organize literature reviews to determine potentially beneficial treatments, discover the patient's healthcare world-view, and assists practitioners from disparate disciplines to communicate effectively. All of this will be explained in the description of the CM model which follows.

Table I. can function as a "map of the terrain" for each step in the process of IHc delivery. This map clarifies all of the interpretive possibilities in healthcare. That is, all ways of looking at and understanding health, illness, and healing are included in Table I. This can be helpful to clinicians as they develop a complete picture of the patient's situation and the possibilities for constructive therapeutic intervention. I suspect few will disagree that this new complex profession we call integrative healthcare is in need of an accurate way of mapping its possibilities.

To continue the analogy to the world of music - just as comprehending the musical scale makes possible reading and playing notes on any instrument, so the Periodic Table of Healthcare makes possible creating order in developing each step in the IHc process.

What the Case Manager Is Not

It should be clear from the outset that the CM exists to *facilitate* the process of IHc delivery. The CM does not determine which treatments are appropriate for a patient. The complexity of IHc calls for *information management* as the central role of the CM. This includes patient education, information flow management, and general facilitation of the clinical process. Managing the steps in the following protocol is the responsibility of the CM, while working closely in conjunction with both the patient and the team of IHc providers.

The Paradigm Change Underlying the Case Manager Model

The CM model is a response to this new complexity, which creates a need for an information management system - and an information manager - to effectively deliver integrative healthcare. The change in thinking that underlies the CM model is that of realizing that the IHc delivery system arises from an information management system. IHc is, at its heart, about delivering a new type of healthcare; and to make this possible it is essential to understand the foundation of decision-making in IHc is an information management system. This will be discussed in detail in Section III.

II. THE CASE MANAGER INTEGRATIVE HEALTHCARE PROCESS – TABLE II

There are five steps in the information management protocol of the CM model.

Step 1. Patient Education - familiarity with the field of treatment options

In situations in which a patient is interested in using integrative healthcare or has been using some CAM treatments, it is important to initially familiarize him with the entire spectrum of options available in IHc, as clarified in Table I. A person's interest in non-conventional and holistic healthcare is an indication that there may be treatment options in previously unconsidered categories of therapeutic influence. (Of course, patient's who would rather be directed solely by practitioners, or have already made a decision as to the treatment they want, may not be interested in an educational conversation and should be treated as they wish, if practitioners are in agreement).

Once the CM has the medical history, Table I. can be explained to the patient so she understands the entire range of possibilities available in IHc. The thrust of this brief educational exercise is to inform the patient of the six ways health and healing can be influenced - the columns in Table I. All that is required is a brief explanation of each of the six modes of therapeutic influence. This introduction is not about making any treatment selections; it is about making certain the person understands the entire scope of possibilities available for addressing health issues.

Also, in some situations a person will be either attracted to, or averse to, a particular mode of therapeutic influence. This is important information when it comes to designing a treatment plan, because having the patient's interest in a type of therapeutic influence, Energy Medicine for example, is an important factor in bringing the patient's healing response into constructive use. Gone are the days of practitioners telling patients what to do, here are the days of patient-centered care and the well-informed 'consumer of healthcare'.

In my consulting practice clients are often very pleased to see the entire range of treatment options shown on a single page. This allows the client to explore any possible openings into new treatment directions, Mind-Body or Energy Medicine for example; and, it allows new treatment directions to be seen in an impartial light. It also removes the confusion that often exists regarding the vast array of treatments people hear about in the media and from relatives, friends, and in health food stores.

This educational discussion can be conducted by the CM as part of the initial intake, or Table I. can be included in a packet distributed to all patients as part of the clinic's intake materials. In the latter case the patient has time prior to the initial meeting to consider the possibilities and develop questions for the CM.

Step 2. Determining the Patient's Healthcare Worldview

The patient's health care world-view is their set of beliefs about what is realistic in terms of treating their health issues. It is what they know and feel regarding the efficacy of the six therapeutic influences. To learn a person's healthcare world-view the CM reviews each of the columns in Table I. with the patient and asks about his experiences and level of interest in each type of therapeutic influence. This results in learning which modes of therapeutic influence are acceptable to the patient.

The point of learning the patient's health care world-view is to begin identifying those forms of treatment in which the patient will be personally invested. This has to do with eventually selecting treatments that will have the best chance of inducing the patient's healing response. A treatment path needs to be developed that is generally consistent with a person's belief system – or is, at least, *not contrary* to their general beliefs about the nature of health, illness, and healing.

This does not need to be a deep or lengthy discussion. After familiarizing the patient with the Periodic Table of Healthcare, the CM simply asks if there are any types of treatment that the patient is particularly inclined towards, and if there are treatments towards which she has a strong aversion. To achieve this, the CM can ask simple questions, "Some people have found non-local approaches such as prayer or Shamanism to be helpful in aiding their healing. How do you feel about such approaches?"

Table II. The Process of Integrative Healthcare

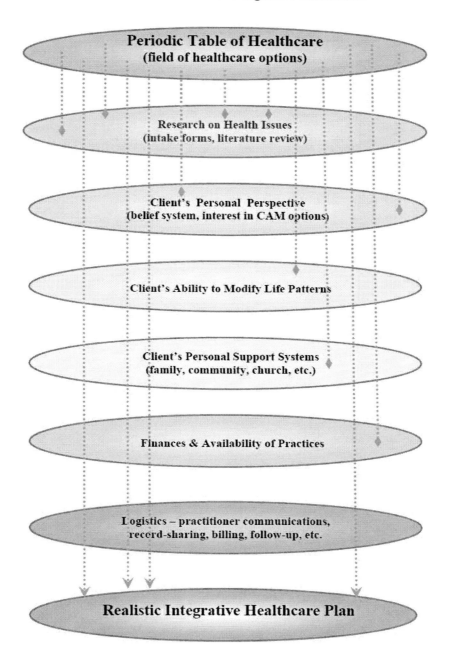

Only if a person is strongly averse to a particular mode of therapeutic influence should that column in the table be removed from consideration for potential treatments. If a patient is non-committal, then the mode of therapeutic influence can be left as a possibility. Using Table I. in this way allows the person to understand that they are an equal partner with the practitioners in determining the healthcare they will receive.

Parenthetically, in the normal clinical intake process Table I. can be used for the patient to chart all of the types of treatment that have been tried in the past. Treatments can be highlighted with separate colors to indicate good, neutral, or poor results (see Creating the Treatment Selection Chart, below). This creates a thumbnail visual history that may inform selection of new treatments. It allows the client to easily see where he has been (past treatments) and where he might go in selecting future treatments.

As the discussion develops the CM should be marking a copy of Table I. with the patient's responses regarding healthcare world-view. This will later be compared to the table on which the patient has highlighted all of the types of treatment they have had in the past. This begins to create an over-view of the world of possible treatment directions for the patient.

Mind-Body-Spirit and Holism in Treatment Selection

Table I. supplies each patient-CM team with all that is needed to insure treatment selections are holistic or mind-body-spirit oriented. By indicating attractions and aversions to types of treatments (using the column headings in Table I.) each patient self-designs the degree of holism that will appear in the treatment plan. Again, patient-centered holism needs to be understood as the holism defined and required *by the patient.*

I suspect one of the reasons the development of IHc is hampered is a public impression that holistic and integrative healthcare might mean being exposed to 'fringe' practitioners that are inclined to unearth the 'meaning' of an illness or are inclined to spiritualistic and/or "energetic" and/or "mentalistic" interpretations of cause and effect. Yes, people are changing in their attitudes toward non-conventional interpretations of health and illness, but many remain largely materialistic and physical illness is often though of as having solely a physical foundation.

In this regard, the beauty of the CM model is that patient's can have input into and direct the degree to which their treatment selection broadens beyond a materialist approach - that is, beyond the first two columns in Table I. Patients can indicate to the CM and treatment team the degree to which more subtle forms of treatment may be personally appropriate. This can be an invaluable tool in the IHc setting.

Step 3. Review of Research on Health Issues and Clinical Trials in CAM

Most people interested in IHc come to the clinic with a conventional western medical diagnosis. Based upon this diagnosis the CM, or office staff, conducts a literature review to determine which CAM therapies, if any, have been shown to be effective in addressing the problem.

Ideally, office staff would conduct this literature review while the CM is conducting the initial interview and make the results available to the CM immediately. Or, this step is done following the initial CM interview. In the latter case, the results of the research review are presented to the patient at their second visit, or they can be mailed to the patient and discussed in a telephone conversation.

Reliable research review sources should be used, such as Medline [6], the Cochrane Systematic Reviews [7], National Council on Complementary and Alternative Medicine (NCCAM) [8]. Also, the Research Council on Complementary Medicine [9] has a good list of research resources. Each IHc clinic will need to discover which set of resources best serves their interests.

The therapies indicated to be effective by a literature review become part of the list of potential therapies for the client. These should be highlighted on Table I. for future reference in the clinical decision-making process.

Step 4. Patients Personal Parameters Relating to Treatment Choices

There are three personal variables that will help a CM and patient develop a list of treatments that are appropriate and realistic. "Appropriate" means the treatment is in keeping with the patient's health care world-view, discussed in Step 2. above. "Realistic" means the treatments will fit into the patient's life situation. Each of these personal variables can be seen as a 'filter' through which treatment choices are made. If a variable excludes a particular type of treatment, so be it. The point of the treatment selection process is to determine the most realistic set of treatment options. The variables that determine a realistic selection of treatment appear as the 4th, 5th, and 6th ovals in the schematic (Table II.) and are as follows.

1. Patient's abilities to modify life-patterns and habits. It is well known that many chronic conditions for which healthcare consumers are using CAM and integrative healthcare are conditions that are either related to or can be influenced constructively by changes in life-style and various personal habits. Dean Ornish's successful work with heart disease employing diet and life-style change is a prime example of this [10].

In this regard, the question for a person interested in IHc is whether or not, in a realistic sense, he is capable of making lasting life-style changes. This needs to be addressed directly with each patient. An honest assessment of these abilities will help the person avoid attempting the impossible, thus steering clear of disappointments and the inevitable setbacks.

Also, the personal assessment thus required (and the patient learning what is at stake) may assist a person in improving their abilities to change. It must always be remembered – achieving health is a *process,* which may require the discomforts of self-assessment and the natural process of incremental change and personal evolution. Directly addressing the person's status as a participant in his healthcare will move the treatment selection process in a realistic direction. That is, there is no point in discovering options that are beyond the patient's ability to make the required life-style changes. The disappointing history of weight-loss and drug rehabilitation programs indicates the need for clarity and honesty in reviewing a person's abilities to alter life-style and habits.

The results of a patient's self-assessment are entered on a copy of Table I, as indicated in the Treatment Selection Process Chart below.

2. The patient's personal support systems. Often medical treatment requires the involvement of a patient's family and personal support system – friends, colleagues, and even neighbors. Such support can make an appreciable difference in a person's ability to fulfill the requirements of any number of therapies, especially those from the mind-body and psychological columns in Table I. "No man is an island", should be kept in mind when selecting therapies that might be better adopted with active personal support in place. If a person is willing and able to begin a new exercise regimen, or to abandon a bad habit, it is certainly advantageous if there is a family member or friend to create a team in taking on such challenges.

It is important for an IHc team to know if a patient has no support systems. Therapeutic approaches can then be selected that do not require such support. Again, having this discussion with the patient moves the exchange towards finding realistic approaches to achieving and maintaining health. Increasing the feeling of autonomy and self-awareness for the patient can only help to establish a constructive atmosphere – at least no one is being deluded as to the conditions within which the patient will be working towards health.

3. The patient's finances. Clearly, a person's ability to pay for a course of treatment is a fundamental parameter within which treatment plans should be designed. Of course, the nature of the IHc clinic and types of insurance coverage available will bear on this. Since much CAM is not covered by conventional medical insurance, the discussion that needs to take place with each patient is in regards to a monthly amount that can be budgeted for healthcare.

3a. Availability of practice. This consideration is very simple – Is the treatment selected available in the patient's geographical locale? Of course, there are rare instances in which a patient can afford to travel for a selected treatment; but, most users of IHc will require treatment be available from local practitioners.

Step 5. Bringing It All Together – the Case Manager's Work of Information Management

The final step is for the CM to review all of the information now at hand and fashion a set of possible therapies that meets the requirements that have been clarified. This is achieved using a copy of the Periodic Table of Healthcare as the template onto which is recorded the indications of all of the information gathered. That is, the patients healthcare world view, the results of the literature review, and the patient's personal parameters establish conditions that may eliminate either particular therapies or entire columns of therapies. The CM works on Table I. to create a graphic summary of the all the information gathered in the patient interview. See the summary page below, "Creating the Treatment Selection Chart".

In general, it may be that the information discovered in the review of research can be combined with the patient's preferences for treatment types to reveal a 'most likely' combination of treatments. These 'most likely' treatments then have to be passed through the 'filters' of the patients personal parameters to reveal a set of possibilities that are both realistic and appropriate.

Review of the results of the decision-making process. Of course, in most clinical settings there needs to be a point at which the Healthcare Director (Medical Director, Treatment

Director) or a Treatment Committee reviews the results of the Case Manager process. This is a question of individual clinical structures and needs to be addressed on a clinic-by-clinic basis. It may be that the CM can present case reviews to the treatment team or written treatment selections can be submitted for review by the Healthcare Director.

Practitioner Communications. Once a course of treatment has begun, sharing of treatment-specific information between practitioners can be achieved by employing an adaptation of the Periodic Table of Healthcare. I have designed a chart for practitioners to communicate with one another. The effects of their various therapeutic interventions-influences are be recorded on a modified version of Table I. Using this chart would require training of practitioners. Interested clinicians can contact me for further discussion.

Creating the Treatment Selection Chart

The sequence below is basically a process of elimination, in which the CM marks a Periodic Table of Healthcare to indicate the therapies and modes of therapeutic influence that are *disqualified* due to each of the parameters in the process, as well as highlighting those treatments preferred by the patient or indicated as effective by literature review.

1. Patient treatment history (H) - from the patient's treatment history on the intake forms the CM marks a copy of the Table I. Using three colored highlighters:
   - mark "green (H)" - treatments that were successful
   - mark "blue (H)" - treatments that were mediocre, or had inconclusive results
   - mark "red (H)" - treatments that were not successful, had no effect
2. Patient's healthcare world-view (W) - as the patient reveals preferences and disinclinations to particular therapies or therapeutic influences, the CM marks the table accordingly:
   - mark "red (W)" - treatments and approaches prohibited by the patients healthcare world-view
3. Research results (R) -
   - mark "green (R)" - treatments showing positive research results
   - mark "blue (R) - inconclusive results
   - research results showing no positive effect are not marked. Should the patient elect such treatment, possibly there will be positive results.
4. Personal parameters (P) - during the discussion the CM marks the chart accordingly.
   - mark "red (P)" - treatments, or columns, disqualified for consideration based on each of the personal parameters
5. Review of the resulting chart. The columns and treatments remaining on the chart (not marked in red) are the field of realistic and appropriate treatments for the patient. This chart can now be compared to the "Local Treatments Chart" [11]. Those treatments that are common to both charts are the field available for final selection.
6. Final selections. The patient makes selections from the available therapies. The CM and patient can create a time-line for treatments considering the expected monthly cost. If all parties agree, this can include a statement by the patient of expectations and commitments required by the treatment selection.
7. Review by practitioner group or Medical Director.

III. DISCUSSION OF SOME ISSUES IN INTEGRATIVE HEALTHCARE DELIVERY

The revolutionary nature of integrative healthcare brings with it a host of issues that will require maturation and development. Space limitations in this setting only allow for beginning a discussion of how the Case Manager model promotes advancement of IHc in relation to these issues. To list some of the major questions: the patient-centered nature of IHc; research-based information in decision-making; scalability of any design proposed for delivering IHc; inducing the healing response; and, financial sustainability of an integrative clinic. Each of these issues will now be discussed, with an intention of casting light on the advantages and disadvantages of the CM model.

1. Patient-centered Care and Integrative Healthcare: Expanding Definitions

"Patient-centered" care has been defined in a variety of ways [12] [13] [14], from including mind-body approaches, assurances that care is based in mind-body-spirit considerations, and as an emphasis on improved practitioner-patient relations. Possibly we need to take a fresh look at defining patient-centeredness in integrative healthcare. The CM model implies we define patient-centeredness as "taking into consideration the patient's definitions of health, illness, and healing in the particulars of the present, thus making the patient's perspectives *central* to consideration of treatment options and development of treatment plans". (It should be said that the human warmth and respect on the part of practitioners is implied by 'patient-centered'.)

Defining patient-centered in this way makes it possible to develop a course of treatment that is fully consistent with the perspectives of each patient. In my consulting practice I often think I see what a person would need in integrative treatment. Yet, the person has no interest whatsoever in the treatments that "seem to be" the best options. Rather, they are attracted to a course of action determined by inner parameters and personal inclinations that are revealed in the course of the consultation.

To define patient-centeredness n. in this way is parting to some degree from the conventional mind-body-spirit or holistic approach. And yet, when a person is selecting their health care, should they not receive treatment addressing their inner-most needs and wants? Just as patients are encouraged to question the suggestions of conventional caregivers, should we not expect IHc patients to carefully examine their options prior to accepting a treatment plan?

The above suggests one of the often unmentioned down-sides of many integrative clinical settings. A stand-alone integrative clinic, not associated with a hospital, is usually a varied group of well trained and well-meaning CAM practitioners, who are willing to treat a broad range of complaints. Often the determination of treatment direction is based upon what is available in the clinic. This is quite natural. Yet, this is selecting treatment based upon practitioners, not based upon patients. It is, in a sense, "practitioner-centered care", rather than patient-centered care. This issue has been pointed out in the literature in a discussion of the "challenge to the new orthodoxy of integrative health care" a very worthwhile read, in my opinion [15].

The CM model allows for a greater emphasis on the patient's perspective in treatment selection; achieved by reviewing the Table I. with the patient and making certain she understands the broad spectrum of therapeutic influences possible. Thus, in conjunction with practitioner's perceptions, a treatment path is developed based upon consideration of the patient's perspective and perceptions. This is not to say that the clinical analysis in which practitioners have been trained will be of limited use. But, it is to place professional analysis in service of the patients understanding of their healthcare needs. That is, one goal of the CM intake is to make the insights of the patient part of the information-set available to the treatment team as the process develops.

For example, I was asked to consult with an 85 year old lady suffering from mental and emotional collapse and physical exhaustion following an automobile accident in which her physical trauma was negligible. She had been well cared for by her conventional physician, but had broken out in hives and was prescribed cortisone cream, which she was not interested in using long term. Due to this general picture, I assumed (to myself) she would want to learn about some stress-reduction techniques and possibly use dietary supplementation to help with the results of the stress of the accident.

When we reviewed the Periodic Table of Healthcare, she mentioned that shortly after her collapse she had some episodes of speaking-in-tongues, and was questioning her own sanity. When I explained there was a world of therapy in which speaking in tongues was a natural occurrence, namely Shamanic Healing and some religious traditions, she insisted this was the path she wanted to follow. Surprised, I could only conclude "So be it". I had done my educational work by explaining the options, and she had made her choice.

Following a single session with a local Shamanic Healer her symptoms improved remarkably, and to this day she has no interest in any additional therapeutic approaches. Had I not witnessed this first-hand, it would have been difficult to believe, in light of my lack of such experience. This strikingly illustrates the unique nature of the type of patient-centered care being proposed in the CM model - with a little bit of education, this lady knew exactly what she needed - and I did not.

The question arises – How is an integrative clinic to take advantage of this type of patient-centeredness with a limited number of CAM modalities available in-house?

A suggestion: In the service of patient-centeredness, make patient education an integral part of the intake process. A discussion of the entire spectrum of therapeutic influence with each patient may reveal directions the practitioner group would overlook due to their inevitable professional paradigm biases. Of course, many integrative practitioners have exposure to, and facility with, a number of types of therapeutic influence – the MD who has learned acupuncture, the Massage Therapist who has learned an energy modality (Healing Touch, Reiki, etc.), and many Naturopaths, among others. So it is very likely that at least *some* therapeutic interventions from each column in Table I. can be offered to clients in-house. If that is not the case, a referral can be made to a local practitioner. See Local Treatments Chart. [11]

2. Research Literature Review: Considering the Data in Integrative Healthcare

Though the amount of clinical research on CAM has increased dramatically in recent years, there remain many therapies and many illnesses for which random controlled trials with CAM have not been conducted. This creates a dilemma for healthcare professionals desiring iron-clad proof of efficacy for CAM treatments. The on-going debates on the issue of standards of proof and study-design are formidable. [16] [17] [18] [19] Are double-blind controlled studies appropriate for many CAM treatments? Does the highly personal nature of IHc cast a shadow of doubt on the relevance of the entire concept of double-blinded proof?

With the above in mind, each IHc clinic must decide the degree to which published reports influence treatment selections. The available information should at least be presented to patients to avoid any suspicion of professional bias on the part of the clinic's practitioners. Then final treatment selections can be made by the patient-practitioner team 'in the light of day', and reviewed by the appropriate protocol established by each clinic.

3. Scalability of a Clinical Model

Scalability means a service or product can be universally reproduced because it depends upon a *teachable process*, rather than being dependent on a particular professional's expertise. For good or ill, McDonalds, Jiffy Lube, and super malls have become ubiquitous in the US. Why? Because the processes on which they operate can be taught widely to appropriately trained individuals. Thus, scalability is possible when a teachable process has been developed, and can lead to wide-spread dispersion of a good or service. It is also true that the quality of a service will always depend upon local talent. Therefore, scalability is not necessarily followed by a reduction in quality, though it is inevitably followed by an increase in availability (quantity).

The influence of integrative healthcare will grow substantially at the point at which a successful *scalable* clinical model is developed and applied. I am of the opinion that at the point at which an IHc model can be reproduced widely with reliable clinical success, we will be approaching a tipping point for the influence of IHc on the healthcare crisis we are facing. [20]

At present, many models of IHc are dependent upon a gatekeeper practitioner or a team of specialty practitioners addressing a particular set of health concerns, such as Midwifery clinics or pain management clinics. Such models, being dependent upon a particular group of practitioners, and/or focusing on a particular population, are difficult to "scale", because local medical expertise is the force that drives and maintains the enterprise. This is understandable in IHc because it is in the early stages of development – many practitioners, conventional and CAM, are educating themselves regarding the nature and difficulty of practicing in an integrative manner.

These clinical settings illustrate that IHc is yet, in a sense, 'practitioner-centered', rather than being fully patient-centered. I understand that some who feel they are practicing patient-centered IHc may not take this statement kindly. But, for a model to be both patient-centered and scalable, it will, *in its design*, need to depend upon an information management system, rather than the expertise of individual practitioners.

In the CM model it is *the process* of determining the range of appropriate treatments that needs to be mastered, not any particular diagnostic or therapeutic skill. Of course, skilled clinicians are required to operate within the CM model, and the past two decades have produced an impressive pool of MDs, RNs, PAs, a multitude of DCs, DOMs, DOs, LMTs and any number of other practitioners who can easily understand Table I. and the nature of the CM model. To achieve scalability, it is *the process* of selecting appropriate treatments that needs to be learned, not any specific diagnostic ability.

To return to the comparison of an IHc clinic to an orchestra: With a conductor or Case Manager involved, the players continue to make the music and practitioners continue to deliver the healthcare. The process of getting the music played is directed by the conductor, while the process of getting the information gathered for making good IHc decisions is overseen by a Case Manager. The role is one of managing information flow and maintaining the patient-centeredness in the clinical decision-making process.

In order to bring IHc into the mainstream, we can no longer afford to limit our conceptualization to "a new mix of practitioners in an exchange with clients". We can begin conceptualizing IHc delivery on a systemic level. If IHc is to expand rapidly we must begin conceptualizing it as grounded in a patient-centered information management system, *because such a system is scalable*. This is a paradigm shift in our thinking about the delivery of integrative healthcare

It cannot be over emphasized that this is *not* to say that the therapeutic exchange between practitioners and patients will no longer be at the heart of healthcare. The point is not to disenfranchise practitioners, but rather to facilitate practitioner's work by creating an efficient system for gathering the formidable amount of information that precedes their work with patients (treatment history, health care world-view, financial position, abilities to change habits, and the strength of personal support systems). This is not information that relies upon any practitioner's training; it is general information that makes an appropriate, realistic treatment plan possible. Should highly trained practitioners use their valuable time gathering this information? Possibly better if they are freed to pursue their passion of practicing healthcare.

To repeat, one way to conceptualize the change to a CM model is to think of IHc delivery as an information management system, as well as a set of new practices. The CM model provides a structure for making the initial patient-centered evaluations, independent of the expertise of any particular practitioner. The CM functions as the facilitator of the patient's decision-making process, which is then presented to the practitioner team or the Clinic Director. The information management system is independent of any particular practitioner, and that creates scalability.

Possible Professional Resistance

Resistance to the CM model may arise amongst some healthcare practitioners because, though professional training creates depth of understanding, it can also create narrowing of perspective. All healthcare professionals are trained within a paradigm to interpret a person's situation and then act in accordance with the determinations dictated by that paradigm. This "paradigm-bias" may become a source of resistance to the decision-making structure of the CM model.

Paradigm-bias is the subtle source of some IHc practices being practitioner-centered, rather than patient-centered, as mentioned above. Most practitioners will rightly claim they are putting the patient's interests first, and this may be true, *from the practitioner's perspective*. Patient-centered healthcare requires decision-making to carefully consider *the patient's perspective*. There is a crucial difference here that cannot be minimized if IHc is to succeed in achieving its goal of delivering patient-centered care in a structure that is scalable. The CM structure creates a systemic safe-guard against practitioner paradigm-bias at the beginning of the process, when a patient's healthcare world-view and personal-parameters are discussed.

4. Inducing the Healing Response

The literature on the relationship of belief (a person's healthcare world-view) and healing is almost exhaustive. From mind-body medicine and the relaxation response, to the experiences of Indigenous Peoples, to spirituality and healing, there is no lack of proof that our belief systems are a factor in our health and healing. To select only those with which I have some familiarity, the writings of Larry Dossey, MD, Herbert Benson, MD, and Caroline Myss, Ph.D. compile a great deal of information on belief and healing. [21] [22] [23] [24].

The goal of the type of patient-centeredness employed in the CM model is to take maximum advantage of the constructive relationship between belief and healing. When the patient's healthcare world-view is considered in the decision-making process, there may be greater likelihood of inducing the healing response during treatments. What is called the 'placebo response' and factored out of conventional medical research can possibly be harnessed to the patient's advantage in each treatment plan in IHc.

This is one of the places of the meeting of the art and the science of healthcare. While each practitioner engages in their science artfully (and their art scientifically), the system that introduces patients to their treatment possibilities can direct the team towards those areas of treatment that will capture the advantages of the healing response with each patient. Clearly there is a scientific advantage to having multiple treatment options; that is, the health-challenge can be addressed from a variety of perspectives, with a variety of 'tools'. There is also an 'artful' advantage to consulting with the patient regarding their healthcare world-view - which is to create greater opportunity for inducing the healing response when treatment begins.

5. Financial Sustainability of an Integrative Clinic

The on-going conversation about financial sustainability of an integrative clinic is complicated. It involves the intersection of the insurance industry, conventional medicine and CAM, clinical decision-making, business practices, and the strained finances of a good portion of our populations. See The Integrator Blog [25] [26], for a good discussion of financial sustainability. One tentative conclusion being: in an integrative clinic there need to be some high-technology (high cost, insurance covered) services provided by MD's to balance the relatively low income producing services of most CAM providers.

One of the goals of the CM model is to reduce the amount of time practitioners spend gathering information and discussing information as a group. The CM model is meant to drastically reduce the time practitioners spend in team meetings. I have never believed, from a business perspective, that practitioner team meetings are a viable option – these meetings simply require too much time. If teams of practitioners meet only to discuss the results of the CM interview, it may be possible to settle on an appropriate treatment plan with greater efficiency.

Basic Requirements of the CM Model

The CM model can be taught to individuals in a variety of IHc settings, where it can be adapted to meet local requirements. The basic requirements are: 1) a CM with solid interviewing skills (insightful, compassionate, unbiased, etc.) and a basic understanding of the six types of therapeutic influence (Table I.); 2) a group of practitioners willing to consider the treatment suggestions revealed by the CM-patient interview; and, 3) an efficient practitioner-communications system in which the medical paradigm-dependent information generated by each practitioner is 'translated' into information that all practitioners can utilize.

Disadvantages of the Case Manager Model

1. *Increased cost.* The CM model adds a staff member to the clinical structure, increasing the clinic's overhead costs. It remains to be seen if increased efficiency in clinical decision-making, reduction of time in team meetings, and increased patient satisfaction leads to greater income to off-set the salary of the CM.
2. *Additional communications structures.* The CM model requires developing a communications system between the CM and the practitioners *and* a new communications system between practitioners. To communicate with practitioners the CM can circulate The Treatment Selection Chart that results from the CM-patient interview, or practitioners can review the chart with the CM in a group meeting.
3. Using these new communications channels will initially require a learning curve and might dissuade practitioner groups from adopting the model. Of course, such learning curves are characteristic of all innovation and systemic evolution.
4. *Practitioner resistance to a new system.* The CM model calls for practitioners to adjust to a new model of patient intake, information gathering, and establishing the broad parameters within which a treatment plan will develop. This may be felt by some practitioners as a reduction of the importance of their role in the clinical setting, though if implemented properly, this need not be the case.
5. *Patients becoming accustomed to the CM model.* Patients may initially not understand the purpose of the CM interview. Overcoming this will require clear instructions to the clinic's clientele and effective marketing.

Advantages of the Case Manager Model

1. *Scalability.* The CM model is universally reproducible (scalable), as explained above.
2. *Common framework.* The model rests on a framework (Periodic Table of Healthcare) that makes possible structuring and connecting patient education, selecting treatments, tracking progress in treatments, and practitioner communications. Having a common framework eventually brings about a foundation for all involved in the process, which makes for smooth long-term clinic operations.
3. *Practitioner time is used efficiently.* The CM model frees practitioner teams from time-consuming meetings discussing patients, as explained above. If discussions in team meetings are confined to the Treatment Selection Chart, an over-all time saving will result.
4. *Reduces patient confusion.* The Case Manager is the focal point of patient education and communications, creating order in the patients' dealings with the clinic and treatment team.
5. *Increased patient empowerment.* Patients have considerable input into the treatment selection process, empowering them and thus enhancing personal 'investment' in their healing journey.
6. *Increases opportunity for inducing patient's healing response.* Because the patient is involved in the decision-making process and their healthcare world-view is engaged, there is an improved opportunity for inducing the healing response during treatments.
7. *Potential Marketability.* When a clinic has established itself offering a Case Manager service, there may be a marketing advantage.

Other Suggestions for Structuring IHc Delivery

The literature on IHc delivery contains a number of suggestions for structuring IHc delivery [27][28][29][30]. To summarize these is beyond the scope of this chapter. What can be said is that often these models lack a comprehensive view of the field of treatment options at the beginning of the process.

For example, in the Frenkel, et.al. article [31], determining CAM use is dependent upon a Medline search. This limits treatment options to the world of randomized controlled trials on CAM, and disregards the patient's possible inclinations toward a great number of therapeutic possibilities. For this reason the Frenkle process may be suited to the uses to which MDs can put some CAM treatments, but it does not appear to be a plan for integrative healthcare in a broader sense.

Heather Boon, et.al. [32] authored an article that summarized the various types of integration now found in healthcare. This is a very informative contribution, mapping seven types of integration, including practices labeled "parallel, consultative, collaborative, coordinated, multidisciplinary, interdisciplinary, and integrative", with discussions of philosophy, structure, process, and outcomes for each type.

In Boon's discussion of "structure" and "process" relating to the "integrative" types of practice there is no mention of decision-making by way of an information management system that would assist practitioners in IHc.

A Swedish primary care clinic developed a model for IHc delivery [33] that employs a physician gatekeeper, a common structure. Although using the NCCAM (NIH) [3] schema for organizing CAM, which has serious limitations [4], the project was admirably designed to meet the needs of a local disadvantaged population and has positive implications for design of similar projects.

Finally, I have found no mention in the literature of a Case Manager model for structuring integrative care. This can only be taken to indicate that such a model has yet to be considered seriously. The reasons for this may be many, and one reason may be that the central concept of the CM model has yet to be considered carefully; namely, understanding an IHc delivery system can be built on an information management system that serves the patients and the practitioners.

CONCLUSION

All indications are that integrative healthcare is a development that will substantially alter the future of healthcare in many countries. Our question becomes one of developing realistic ways in which IHc can grow to fulfill its service mission as quickly as possible. The dual qualities of IHc, namely, offering a new range of treatments and being patient-centered, creates additional complexity that challenges all concerned to work towards delivery models that will both satisfy the health needs of patients (consumers of healthcare) and make possible rapid expansion of integrative healthcare.

The Case Manager model presented here is a process designed to meet the above challenges while serving time-pressed practitioners. The CM model makes it possible for practitioners to focus on the daily challenges of delivering quality services, while they operate within an information management system that accurately represents their services to patients. (The evolution of a business model to serve a clinically successful IHc delivery model is an issue fraught with additional complexity, a subject for a future discussion.

The change to operating within an information management system is an avenue for bringing greater efficiency into the IHc delivery process, which, given the healthcare crisis in which we find ourselves, could be part of unlocking the great potential of integrative healthcare. Let us hope the development described here will be applied, refined, and found to be of assistance in creating the 'symphony' that we all foresee as the future of integrative healthcare.

REFERENCES

[1]   Stumpf S, Shapiro SJ, Hardy ML. Divining Integrative Medicine. Evidence Based Complementary and Alternative Medicine. eCAM Advance Access. September 26, 2007. Available from: www.ecam.oxfordjournals.org.

[2]   Kaptchuk TJ, Eisenberg DM. Varieties of Healing: A Taxonomy of Unconventional Healing Practices. *Annals of Internal Medicine* 2001. Vol. 3. 196-204.

[3]   Tataryn JD. Paradigms of Health and Disease: A Framework for Classifying and Understanding Complementary and Alternative Medicine. *Journal of Alternative and Complementary Medicine*, 2002. Vol.6. 877-892.

[4]   National Institutes of Health. Health Information: Understanding Alternative and Complementary Medicine. *National Center for Complementary and Alternative Medicine*. www.nccam.nih.gov. Sept. 2004.

[5]   Jones, CH. The Spectrum of Therapeutic Influences and Integrative Healthcare: Classifying Health Care Practices by Mode of Therapeutic Action. *The Journal of Alternative and Complementary Medicine*, Oct. 2005 Vol. 11. No. 5. 937-944.

[6]   Medline. Available from: www.nlm.nih.gov/medlineplus/ *Resource of the National Library of Medicine*, USA.

[7]   Cochrane Database of Systematic Reviews. Available from: www.cochrane.org/reviews.

[8]   National Council on Complementary and Alternative Medicine (NCCAM). Available from: www.nccam.hih.gov.

[9]   The Research Council on Complementary Medicine, Available from: www.rccm.org.uk Note: see also, The National Library for Health Complementary and Alternative Medicine Specialist Library (NeLCAM). Available from: www.library.nhs.uk/cam/.

[10]   Ornish D. Dr. Dean Ornish's Program for Reversing Heart Disease: The Only System Scientifically Proven to Reverse Heart Disease Without Drugs or Surgery. New York: Ivy Books, 1996.

[11]   To create a chart of treatments that are available locally, use a copy of the Periodic Table of Healthcare that has *blank* columns – just the headings remain. In each column write the treatments that can be found locally. This creates an overview of the treatment selection available for patients in their geographical area.

[12]   Shaller D. Patient-Centered Care: What Does It Take? The Commonwealth Fund, Oct. 2007. Vol. 74. Available from: www.thecommonwealthfund.org.

[13]   The Planetree Model. Available from: www.planetree.org/about.

[14]   The Continuum Center for Health and Healing at Beth Israel Medical Center. Available from: www.healthandhealingny.com.

[15]   MacKenzie-Cook PD. Challenging the New Orthodoxy in Integrative Medicine. *The Journal of Alternative and Complementary Medicine*. September 1, 2006. Vol. 12. No. 7. 679-683.

[16]   Park CM. Diversity, the individual, and proof of efficacy: complementary and alternative medicine in medical education. *The American Journal of Public Health*. Oct. 2002, Vol. 92. No. 10. 1568-73.

[17]   Ventegodt S, Andersen NJ, Merrick J. The square curve paradigm for research in alternative, complementary, and holistic medicine: a cost-effective, easy, and scientifically valid design for evidence-based medicine and quality improvement. *Scientific World Journal*. Nov. 2003 Vol. 13. No. 3. 1117-27.

[18]   Borgerson K. Evidence Based Alternative Medicine? *Perspectives in Biology and Medicine*. Vol.48. No. 4. Autumn 2005.

[19]   Wayne PM, Kaptchuk TJ. Challenges Inherent to T'ai Chi Research: Part I - T'ai Chi as a Complex Multicomponent Intervention. *The Journal of Alternative and Complementary Medicine*. January 1, 2008, Vol. 14. No. 1. 95-102.

[20] Pellitier K. Corporate Health Improvement Program. 2008. Available from: www.drpellitier.com/chip.

[21] Dossey L. Meaning and Medicine: Learning from a Doctor's Tales of Breakthrough and Healing. Bantam Books. November, 1992.

[22] Benson H. The nocebo effect: history and physiology. Preventative Medicine, 1997. *BMC Health Services Research*, 2007, Vol. 7. No. 26. 612-5.

[23] Myss C, Shealy CN. Anatomy of the Spirit: the Seven Stages of Power and Healing. Crown Publishing Group. 1997.

[24] Rosenweig P, Brohier S, Zipfel A. The placebo effect in healthy volunteers: influence of the experimental conditions on the adverse events profile during phase I studies. *Clin. Pharmacol. Ther.* 1993. Vol. 54. 578-83.

[25] Weeks J. The Integrator Blog. Issues 40 (and34). Feb. 5, 2008. Available from: www.theintegratorblog.com Note: Use the blog search engine for "Peter Amato" to find the full discussion.

[26] Weeks J. Integrative Healthcare Businesses in Patient Advocacy: The Yellow Courtyard and Lynxcare Models www.integratorblog.com. Aug. 29, 2007.

[27] Mulkins A, Eng J, Verhoef M. Working towards a model of integrative health care: Critical elements for an effective team. *Complementary Therapies in Medicine*, Vol. 13, No. 2, 115-122.

[28] Leach, Matthew J. "Integrative Health Care: a Need for Change?," *Journal of Complementary and Integrative Medicine:* 2006. Vol. 3. No. 1. Available from: www.bepress.com/jcim/vol3/iss1/1.

[29] Integrative Healthcare Clinics. Dr. Adiel Tel-Oren. Minneapolis, Minnesota, USA. Available from: www.integrativehealthcare.org.

[30] Launso L, Skovgaard L. The IMCO Scheme as a Tool in Developing Team-Based Treatment for People with Multiple Sclerosis. *The Journal of Alternative and Complementary Medicine.* January 1, 2008, Vol. 14. No. 1. 69-77.

[31] Frenkel MA, Borkan, JM. An approach for integrating complementary– alternative medicine into primary care. *Family Practice*, 2003, Vol. 20. No. 3. 324-332.

[32] Boon H. From parallel practice to integrative health care: a conceptual framework. *BMC Health Services Research* Feb. 20 2008, Vol. 4. No. 15. Available from: www.biomedcentral.com/1472-6963/4/15.

[33] Sundberg T, Halpin J, Warenmark A, Faslkenberg T. Towards a Model for Integrative Medicine in Swedish Medicine. BMC Health Services Research, 2007. Vol. 7. Available from: http://www.biomedcentral.com/1472-6963/7/107.

In: Integrated Health Care Delivers
Editor: Leonie A. Klein and Emily L. Neumann

ISBN 978-1-60456-851-6
© 2008 Nova Science Publishers, Inc.

Chapter 7

INTEGRATED CARE DELIVERY: PROCESS REDESIGN AND THE ROLE OF RULES, ROUTINES AND TRANSACTION COSTS

A. J. A. van Raak, A. T. G. Paulus and S. Groothuis*

Maastricht University, Care and Public Health Research Institute (CAPHRI)
Faculty of Health, Medicine and Life sciences,
Department of HOPE, P.O. Box 616,
6200 MD MAASTRICHT, The Netherlands

ABSTRACT

In many countries, managers are making efforts to organize integrated health care and social care. The managers need information from research that they can use in order to understand the situation they are facing and to make decisions about the implementation of integrated care. In this chapter, we present an approach that, when applied by researchers, will provide this information. The approach covers four parts: a *systematic analysis* of the existing care delivery processes and the waste of resources that occur during these processes; the *redesign* of these processes into a tailor-made, optimized integrated care delivery process where waste is reduced; use of knowledge about *rules for actions* and *routines* (action patterns) of care providers, which rules and routines can hamper implementation of integrated care; use of knowledge about *transaction costs,* which occur during the implementation of integrated care, especially when routines of care providers must be changed. We illustrate the approach on the basis of data about care delivery to HIV/AIDS patients in Botswana (Africa). We selected this case because it concerns an illness that is widely spread across the continents, and therefore is recognizable for an international readership. In addition, cooperation among care providers in the case is in its infancy, and therefore brings to light the problems and challenges of redesigning and implementing integrated care. In the final section we discuss how our approach might help managers to decide whether or not to initiate change towards integrated care.

---

[*] Tel.: +31 43 3881699, Fax: +31 43 3670960, E-mail: a.vanraak@beoz.unimaas.nl

INTRODUCTION

Across the globe, in many countries including the US, Canada, Columbia, the UK, The Netherlands, Italy, India, South Africa, Botswana and Australia, governments and other agencies are taking initiatives to promote integrated care for disabled persons, chronic ill persons who suffer from, e.g., Alzheimer's disease, cardiovascular disease, rheumatoid arthritis or diabetes mellitus, and other target groups [Van Raak et al., 2005]. We consider 'integrated care' as a coherent and coordinated set of health and social services which are delivered by a range of organizations and professionals [Leichsenring and Alaszewski, 2004; Van Raak et. al., 2003]. Examples of providing agencies are GPs, nursing homes, homes for the elderly, home care agencies, social work organizations, hospitals, public health authorities, housing corporations and transport companies [Van Raak and Paulus, 2008]. Integrated care requires interorganizational cooperation. The problem for managers is that, often, it is very difficult to bring about cooperation. Among the causes that are mentioned by studies are inconsistent government policy and legislation, lack of funding, the existence of separate budgets for different services, organizational fragmentation, conflicts of interests among providers, domain issues and an unclear division of tasks and communication among agents [for an overview, see Van Raak et al., 1999, 2003]. Implementation of integrated care therefore is facing many problems. It is critical that managers are offered information from research, which they can use in order to understand the situation they are facing and to make decisions about implementation of integrated care.

A closer look at the available studies of integrated care shows that an approach is largely neglected, which contains the following four parts:

1. The first part is a *systematic analysis* of the existing care delivery processes and the waste of resources that occur during these processes.
2. The second part is the *redesign* of these processes into a tailor-made, optimized integrated care delivery process where waste is reduced. Process redesign, originating from the industrial sectors, is increasingly applied and appreciated in hospitals. However, for integrated care this is not yet the case.
3. The third part is use of knowledge about *rules for actions* and *routines* (action patterns). Implementation of integrated care often breaks down on existing rules and deeply rooted professional routines, a topic which deserves more attention in the organizational literature about integrated care.
4. The fourth part concerns use of knowledge about *transaction costs*. Although it is assumed that integrated care saves costs [Kodner and Spreeuwenberg, 2002], there is little evidence on its actual cost-saving potential [Newhouse et al., 2003; Paulus et al., 2008; Segal et al., 2004; Tjerbo and Kjekshus, 2005; Vondeling, 2004; Wan et al., 2001]. Knowledge about the types of costs that are involved in the development and implementation of organizational changes — including redesigns — towards integrated care delivery is virtually absent.

In order to explain this approach and to indicate the insights it might produce, we use information about a case of integrated care delivery, which is set in Botswana (Africa). In the upcoming sections, following a brief description of integrated care, we first analyze the existing care delivery processes in the case with the aid of 'process mapping'. Next, based on principles of Business Process Redesign, we consider the issue of waste of resources, and we redesign the care delivery processes into an integrated care delivery process.

Then, we describe the issue of rules and professional routines. We argue that if a redesign does not match the existing rules and patterns of care delivery, implementation of the redesign will encounter major difficulties, particularly the emergence of transaction costs. The development and implementation of organizational changes, including redesigns, involves a range of transactions, which are accompanied by several types of transaction costs. We describe these transactions and transaction costs in the penultimate section.

In the final section, we discuss the insights from the case analysis and the relevance of the presented approach.

A CASE OF INTEGRATED CARE

Integrated care is a collective noun for a wide range of cases, including examples of programs for disease management, shared care and primary care. On the surface these cases tend to be rather similar – i.e. they share a common feature, which is the need for cooperation and coordination between different providers. When we look more closely, in many respects the cases are very different.

In order to give an impression of the variety, if only in Europe and Africa, table 1 presents a sample of five cases from the Netherlands, Italy, United Kingdom, Botswana, and South Africa. In terms of their overall purpose, the cases pursue a similar general goal: better integration of care to their target groups.

The specific goals vary, while the target groups are different in terms of their age and illness. The cases involve different collections of providers, and the organizational characteristics of care delivery differ among the cases as well. The features of the national health and social care system, together with the types of illness, probably provide the best explanation of the similarity with regard to the general goal and the differences regarding the other topics.

Particularly, all national systems suffer from fragmentation, which in these systems has raised a similar need for integrated care. However, different types of illness require the involvement of different health and social care providers because the needs of the service users are different.

In addition, the division of authority between the providers varies among the types of systems, which is one of the reasons that the organization of care delivery varies. For instance, in the UK, local and regional authorities dominate the organization of care delivery, whereas in the Netherlands, private providers are prominent [Van Raak and Paulus, 2008].

The Case of Botswana

From the many cases of integrated care delivery, we have selected one case for the purpose of illustrating the four-part approach that we introduced earlier. We do not suggest the case is representative of integrated care in general, nor should it be.

Table 1. Cases of integrated care delivery in Europe and Africa

Case and Country	Goals (main)	Target groups	Providers	Organizational characteristics of care delivery
The Netherlands: Trynwalden [Sustainable Trynwalden, n.d.]	1. To revitalize the rural community through rebuilding local infrastructures. 2. To provide services that enable older people to remain independent and to stay in their community.	Older inhabitants from Trynwalden (a rural region in the North-East of the Netherlands, province of Friesland).	Local authorities, health insurance company, housing corporations, nursing home, social work agencies, home care agencies, advisory council of older people.	1. A separate, independent and private organization, 'Sustainable Trynwalden', was created to organize the care delivery process. 2. Demand-oriented and decentralized service delivery to older people (a 'supermarket') instead of centralized, provider oriented care delivery. 3. Older people get the care when and where they need it, particularly in the community instead of e.g. nursing homes. 4. Involvement of brokers in housing, welfare and care. 5. Multidisciplinary teams.
Italy: The Working Unit of Continuous Care [Nesti et al., 2003]	To guide older persons from the hospital to appropriate care services.	Older persons who are discharged from the hospitals in Health District ASL 4 (municipalities of Alto Vicentino, North-East Italy)	Hospitals (physicians, geriatrician, physiotherapists, nurses and social worker), general practitioners, community care providers, nursing homes.	1. Intake and needs assessment by the WUCC (a geriatric assessment unit located in (and staffed by) the hospitals) and planning of care. 2. Shared information system and monitoring of care delivery process. 3. Provision of home care, admission to a nursing home, etc. 4. Social worker is the interface between hospital and the region.
United Kingdom: Community Care by Rapid Response Teams [Alaszewski et al., 2003]	1. Prevention of inappropriate hospital admission. 2. Promotion of early hospital discharge. 3. To work in partnership with existing agencies.	Hospital patients in Cumbria (North-West England) who are eligible for discharge and who are awaiting social care; patients at home who experience an acute period of illness.	Health authority, acute NHS hospital wards, local social care agencies.	1. Needs assessment by teams of nurses. 2. Purchase by the team of social care from local agencies. 3. Liaisons with social service agencies to establish continuing care.

Table 1. Cases of integrated care delivery in Europe and Africa (continued)

Case and Country	Goals (main)	Target groups	Providers	Organizational characteristics of care delivery
Botswana: Community Home-Based Care (CHBC) [Fogstad, 2002]	1. Implementation of Community Home-Based Care in the entire country as a key strategy to sharing and harmonizing care tasks between providers.	Persons with HIV/AIDS who need Community Home-Based Care.	Hospitals, District Health Teams, welfare agencies (food, shelter, clothing), hospices, NGO's, community based organizations (CBOs), daycare centers, community volunteers, family members.	1. Division of tasks and authority between: -AIDS/STD unit within the Ministry of Health (national coordination and monitoring/surveys). -District Health Teams: overall supervision and coordination of Community Home-Based Care for their district. -Providers. 2. Linkages between these agents, particularly to strengthen the referral system and communication in order to ensure continuity of care.
South Africa: Tuberculosis Treatment Team (TTT) [Wilkinson, 2002]	1. To deliver tuberculosis diagnosis and treatment services. 2. Sustainable integration of the services of the TTT into the district health system.	All residents in the Hlabisa Health District (Eastern part of South Africa), who are suspected of, or suffering from Tuberculosis.	Hospital's outpatient department, acute medical services, tuberculosis ward, village primary care clinics, community health workers, private doctors, traditional healers, volunteers.	1. Screening at the outpatient department. 2. Stabilization of condition by the acute medical services. 3. Arrangement of community care and discharge from the hospital to the community. 4. Coordination and organization of care delivery by the TTT.

It was sufficient that the case met the following two criteria: the case should concern an illness that requires the delivery of integrated care and which is widely spread across the continents, in order that the issue is immediately recognized by readers from different national backgrounds; the case should concern a cooperative of providers in its infancy, because this would bring to light the problems and challenges of redesigning and implementing integrated care. The selected case concerns integrated care delivery to HIV/AIDS patients in Botswana.

Botswana is a country in the center of the Southern African plateau. The total land area is approximately 582,000 square kilometers, 87% of which is occupied by the Kgalagadi (Kalahari) Desert. In 2004, the country had a population of 1,77 million people and is one of the least populated African countries. Approximately 89% of the population lives in the eastern part of Botswana where the soil is more fertile. Although the economy of Botswana is among the strongest in Africa, poverty is a major problem. According to the 1997 Botswana Poverty Study, 47% of the population lives below the poverty line [Fogstad, 2002; Shaibu, 2006; WHO, 2005; WHO, n.d.].

Botswana is subdivided into 24 health districts. The central level formulates policies, programs and guidelines, which are implemented by the district and local levels. 90% of the health services are provided directly by the government or by state subsidized facilities. The remaining 10% are provided by private hospitals and private practitioners [WHO, n.d.].The national government of Botswana has encouraged the development of a decentralized health care referral system, in which the local governments (i.e. district or town councils) are running the primary health care system [Fogstad, 2002].

HIV/AIDS is considered the biggest threat to Botswana's development. The first case of HIV/AIDS in Botswana was diagnosed in 1985 and since then the prevalence has increased rapidly. Nowadays Botswana is among the countries with the highest prevalence of HIV/AIDS [WHO, 2006]. Up to 70% of all in-patients in medical wards of referral hospitals are HIV-related cases [WHO, n.d.]. Due to the increase of the numbers of HIV/AIDS cases, the occupancy of hospital beds and the use of home-based care have increased significantly, while financial and human resources for cure and care were already under pressure. As a response to the emerging HIV/AIDS epidemic, the national government of Botswana has launched two Medium Term Plans for HIV/AIDS (MTP I and MTP II), followed by the National HIV/AIDS Strategic Framework 2003-2009. One of the purposes of the Framework is to provide clear guidance for Ministries, districts, NGOs (nongovernmental organizations that provide support to people living with HIV/AIDS), and the private sector to enable them to work in a collaborative manner in reducing the impact of AIDS in Botswana. Several bodies are assigned the task of coordinating the implementation of the government policies on HIV/AIDS. The highest body, at the national level, is the National AIDS Council (chaired by the Head of State), which coordinates the multi-sectoral responses to HIV/AIDS. The National AIDS Coordinating Agency acts as the secretariat of the Council. Together with the National AIDS Council, this agency provides leadership in delivering HIV/AIDS services. Coordination at the district level, which is the primary implementation level, is assigned to the District Multi-Sectoral Aids Committees and the District Aids Coordinators. At the lowest level, in a number of villages, Village Multi-Sectoral AIDS Committees have been established [NACA, 2003]. Among others, the National Strategic Framework is guiding the Community Home-Based Care (CHBC)-Program, which is considered as an important approach to deal with HIV/AIDS in the districts. This Program aims to ensure an optimum level of care for terminally ill patients, to provide clinical care, nursing care, counseling services to patients and their families at home, and to establish a functional referring system among hospitals, District Health Teams and clinics. The latter aim involves sharing care tasks between hospitals, welfare agencies (food, shelter, clothing), hospices for palliative care, NGOs, village health committees, community based organizations (CBOs, mostly church organizations and women groups), daycare centers, community volunteers, families and the community (informal care). Community Home-Based Care is available through District Health Teams, which are coordinated by the AIDS/STD Unit in the Ministry of Health [NACA, 2003; Shaibu, 2006, WHO, 2005].

The National Strategic Framework shows that district responses to HIV/AIDS tend to be fragmented. The responses produce duplication and overlap and generally lack the cohesiveness and direction that strong coordination might provide. While the response at the district level has made some progress in terms of establishing e.g. coordination mechanisms, these remain somewhat fragmented [NACA, 2003]. It appears that the linkages between the agents, at least in a number of districts, are weak. For example, according to Shaibu [2006], in the village of Mmopane there is lack of coordination from the referral hospitals to other agencies, and as a result there is no continuity of care for patients who are discharged from the hospital or who move back and forth between health services. Fogstad [2002] has observed that services were delivered in a piecemeal fashion by the different providers, who neglected the need for linkages between provisions and harmonization of services.

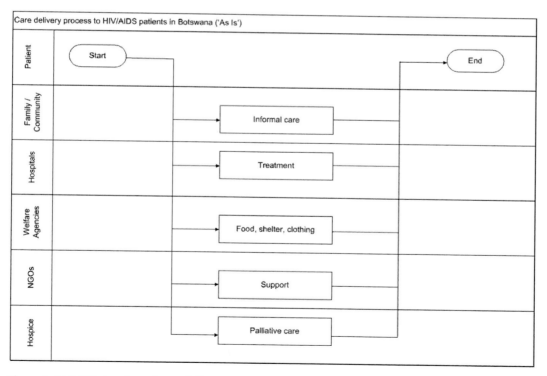

Figure 1. 'AS IS' situation of care delivery to HIV/AIDS patients in Botswana.

Figure 1 shows a process map [Harmon, 2003; Hunt, 1996], which represents the summary of the above description of the existing care delivery process to AIDS/HIV patients

('AS IS'). The 'Start' indicates the entrance of the HIV/AIDS patient into the care delivery process, while the 'End' indicates the patient's death. The rectangles represent the care activities by the providers, i.e. 'Functions' in each so-called 'Swim Lane'. The arrows represent the patient's move through the process. The process map also shows the lack of linkages between the providers. Basically, depending on the local situation, the patient can use any of the provisions and move back and forth between the providers. The second Swim Lane –family/community- includes traditional healers.

The traditional healers are a force to be reckoned with, as is indicated by Shaibu's [2006] report that some patients in the village of Mmopane at some point abandoned Western biomedicine for traditional healing methods.

REDESIGNING THE CARE DELIVERY PROCESS

When we are convinced that the current situation (in the case of Botswana the 'AS IS' situation in figure 1) is not the desired situation ('SHOULD BE'), we need to make a systematic assessment of the existing situation. This requires that we identify the central entity, in this case the patient with HIV/AIDS, and the actors in the process of care delivery. In addition, to judge whether a process in the 'AS IS' situation needs to be improved, ideally performance indicators and their measures are set [Van Merode et al., 1999]. Particularly in the cure sector of the health care system, known performance indicators are the cost effectiveness of service delivery, the time the patient spends in the delivery process or the percentage of patients who have complications after surgery. Once the performance indicators and measures for this are set their values have to be determined. This has to be done during a fixed time interval in which the environment of the process is stable. In the care sector, unambiguous performance indicators are mostly not available or reliable measures are missing. In addition, there are many instances of integrated care which are facing continuously changing processes and environments, while the outcomes of coordination and cooperation are uncertain. Furthermore, because integrated care aims at delivering tailor-made care, there are no generalized or standardized outcomes [Paulus et al., 2002]. Under these circumstances, one should concentrate on process indicators rather than performance indicators.

There are several examples of process indicators, including the presence of waste and the simplicity of the process. According to Fogstad [2002] and the WHO [2005], there is a great need to strengthen coordination among partners and stakeholders in Botswana, in order to ensure timely, efficient and effective service provision. Lack of linkages usually indicates or causes waste. Therefore at least some types of waste will probably occur in the Botswana case. The 'AS IS' process map is the input for a waste analysis. During a waste analysis steps within the process are identified that do not add value to the process. Waste analysis has its roots in the Toyota production system and seven different types of waste are distinguished [Liker, 2004: 27-34] (table 2). The eighth type of waste is the 'unused employee creativity' [Liker, 2004; Van Merode et al., 2004]. Employees often have ideas about how to improve the efficiency of their work.

Table 2. Different types of waste and examples in health care [after Liker, 2004]

Types of waste	Examples in health care
1. Overproduction	Too much medication, space
2. Waiting	Waiting of patients, staff
3. Unnecessary transport	Documents, laboratory results
4. Over processing	Making invoices, dictating
5. Excess inventory	Documents, inventory
6. Unnecessary movement	Looking for a patient file
7. Defects	Offering excuse for long waiting, new appointments

Common examples of waste that occur in integrated care are *overproduction* by providers (indicated by duplication and overlap of services), patients who are *waiting* unnecessarily for services due to e.g. lack of coordination and communication between providers, *unnecessary movement* of patients (e.g. when patients have to move back and forth between providers), unnecessary steps in the process such as duplication of tests (*over processing*), and *defects* such as poor outcomes of service delivery.

When process indicators are used, one has to ask oneself: "Why are we doing it and why are we doing it in this way?". By asking the first part of the question we try to find the fundamental goal of the process. In our case this is to provide the needed care to a patient who has HIV/AIDS. The answer to the second part of the question ("why are we doing it in this way?") is often: for historical reasons. The process has developed into its current state over the years. In a redesign the next question is: "What should the process look like?" A redesign starts with a blank sheet. A redesign does not intend to modify an existing process but to develop a totally new designed process from scratch, which process should be as simple as possible.

In our case we see in figure 1 that coordination between providers is lacking, which might ultimately paralyze the provision of care. To give some examples, a GP can assess which kind of care is needed from a medical point of view. The hospital as well may play a role in assessing the need for care from a medical perspective. A social worker is able to determine (in discussion with the patient and his relatives) whether or not non-medical support is needed. Both the need for medical care and the need for non-medical care must be assessed on a regular base. Chances are that neither of these providers has an overall view of the total domain of integrated care to their patient, because assessment by each of them will cover only their part of the care delivery process. Therefore, in the redesign an agent is needed who is able to overlook the full spectrum of care delivery and who can coordinate all contributions to the provision of care to the HIV/AIDS patient, in order to bring about integration. The coordinator has to have regular meetings for example with the GP concerning the medical status and with the social worker concerning the non-medical status of the patient. The time intervals between these meetings will depend on the medical status and the social well-being of the patient. The coordinator also has to provide information to all care providers involved about their work and mutual contributions to integrated care. In case of absence of the coordinator a substitute coordinator has to be available in order to cover for the coordinator.

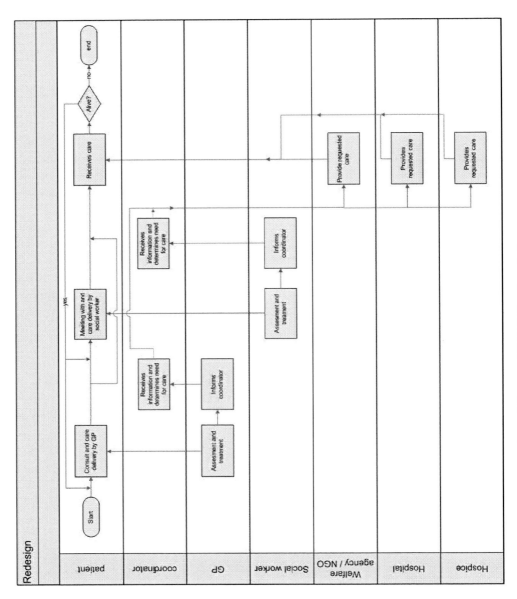

Figure 2. The redesign: 'SHOULD BE' situation of care delivery to HIV/AIDS patients in Botswana.

Although the redesign in figure 2 includes a crucial resource, i.e. the coordinator, we kept the redesign as simple as possible. Particularly, we decided not to include a coordination team (in Botswana, District Health Teams in fact fulfill this role) instead of a single coordinator, as the performance of such a team itself would depend on the presence of a well-functioning internal coordination system among the team members. This might make the redesign more complicated than necessary.

The redesigned process -the actual care delivery is not a subject of this redesign- starts with the patient who has HIV/AIDS making his/her entrance. The patient has a consultation with the GP, the health condition of the patient is determined and an assessment is made as to whether medical care is required, and, if so, which medical specialty is needed. If the required care can be provided by the GP, the GP provides it during the consultation. The GP discusses the results of the assessment with the coordinator, as well as the actions that have to be taken by the coordinator, such as arranging the involvement of other providers. The coordinator takes action and communicates with the care providers (the hospice, hospital, welfare agencies and NGOs; although informal care from the family/community may be needed as well, they are not included in figure 2). In case of medical care, for legal reasons, the communication with the care provider might have to be done by the GP instead of the coordinator. The social worker also has an appointment with the patient, in order to make an assessment of the services needed, and, if possible the social worker provides those services. The social worker informs the coordinator about the results of the assessment and based on the discussion the coordinator contacts the appropriate care providers in order to make further agreements about the delivery of the required care. There has to be a continuous monitoring of the patient, but the pace of the visits of the GP and social worker may differ. The social and medical status of the patient determines the intervals between visits and consultations. In addition, the patients or his/her relatives may ask the GP for a consultation or the social worker for a visit if they think this is needed.

In western countries, an ICT-system should facilitate the redesigned process. An example of an ICT-system is an electronic record system in which care providers share information about the patient within the boundaries that are set by legislation. In such an ICT-system, all involved care providers can find information as to which kind of care was already provided and how the patients responded to this. In developing countries, implementation of such ICT systems will not always be feasible. From a Western point of view this can be regarded as waste. Instead, the coordinator and the providers must rely on the exchange of oral or – preferably- written information. Information about the situation of the patient or actions that were taken, and agreements between the coordinator and individual care providers must be committed to paper in order to enable dissemination of the same information to different care providers.

RULES AND ROUTINES VERSUS INTEGRATED CARE

In the previous section, we indicated that processes of care delivery in health and social care and their context have a historical dimension. During years of training and education, professional care deliverers have grown accustomed to particular procedures for providing care. Working according to these procedures has become a habit. Some methods, particularly those which are applied by traditional healers, are transferred from generation to generation through processes of socialization and are preserved in their original shape as much as possible. These habits, or routines, represent an important concept for the study of processes of health and social care, because a large proportion of the work of providers is performed through routines. Based on Feldman [2000] we consider routines as repetitive, recognizable patterns of interdependent actions, which are carried out by multiple agents, are bound by rules and do not change very much from one iteration to another [Van Raak et al., 2007]. These habits, as experience shows, are difficult to shake off, because they are confirmed and fixed by formal and informal rules that have developed during years, decades and sometimes even centuries. The rules structure, constrain, guide, or constitute the behavior of persons (individuals and groups) and can allow, oblige, or prohibit particular actions and interactions. Rules are laid down in legislation, policy structures, contracts, protocols, job descriptions, organizational guidelines, agreements, professional standards, and, not to be ignored, longstanding traditions.

Rules are developed and operate on different levels, especially the national, regional, local and even the individual level. In the case of Botswana, for example, the National HIV/AIDS Strategic Framework 2003-2009 constitutes a collection of rules that is developed on the national level and guides the actions of the District Multi-Sectoral Aids Committees. The Framework stipulates that the committees must coordinate the execution of the HIV/AIDS policy in their districts. If these committees comply to the rules in the Framework and continue to do so, providing coordination becomes one of their routines. Some rules, especially legislation, work from outside the person when they are enforced through sanctions and control. Others work from inside, when they have become internalized as a part of the persons' mind set during training and socialization, and they have become entrenched through repeated use [Clemens and Cook, 1999; Hall and Weaver, 2001; Hargrave and Van de Ven, 2006; Ingram and Clay, 2000; Scott, 2001]. Typical examples of the latter rules are the often observed, persistent inclination among professionals to provide monodisciplinary care rather than multidisciplinary care, or tendencies among African villagers to visit traditional healers.

The outcome of these historical processes at a given time is a particular configuration of rules and routines. Health care systems across the world can be thought of as collections of such configurations. The development of each of these configurations has taken its own course, and resulted in each configuration as having its own, sometimes even unique set of features [Van Raak et al., 2007; Van Raak and Paulus, 2008; Thelen, 1999]. Each of these configurations has slowly developed over the years and cannot be changed overnight.

Typical of any process redesign is that it represents a proposal for a new set of rules for actions. If these rules are followed on a regular basis, they result in new routines. In the case of our redesign the new routines mainly concern bringing about coordination and holding meetings between the coordinator and service providers, which implies a change of tasks among the involved agents. However, the more the redesign deviates from the features of the existing configuration, the harder it will be to implement the redesign. On the other hand, the better the match, the more feasible the implementation. Kümpers et al. [2002, 2006] observed that it is possible to incorporate new organizational procedures quite smoothly into existing service delivery processes in a region, provided that the procedures match with the characteristics of the region. Otherwise, processes can be severely interrupted, delayed or riddled with conflict. Consequently, in order to assess the feasibility of implementation of a redesign, we have to determine whether and where the redesign matches or deviates from the existing configuration of rules and routines.

To determine matches and deviations, the first step is to map out the existing rules (particularly legislation, but also organizational rules), and routines. The latter can be identified by e.g. observing behavior or by asking workers about their daily work program. Next, the rules for actions in the redesign are compared with the existing rules and routines. Finally, the match is determined. Obviously, if there is no match with legal rules, there is no point in proceeding with the redesign, unless the redesign is altered. If there is a match with the legislation (and organizational rules), and the routines as well, implementation of the redesign has a very good chance of succeeding. If the redesign happens to deviate from particularly the existing routines, there are two options. One option is to change the redesign towards the existing routines. This will make implementation much easier, but will result in a redesign that strongly deviates from the original intentions. The other option is more ambitious, as it requires a change of existing routines towards the rules in the redesign.

A comparison between the original situation in our case (figure 1) and the redesign of the care delivery process in figure 2 shows that the redesign is less simple than the existing situation. (From the perspective of Business Process Redesign this is rather unusual.) The reason is that we had to add an element to the redesign, which is indispensable for integrated care and was missing in the 'AS IS' situation, namely coordination. The comparison also shows that the redesign differs strongly from the current practice in the Botswana case, including the routines of the providers involved. Particularly, in the 'AS IS' situation, the providers are used to working independently and in isolation from each other, whereas in the 'SHOULD BE' situation, they are supposed to communicate and cooperate with a coordinator and other providers. If we want to continue with the implementation of the redesign for integrated care in its original form, we must change the existing situation. This is part of a process of organizational change, which includes a range of transactions and transaction costs.

TRANSACTION COSTS OF INTEGRATED CARE

As became clear so far, the realization of integrated care in cases such as Botswana requires the development and implementation of a drastic redesign of existing care delivery processes, which strongly deviates from existing routines. Consequently, a pain-staking, time consuming process of organizational change, requiring many resources, usually precedes the actual introduction of integrated care. Each process of organizational change, such as the development and implementation of a redesign, encompasses a substantial number of different transactions including changing the status quo [Lewin, 1952] and creating relevant circumstances. Transactions, i.e. exchange activities between two or more units, generate costs. Hamilton et al. [2005] show that these costs can be formidable due to the complexity of the change process and the long set-up period that is required to organize integrated care. For managers, detailed information on these costs is considered necessary to make decisions on whether or not to invest in a redesign or another type of change, to continue or re-direct change (if necessary) and to better understand, predict and control organizational change [Cummings and Worley, 2005].

Table 3. Redesign/change process in theory: transactions and transaction costs [based on Paulus et al, 2003]

Phase	Steps	Type of transactions	Type of transaction costs			
			Search	Contract	Maintenance	Completion
1. Introduction	1.1 Recognition of the problem	1. Gathering information	+			
		2. Linking information data			+	+
		3. Monitoring outcomes			+	+
		4. Comparing to standards	+			
	1.2 Specification of the nature of the problem	5. Detecting causes for faults in current organizational structure	+		+	+
		6. Identifying necessary changes		+		
2. Planning	2.1 Developing alternatives	7. Searching alternatives	+			+
		8. Developing alternatives	+			+
	2.2 Selecting alternatives	9. Considering how to implement alternatives			+	
		10. Choosing the best alternative			+	
	2.3 Developing a change approach	11. Brainstorming on the overall approach	+			+
		12. Selecting the overall approach		+		
	2.4 Selecting techniques	13. Developing techniques supportive for change	+			+
		14. Selecting techniques supportive for change		+		
		15. Reducing resistance against change (before implementation)	+			+
3. Implementation	3.1 Unfreezing the status quo	16. Preparing persons involved for change	+			+
		17. Making persons involved aware of change	+			+
		18. Reducing resistance (after implementation)	+			+
	3.2 Introduction of actual change	19. Implementing concepts		+		
		20. Beginning with the use of concepts			+	
	3.3 Refreezing the situation after change	21. Making the situation stable again		+		
		22. Realizing conditions			+	+
		23. Keeping an eye on maintaining change			+	+
4. Evaluation	4.1 Comparing the actual results with planned results	24. Assembling relevant information	+			+
		25. Realizing conditions			+	+
		26. Keeping an eye on maintaining change			+	+
	4.2 Explaining the differences between actual and planned results	27. Exploring causes for differences			+	+
	4.3 Using information for future activities	28. Using information for the future				+

This is particularly important because change seems to increasingly become a characteristic feature of health and social care, while the means to achieve such a change seem to become scarcer and scarcer due to ageing and a reduced spending on health care.

Nevertheless, as Fulop et al. [2002] indicate, the costs of change processes are barely part of current research. The same is true with respect to research on the implementation of integrated care [Hébert and Veil, 2004]. Hence, a model that can be used to assess the costs of organizational change will increasingly become important. Below, we present the outline of a model, which is still being developed, and which can be used to identify and determine these costs. We unravel the most important costs and transactions which are involved in processes of organizational change that are intended to produce integrated care.

We make use of a self-composed theoretical framework [Paulus et al., 2003] and the insights gained from the application of this framework to actual integrated care cases. Our theoretical framework combines insights from organizational change models [for an overview see Cummings and Worley, 2005] and transaction cost theory [Kaplan, 1995, see James, 2005, for an overview; Williamson, 1979]. The main elements of this framework are summarized in table 3.

Table 3 shows a linear process of planned change [Cummings, 1984; Lewin, 1952]. The process is based on the 'model of the Process of Managing Organizational Changes' of Duncan, Ginter and Swayne [Duncan et al., 1998; Longest, 1998]. This model represents different phases and steps that take place before, during and after change. The phases and steps are commonly distinguished in the literature on organizational change processes. According to the model, each change process has four consecutive phases:

1. Introduction (identification of a problem);
2. Planning (selection of alternative solutions, e.g. process redesigns);
3. Implementation of the solution (in our case the redesign);
4. Evaluation of change.

Each phase requires different steps and transactions to successfully effectuate the total change process [Paulus et al., 2003]. On the basis of the literature on organizational change and our own empirical analyses of change processes, we identified 28 key transactions for the total change process (see table 3). These transactions range from gathering information to identifying necessary changes, developing techniques supportive for change and realizing necessary conditions. A study of six change processes aimed at the implementation of integrated care in the Netherlands indicates that relatively many transactions take place in the planning phase and implementation phase [Paulus and Van Raak, 2007]. The same study shows that gathering information (#1), developing alternatives (#8), selecting techniques supportive for change (#14), reducing resistance against change (#15), realizing conditions (#22), assembling relevant information (#24) and using information for the future (#28) are among the most frequently conducted transactions during change [Paulus and Van Raak, 2007]. In the case of our redesign, #1 and #8 would concern the analysis of the existing situation ('AS IS'; figure 1) and the development of the redesign, whereas #15 and #22 would concern the implementation of the redesign.

We assume that each of the 28 transactions generates transaction costs. According to Rao [2003], transaction costs among other things include the costs of information, bargaining/negotiation over transactions, contracting (formal or informal), monitoring and enforcement of agreements, and search and information costs. Since there are various transaction costs, there are also different classifications of these costs [see James, 2005; Williamson, 1979]. Following Kaplan [1995], we distinguish between four types of transaction costs:

1. Search costs (i.e. the costs of seeking and finding contract parties);
2. Contract costs (i.e. the costs of actual contract-making);
3. Maintenance costs (i.e. the costs of controlling progress or maintaining certain procedures);
4. Completion costs (i.e. the costs of completing a transaction).

Each transaction can involve more than one type of costs (see table 3). Table 3 shows that the bulk of the costs of change, in theory, are related to transactions that take place in the planning phase and implementation phase. Costs mostly concern completion costs, search costs and maintenance costs. Empirical studies indicate that the actual costs of the change processes that are aimed at integrated care are related to transactions that take place in the planning phase. They mainly include search costs and maintenance costs [Paulus and Van Raak, 2007].

Our brief overview shows that, in order to control the costs of change, a focus is required on the planning phase and containment of the costs of developing and selecting the proper techniques supportive for change. Containing the costs of unfreezing the status quo and refreezing the situation after change in the implementation phase is equally important. Unfreezing and refreezing in our case concerns routines and the rules that fix these routines, such as organizational procedures and mind sets of the providers. The participants in the Botswana case must break away from old routines in order to make new routines viable, core of which are coordination and working according to a new task division. The larger the gap between old and new routines, the more transaction costs can be expected. For example, in order to have the providers in the Botswana districts work according to the redesign, District Health Teams may need to negotiate with the providers about new working procedures. In addition, they might decide to apply a number of techniques of management control, such as codes of conduct and role model behavior by authoritative persons (cultural controls); the making of job designs, selection of new staff and assignment of staff to new positions, training and education (personnel controls); use of protocols (action controls); monitoring of performances and handing out sanctions (result controls) [Merchant and Van der Stede, 2003]. All these techniques that are used to unfreeze and refreeze routines and rules will produce transaction costs, especially maintenance costs.

CONCLUSION

The approach that we presented in this paper combines a number of established perspectives. A combined application to integrated care however is a first-ever approach, which opens new directions for future research. Application of the approach provides managers information which they can use to make a number of decisions about the implementation of integrated care. The analysis of the existing situation ('AS IS') helps managers to determine whether or not this situation corresponds with their goals and the patients' needs, and to decide whether change is needed. The making of a redesign ('SHOULD BE') helps managers to identify the similarities and differences between the existing situation and the desirable situation, and to determine where changes are required. Managers must then decide whether they are willing to pay for the transaction costs that will emerge during the processes of change. If they know in advance that the costs of change will exceed the benefits (i.e. reduction of waste), it will be easy to make a decision. They will probably decide to maintain the situation as it is. Conversely, when the expected benefits will exceed the costs, they will probably decide to change the 'AS IS' situation into a 'SHOULD BE' situation. In case the costs and benefits might be balanced, it is more difficult to make a decision (figure 3).

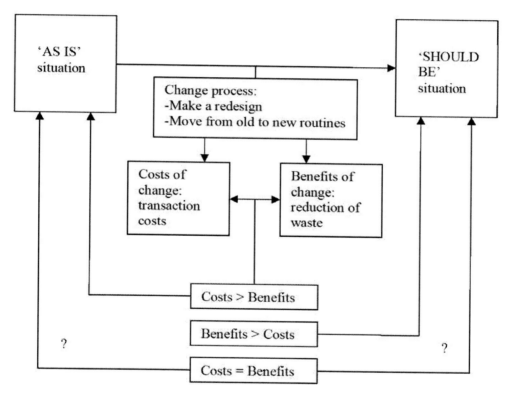

Figure 3. Change towards integrated care: information and decision making by managers.

In real life, decision making will be difficult anyway. This is because the managers will not have all the necessary information for decision making in advance. Experienced managers are used to this. Nevertheless, use of our approach will provide the managers at least a certain amount of information that they can use to make a balanced decision. From the comparison of the 'AS IS' situation and the 'SHOULD BE' situation, managers will know whether there is a gap between both. The wider the gap, the more efforts will be needed to change existing rules and routines and the more transaction costs are produced. If in the current situation the amount of waste is unacceptably high, managers have no other option but to decide that change must be initiated. Otherwise, it depends on the self-confidence and 'gut feeling' of the managers whether they dare to make a decision and are able to make the right decision. If they feel not sufficiently confident, and if they are concerned that achieving the 'SHOULD BE' situation might be too ambitious, we can offer a way out. Managers can also decide to strive for a 'COULD BE' situation instead. 'SHOULD BE' refers to the ideal situation, whereas 'COULD BE' concerns a situation that is less optimal, but perhaps more feasible, because the differences between the 'COULD BE' situation and the 'AS IS' situation are smaller. Perhaps, striving for a 'COULD BE' situation for integrated care is better in any case. After all, the interests of patients are not served when efforts to create the ideal situation are stranded.

REFERENCES

Alaszewksi, A., Baldock, J., Billings, J., Coxon, C., and Twigg, J. (2003). Providing integrated health and social care for older persons in the United Kingdom [E-report]. National Report. Canterbury, UK: CHSS. www.euro.centre.org/procare.

Clemens, E. S., and Cook, J. M. (1999). Politics and institutionalism: explaining durability and change. *Annual Review of Sociology, 25,* 441–466.

Cummings, T. G. (1984). Transorganizational Development. In B. M. Straw, and L. L. Cummings (Eds.), *Research in Organizational Behavior* (Vol. 6, pp. 367-422). Greenwich, CN: JAI Press.

Cummings, T. G., and Worley, C. G. (2005). *Organizational development and change* (8th edition). Mason, Ohio: Thomson/South Western.

Duncan, W. J., Ginter, P. M., and Swayne, L. E. (1998). *Handbook of health care management.* Oxford, UK: Blackwell Publishers.

Feldman, M. S. (2000). Organizational Routines as a Source of Continuous Change. *Organization Science, 11 (6),* 611 – 629.

Fogstad, H. (2002). Community home-based care for people with AIDS in Botswana: operational guidelines, staffing methodologies and norms [E-report]. Maastricht, The Netherlands: The Network-TUFH www.the-networktufh.org.

Fulop, N., Protopsaltis, G., Hutchings, A., King, A., Allen, P., Normand, C., and Walters, R. (2002). Process and impact of mergers of NHS trusts: multicentre case study and management cost analysis. *BMJ, August 3, 325 (7358),* 246.

Hall, P., and Weaver, L. (2001). Interdisciplinary education and teamwork: a long and winding road. *Medical education, 35,* 867–875.

Hamilton, K. E., Sullivan, F. M., Donnan, P. T., Taylor, R., Ikenwilo, D., Scott, A., Baker, C., and Wyke, S. (2005). A managed clinical network for cardiac services: set-up, operation and impact on patient care. *International Journal of Integrated Care* [On-line journal], Vol. 5 (July-September). www.ijic.org.

Harmon, P. (2003). *Business Process Change. A manager's guide to improving, redesigning, and automating processes.* Amsterdam, The Netherlands etc.: Morgan Kaufmann Publishers.

Hargrave, T. J., and Ven, A. H. van de (2006). A collective action model of institutional innovation. *Academy of Management Review, 31(4),* 864–888.

Hébert, R. R., and Veil, A. A. (2004). Monitoring the degree of implementation of an integrated delivery system. *International Journal of Integrated Care* [On-line journal], Vol. 4 (July-September). www.ijic.org.

Hunt, V. D. (1996). *Process Mapping: How to Reengineer Your Business Processes*. New York, NJ: Wiley.

Ingram, P., and Clay, K. (2000). The choice-within-constraints new institutionalism and implications for sociology. *Annual Review of Sociology, 26,* 525–546.

James, J. S. (2005). Annotated bibliography on transaction cost economics; theoretical, empirical and institutional issues with some applications [E-paper]. http://dass.missouri.edu/faculty/hjames/TCE/.

Kaplan, B. (1995). *Organizations specialization examined: Transaction costs vs. Agency theory*. Riverside, California: University of California.

Kodner, D. L., and Spreeuwenberg, C., (2002). Integrated care: meaning, logic, applications, and implications – a discussion paper. *International Journal of Integrated Care* [On-line journal], Vol. 2 (October-December). www.ijic.org.

Kümpers, S., Raak, A. J. A. van, Hardy, B., and Mur-Veeman, I. (2002). The influences of institutions and culture on health policies: different approaches to integrated care in England and The Netherlands. *Public Administration 80 (2),* 339-358.

Kümpers, S, Mur-Veeman, I., Hardy, B., Raak, A. van, and Maarse, H. (2006). Integrating dementia care in England and The Netherlands: Four comparative local case studies. *Health and Place 12 (4),* 404-420.

Leichsenring, K., and Alaszewski, A. M. (Eds.) (2004). *Providing integrated health and social care for older persons. A European overview of issues at stake*. Aldershot, UK: Ashgate Publishing Ltd.

Lewin, K. (1952). Group Decision and Social Change. In T. M. N. G. E. Swanson, and E. L. Hartley (Eds.), *Readings in Social Psychology* (pp. 459-473). New York, NJ: Holt, Rinehart.

Liker, J. K. (2004). *The Toyota way: 14 management principles from the world's greatest manufacturer*. New York, N.J., etc.: McGraw-Hill.

Longest, B. B. (1998). Organizational Change and Innovation. In W. J. Duncan, P. M. Ginter and L. E. Swayne (Eds.), *Handbook of health care management* (pp. 369-398). Oxford, UK: Blackwell.

Merchant, K. A., and Stede, W. van der (2003). *Management control systems: performance measurement, evaluation and incentives* (1st edition). Harlow, England etc.: Prentice Hall.

Merode, G. G. van, Groothuis, S., and Goldschmidt, H. M. J. (1999). Workflow management: changing your organization through simulation. *Accreditation and Quality Assurance, 4 (9-10),* 438-442.

Merode, F. van, Molema, H., and Goldschmidt, H. (2004). GUM and six sigma approaches positioned as deterministic tools in quality target engineering. *Accreditation and Quality Assurance, 10,* 32-36.

NACA (2003). National HIV/AIDS Strategic Framework 2003-2009 [E-policy paper]. www.naca.gov.bw/documents/.

Nesti, G., Campostrini, S., Garbin, S., Piva, P., Di Santo, P., and Tunzi, F. (2003). Providing integrated health and social care for older persons in Italy. National Report [E-report]. www.euro.centre.org/procare.

Newhouse, R., Mills, M., Johantgen, M., and Pronovost, P., (2003). Is there a relationship between service integration and differentiation and patient outcomes? *International Journal of Integrated Care* [On-line journal], Vol. 3 (October-December). www.ijic.org.

Paulus, A., Raak, A. van, and Keijzer, F. (2002). ABC: The pathway to Comparison of the Costs of Integrated Care. *Public Money and Management, 22 (3),* 25-32.

Paulus, A. T. G., Boumans, N., Keijzer, F., Vijgen, S., and Mur, I. (2003). *Geïntegreerde vraaggestuurde verpleeghuiszorg. Een longitudinaal en transversaal onderzoek naar de effecten, kosten en het proces van verandering van aanbod- naar geïntegreerde vraaggestuurde vormen van verpleeghuiszorg* (Integrated nursing home care. A longitudinal and transversal research of the effects, costs and the process of change from supplier-oriented to demand-oriented integrated nursing home care). Maastricht, The Netherlands: Maastricht University.

Paulus, A. T. G., and Raak, A. J. A. van (2007). *Change processes in health care: a transaction cost perspective* (unpublished manuscript). Maastricht, The Netherlands: Maastricht University.

Paulus, A., Raak, A. van, and Maarse, H. (2008). Is integrated nursing home care cheaper than traditional care? A cost comparison. *International Journal of Nursing Studies* (accepted for publication).

Raak, A. van, Mur-Veeman, I., and Paulus, A. (1999). Understanding the feasibility of integrated care: a rival viewpoint on the influence of actions and the institutional context. *The International Journal of Health Planning and Management, 14,* 235-248.

Raak, A. van, Mur-Veeman, I., Hardy, B., Steenbergen, M., and Paulus, A. (Eds.) (2003). *Integrated care in Europe. Description and comparison of integrated care in six EU countries.* Maarssen, The Netherlands: Reed Business Information, Elsevier Gezondheidszorg.

Raak, A. van, Paulus, A, and Mur-Veeman, I. (2005). Why do health and social care providers co-operate? *Health Policy, 74,* 13-23.

Raak, A. van, Paulus, A., and Made, J. van der (2007). The conditions for health and social care policy: routines and institutions in the Dutch case of need assessment. *Public Administration, 85 (4),* 1077–1095.

Raak, A. van, and Paulus, A. (2008). The emergence of multidisciplinary teams for interagency service delivery in Europe: Is historical institutionalism wrong? *Health Care Analysis* [Online First] www.springerlink.com.

Rao, P. K. (2003). *The economics of transaction costs. Theory, methods and applications.* Basingstoke, England: Palgrave Macmillan.

Scott, W. (2001). *Institutions and organizations* (2nd edition). Thousand Oaks, California: Sage Publications.

Segal, L., Dunt, D., Day, S. E., Day, N. A., Robertson, I., and Hawthorne, G. (2004). Introducing co-ordinated care (1): a randomised trial assessing client and cost outcomes. *Health Policy, 69 (2),* 201-213.

Shaibu, S. (2006). Community Home-based care in a rural vilage: challenges and strategies. *Journal of Transcultural Nursing, 17,* 89-94.

Sustainable Trynwalden (n.d.). Case study – Sustainable Trynwalden [E-paper]. www.skewiel-trynwalden.nl/engels/Downloads.htm

Thelen, K. (1999). Historical institutional institutionalism in comparative politics. *Annual Review of Political Science, 2,* 369–404.

Tjerbo T., and Kjekshus, L. E. (2005). Coordinating health care: lessons from Norway. *International Journal of Integrated Care* [On-line journal], Vol. 5 (October-December). www.ijic.org.

Vondeling, H., (2004). Economic evaluation of integrated care: an introduction. *International Journal of Integrated Care* [On-line journal], Vol. 4 (January-March). www.ijic.org.

Wan, T. T. H., Ma, A., and Lin, B.Y. J. (2001). Integration and the performance of healthcare networks: do integration strategies enhance efficiency, profitability, and image? *International Journal of Integrated Care* [On-line journal], Vol. 1 (April-June). www.ijic.org.

WHO (2005). Botswana – Summary country profile for HIV/AIDS treatment scale-up [E-report]. www.who.int.

WHO (2006). Botswana – Country Health System Fact Sheet 2006 [E-report]. www.who.int.

WHO (n.d.). Country Cooperation Strategy Botswana 2003-2007 [E-report]. www.who.int.

Wilkinson, D. (2002). Integrating tuberculosis diagnostic and treatment services into the district health system: towards unity in health in rural South Africa [E-report]. Maastricht, The Netherlands: The Network-TUFH. www.the-networktufh.org.

Williamson, O. E. (1979). Transaction cost economics: the governance of contractual relations. *Journal of Law and Economics, 22*, 233-261.

In: Integrated Health Care Delivers
Editor: Leonie A. Klein and Emily L. Neumann

ISBN 978-1-60456-851-6
© 2008 Nova Science Publishers, Inc.

Chapter 8

WHYS AND WHEREFORES OF INTEGRATED HEALTH CARE

Bengt Ahgren

Nordic School of Public Health, Gothenburg, Sweden

ABSTRACT

The development of health care systems can be described in terms of an escalating differentiation of roles, tasks and responsibilities. There are three main forces behind this development: decentralisation, specialisation and professionalization. The outcome can, on one hand, be regarded as a success story. On the other hand, there is also a flipside of this development. The three driving forces, individually and together, have contributed to a state of differentiation, often described as fragmentation. This state can be divided into different categories, depending on the interaction between the three driving forces: organisational fragmentation, clinical fragmentation and cultural fragmentation, which, in turn, may lead to patients becoming lost in health care delivery systems. This phenomenon can metaphorically be described as a Patient Bermuda Triangle.

Integrated health care is an issue addressed in many countries. Furthermore, there are many different approaches and their scopes are quite different. Some approaches aim to eliminate professional and departmental boundaries and develop multiprofessional teams, while others have the objectives to integrate different sectors of health care, i.e., to link primary, secondary and tertiary health care. Integrated health care should therefore be regarded as a concept of organising between different health care providers. Moreover, the dominating motive for creating integrated health care is to bring order in the chaotic condition of a fragmented health care.

It seems possible to diminish the clinical and organisational fragmentation in health care organisations by developing clinical guidelines and integrated health care network. However, the cultural fragmentation is probably the biggest challenge when creating integrated health care. It is proven to be difficult to change the values of health care professionals by top-down actions. Moreover, physicians tend to listen more to patients than to politicians or health care managers. A major breakthrough for patient empowerment may therefore imply that existing sets of professional values will be combined with demands emerging from consumer behaviour. Thus, political and top management rhetoric of integration will perhaps not be realised until articulated demands from patients and carers are channelled to health care professionals. By creating change bottom-up and also integrating the patients as resources and change-agents may thus increase the possibilities to diminish cultural fragmentation.

To conclude, the challenge of the future is to simultaneously promote integrated health care networks, clinical guidelines, patient empowerment, and change bottom-up, so as to ensure that the patients not are lost in a "Bermuda Triangle" of a health care system.

THE ESCALATING DIFFERENTIATION

The development of health care systems can be described in terms of an escalating differentiation of roles, tasks and responsibilities. Following Lawrence and Lorsch (1967), differentiation means differences in orientation as well as in structure between groups or organisational units. In health care, there are three main forces behind this development.

Decentralisation

Tighter economic conditions in health care during the last decades have created a need for rationalisation. There have been different strategies employed for this purpose. In the 1980s, an extensive decentralisation was implemented in most public health care organisations, which can involve *delegation* of responsibilities to a lower organisational level, *deconcentration* to a lower administrative servant, *devolution* to a lower political level; and *privatisation* of former public production (Rondinelli 1983). Following Saltman and Figueras (1997), most Western health care systems represent a hybrid of these four categories of decentralisation.

The rationale behind decentralisation is usually regarded as attractive because it brings decision-making closer to the health care staff. The decentralised organisation can, thereby, act more flexible and innovative than centralised institutions in the response to local needs and conditions. Furthermore, it can be more effective than a centralised organisation, as the frontline workforce has better ability to identify local problems and opportunities (Saltman and Figueras 1997).

Decentralisation can thus be seen as an alternative to provide public health care services in a more cost effective way. As a consequence of this strategy, extensive responsibilities, including budgetary tasks, were delegated/deconcentrated to frontline managers. In this connection, there was also an increasing sense of economy and awareness of costs within the frontline of public health care.

In the 1990s, the decentralised organisation has in some Beveridge-like health care systems (that is those financed mainly by general taxation and with a public supervision of the provision), been reinforced by a purchaser-provider split creating internal markets with performance-related reimbursement for health care providers (Ham and Brommels 1994). Increased privatisation of health care production accompanied this development.

Specialisation

Parallel to the decentralisation process, but with a somewhat earlier start in the post-war period of the 1940s, there has also been an accelerating specialisation in health care. For instance, in 1960 Swedish health care contained 29 official clinical specialities. Five years later this number had increased to 44 and in 1996 it reached the amount of 62 (National Board of Health and Social Welfare 2003). After the latest revision in 2006, 56 specialities are included in the official classification. In addition, most clinical specialities are internally divided in sub-specialities and also differentiated into levels of specialisation, that when general skills and knowledge are supplemented by a concentration of rare competences to regional and sometimes also country levels of the health care delivery system.

In Sweden as well as in other health care systems, this increasing specialisation is predominantly due to the clinical development, whereby health care personnel need to acquire more in-depth medical knowledge in an ever-decreasing area, but at the same time it has also led to diminished knowledge of other clinical specialities. The specialists have become encapsulated, and "*it is difficult get word from one cocoon to the other*" (von Bertalanffy 1968, p. 30).

Of equal importance has been the development of different types of health care occupations. By analogy with the specialisation of physicians, the nursing profession, for example, has increased the areas of specialisation for which nurses require specific training (Jordan 1985).

Professionalisation

The development of health care has also been characterised by an increasing professionalisation. Such a process embodies the principles of professionalism, which is founded on autonomy and self-regulation in setting standards of practice, the content of education, entry into and exit from the profession. As a result of this development, vast responsibilities have been put on physicians and other professional groups, who are working with great independence and personal responsibility towards the patients. If anything goes wrong these professionals risk their certificates or could get reprimands from the authority of supervision. The Health Care Executives are rarely held responsible in these situations.

Following Abbot (1988), the focus of a profession is its work and not its organisation. Furthermore, in a professional organisation there is usually also a competition for power and influence between the different professional groups (Mintzberg 1979). In addition, professional groups predominantly disallow management by an outsider. To be accepted as a manager in such groupings you usually need to have the same profession as those you manage, and also to give proof of high-quality professional skills. These conditions are important parts of the organisational culture of a health care organisation (Johnson *et al.* 2003), which, in turn, determines the impact of common policies on the local level.

The three driving forces behind the increasing differentiation of the health care systems and their organisational, clinical and cultural contexts are summarised in Box 1.

Box 1. The increasing differentiation: three driving forces and their contexts in health care

- Organisational
    - *Decentralisation* where extensive responsibilities and authorities have been delegated/deconcentrated to the frontline organisation.
- Clinical
    - *Specialisation* where health care personnel have acquired in-depth clinical knowledge in an ever-decreasing area.
- Cultural
    - *Professionalisation* where extensive responsibilities have been placed on groups working with great independence and personal responsibility towards the patients.

THE PATIENT BERMUDA TRIANGLE

The outcome of this development of the health care systems can on one hand be regarded as a success story. Specialisation has proven to decrease mortality rates and prevent ill-health. Decentralisation is commonly regarded as a successful condition to rationalise the activities. Furthermore, the principle of a professional organisation of management is today deeply embedded in the organisation of health care. On the other hand, there is also a flipside of this development.

Decentralisation, founded on constitutional devolution of power, deconcentration, and administrative delegation of authorities from on one level to another, is reinforcing a local identity and rationality (Brunsson and Sahlin-Andersson 2002), which may lead to suboptimisations at the expense of the overall organisational effectiveness and a holistic view of the patient. Thus, the personnel may be concerned with carrying out their tasks in the right way, but not equally concerned with whether they are carrying out the right tasks.

The specialisation has also had an influence on the organisation of health care. Throughout, broad departments have been divided into smaller specialised units of common structure and approach. This process of organising through imitation has been described by DiMaggio and Powell (1983) as "institutional isomorphism". Health care organisations have thus become more differentiated but at the same time not more dissimilar to one other. If this standardising of organisational development has led to increased efficiency or not has rarely been considered. Instead, professional regulation, imitation and political influence seem to have had greater impact on the organisation of health care.

According to the definition of Lawrence and Lorsch (1967), differentiation implies differences in culture and also differences in behaviour among different groups or units. In the organisational culture of health care, which is strongly influenced by professional values and ethics, it is therefore difficult to establish and implement common visions and objectives including political, management, and clinical perspectives.

Thus, all the three driving forces, individually and together, have contributed to a state of differentiation with manifold negative consequences for the health care system as a whole. This is often described as a state of fragmentation, which can be defined as a state of differentiation without the integration that is required to achieve a unity of effort (Axelsson and Bihari Axelsson 2006). Furthermore, it can be divided into different categories, depending on the interaction between the three driving forces described.

First, *organisational fragmentation* makes it difficult to manage and organise between organisational units. This form of fragmentation is mainly due to the decentralisation of health care organisations adapted to the specialisation process, where large departments are split up into smaller clinical units. An organisational configuration of this type is characterised by a high degree of autonomy for the different units, but a weak integration between them. This fragmentation is reinforced when it is founded on different authorities (Hardy *et al.* 1999).

Second, *clinical fragmentation,* is primarily a result of the specialisation in health care and its disintegrative pressures (Glendinning 2003). In addition, within a specific speciality there are variations in clinical procedures (Berrow *et al.* 1997), which can be explained by the sovereignty of individual professionals and their reluctance to accept new evidence considering their own clinical experience (Vallgårda 1996).

Third, professionalisation together with decentralisation reinforces a *cultural fragmentation* that preserves "tribal values" (Glendinning 2003), which makes it difficult to develop and share common values among the health care personnel. Health care professionals tend to do what they consider to be best for the patient and not what is beneficial for the health care organisation as a whole. A health care system can therefore have strong cultures, but it often lacks a common culture and similar understandings of the health care professionals (Glouberman and Mintzberg 2001; Henriksen 2002).

Figure 1 illustrates the three driving forces of health care development in connection with the mentioned categories of fragmentation.

The importance of the three driving forces may vary from one health care organisation to another, depending on their contexts. However, it seems that the cultural context is generally more important than the organisational and the clinical context (Godfrey *et al.* 2003).

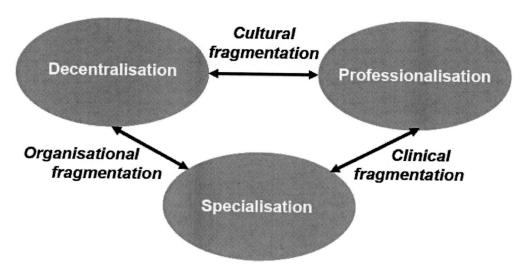

Figure 1. Fragmentation of health care: a result of three major driving forces in health care development.

For that reason, there is a need to understand the mechanisms of professional behaviour, often built upon autonomous positions, to be able to replace fragmentation by integration with professionals continuing as creators and carriers of the organisational culture. On the other hand, this is most likely not enough. The complexity of health care fragmentation demonstrates the need also to focus on organisational and clinical fragmentation. Otherwise, the development work will probably lack the synergies that once reinforced the fragmentation and which should be exploited the other way around to eliminate barriers to integrated care.

Following Gröne and Garcia-Barbero (2001), a fragmented health care system is characterised by patients often being transferred to other departments or institutions without complete information about the patient's condition, medical history, services provided in other settings, or medications prescribed by other clinicians. A situation like this is particularly problematic in the cure and care of older persons, due to their complex and complicated needs.

These kinds of conditions may lead to waiting times and delays for the patients, and, furthermore, duplications of tests causing additional costs to the health care system. In this way, fragmentation may cause difficulties in the co-ordination of activities for patient treatment. Or, to follow Berwick (1991), patients are lost due to the fragmentation of health care delivery systems. This phenomenon can metaphorically be described as a "Patient Bermuda Triangle[1]" and illustrated as in figure 2.

A global perspective on this matter shows that the health services within a Beveridge-like health care system are generally regarded as integrated, since it is set up by common taxation and has a comprehensive range of services for the population. As been commented above, a closer look at these kinds of health care systems shows, however, that they are not as integrated as usually perceived.

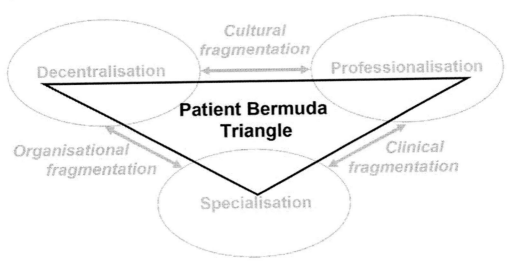

Figure 2. Symbolic description of the metaphor "Patient Bermuda Triangle" in the context of a fragmented health care delivery system.

---

[1] The "Bermuda Triangle" is an imaginary area located off the southeastern Atlantic coast of the United States, which is noted for a high incidence of unexplained losses of ships, small boats, and aircrafts. The triangle stretches from the east coast of Florida to the island of Bermuda and back to Puerto Rico.

Furthermore, studies comparing performance of the National Health Service in the UK, with a Health Maintenance Organisation and a Veteran's Health Care Administration in the USA (Feachem *et al.* 2002; Ham *et al.* 2003), show that the US health care organisations have a better performance, particularly in aspects of responsiveness to patients, mainly due to a more integrated care for patients with chronic diseases. This is achieved in a country known for disintegrated health care services (Woods 2004), which indicates that there are complex and multidimensional reasons behind the fragmentation of health care. Thus, fragmented health care systems are able to perform integrated care, at the same time as integrated health care systems are not a guarantee for an integrated performance.

BRINGING ORDER OUT OF CHAOS

The word integration originates from the Latin verb integrare, that is, *"to make a whole"*. The dictionary defines the adjective integrated as *"uniting in one system several constituents previously regarded as separate"*, and it is mainly used to articulate the bringing together or merging of separated elements or components. Integration means *"the making up or composition of a whole by adding together or combining the separate parts or elements"* (Oxford English dictionary 1989), implying purposeful working together of independent elements in the belief that the resulting whole is greater than the sum of individual parts (Berwick 1997). Integration is not only about forming a well functioning collaboration. According to Lawrence and Lorsch (1967, p. 11) the outcome must also satisfy customer needs: *"integration is the quality of the state of collaboration that exits among departments that are required to achieve unity of effort by demands of the environment"*.

The antonym of integrate is segregate: *"to set apart, isolate, divide"* (Oxford English dictionary 1989).

Major Approaches towards Integrated Health Care

In general, the discourse on integrated care embraces two major approaches. The health management approach to integrated care is in many cases emanating from a health care perspective. Up till now, this has been the dominant approach, manifested not only in the literature but also in experiences from implementation of various forms of integrated care. Within this approach, two main directions can be observed: a *"Public health"* approach and a *"Managed care"* approach (Leichsenring 2004a). The managed care approach is focusing on ways to increase the efficiency of the health care system by improving integration at different organisational interfaces within the system, while the public health approach is focusing on means to deliver good health care for a population by integrating various health care providers.

On the other hand, there are also efforts to broaden the concept of integrated care and to increase the importance of social services, particularly in the provision of services for older people. By and large, older people have more chronic diseases and are subject to multi-morbidity, which means that complex needs has to be met over a long period of time. Together health and social care can play an important role to meet multiple needs among older people, which accentuates the necessity to have a diversified concept of integrated care including all important sectors in a welfare system (Leichsenring 2004b).

Box 2. Major approaches towards integrated care

- Health care orientation
  - *Managed care* aims to increase efficiency by focusing on integration at organisational interfaces within the health care system.
  - *Public health* in general terms refers to demand-orientation and continuity of care, which are achieved by collaboration between health care providers both vertically and horizontally.
- Welfare orientation
  - The *person centred* approach is close to public health, although it underlines the interdependency between health care and other sectors also embedded in a welfare system, e.g. social welfare, housing, labour market, education, etc. This approach focuses clearly on the "demedicalisation" of integrated care.
  - The *institutional* approach is about organisational strategies to achieve integration of the sectors in a welfare system.

According to Leichsenring (2004a), integrated care in a welfare context can have a "*person centred*" or an "*institutional*" approach. The later approach includes ways of working together, for instance by implementing co-ordination, co-operation and networking, within as well as between the sectors in a welfare system. The different approaches towards integrated care are described by some general characteristics in box 2.

According to the WHO programme of Integrated Health Care Services, many countries have introduced mechanisms to achieve better integration and reduce fragmentation in their health care delivery systems. There is however a lack of a common terminology and these mechanisms are therefore labelled with different terms, such as: "local health care", "managed clinical networks", "shared care", "transmural care" (*bridge the wall in Dutch*), "comprehensive care", "intermediate care", "seamless care", "disease management", "case management", "continuing care", "integrated delivery networks", "chains of care" and "integrated care pathways", et cetera, somewhat indicating the countries of origin and the differentiations in scope and approach.

Despite these differences in terminology, a large amount of the examples seems to originate from the theory of inter-organisational relations, which includes several collaborative arrangements, e.g. networks, partnerships, coalitions and alliances. These are more "loosely coupled" than traditional hierarchical organisations due to the absence of a common management hierarchy (Weick 1979). Instead, collaboration is founded on more or less voluntary agreements. Actors individually retain control over their resources, yet periodically negotiate, sometimes even jointly decide on, their use. Using the terminology of Mintzberg (1993), this kind of condition could be described as an "adhocracy", which is a highly organic structure with a minimum of formalised behaviour. Furthermore, in this adhocracy, professionals are expected to integrate their efforts and bridge obstacles of specialisation and differentiation.

Inter-organisational relationships involve thus bilateral, rather than unilateral, co-ordination of activities. Moreover, these arrangements can be placed along a continuum of integration based on the degree or intensity of connections between services or organisations: full segregation, linkage, coordination in networks, cooperation and full integration (Ahgren and Axelsson 2005).

Segregated health care involves patients with rare and distinct needs, who require treatment from a few health care professionals. This concentration of skills and knowledge makes the delivery of health care segregated from other parts of the health care system. Though, segregated health care is not the same as fragmented health care. In segregated health care, the degree of differentiation is low and the need for integration is therefore also low. Integrated and segregated health care are indeed based on quite different logics, but both must be addressed in the creation of a balanced health care system which shall fulfil different kinds of needs in a population.

Integrated health care is thus an issue addressed in many countries. Furthermore, there are many different approaches and their scopes are quite different, but what they have in common is the purpose to improve the integration of fragmented health care services. Some approaches aim to eliminate professional and departmental boundaries and develop multiprofessional teams, while others have the objectives to integrate different sectors of health care, i.e. to link primary, secondary and tertiary health care. In all of these approaches, integrated health care is regarded as a means to an end, i.e. a desired outcome like for instance improved health, quality of care or service efficiency.

Integrated health care should therefore be regarded as a concept of organising between different health care providers. Moreover, the major driving force for creating integrated health care is to bring order in the chaotic condition of a fragmented health care, where the level of integration is not corresponding to the level of differentiation, which may lead to an overall service delivery out of patient focus and also to inefficiency in overall service performance.

Strategies of Use

The fragmentation of health care is thus caused by several reasons. This chapter has illuminated three principal dimensions of this fragmentation: clinical, organisational and cultural. It is apparent that, even if the fragmentation has this multidimensional content, to develop the right mix of differentiation and integration, solutions should emanate from the prime motivation of professionals: to improve the quality of care. Thus, by developing clinical guidelines and health care agreements, what shall be done and by whom for a specific patient group, the clinical fragmentation is expected be reduced (see e.g. Goodwin *et al.* 2004). However, it is important to point out that full clinical integration is usually not the target, as there is always a need for clinical differentiation, i.e. specialisation (Ahgren and Axelsson 2005).

Clinical guidelines have potentials to take integration one step further. On the basis of an agreed division of tasks and responsibilities, it is possible to develop an inter-organisational co-ordination between the service providers involved (Konrad 1996). This form of organising between health care organisations is mostly done with the help of integrated care pathways, chains of care and similar health care network collaboration. If they are supervised by network managers, it is likely that organisational integration can be transformed into a higher degree of integration. However, once again, integration efforts must always be balanced against the needs for differentiation.

Thus, it seems possible to diminish the clinical and organisational fragmentation in health care organisations. However, the cultural fragmentation is probably the biggest challenge when creating integrated health care. It is proven to be difficult, almost impossible, to change the values of health care professionals by top-down actions. An organisation founded on professional values makes it difficult to communicate common visions and targets and, furthermore, to create support for this kind of top management initiatives (Abbott 1988). Then, how are malignant cultural fragmentation eliminated?

Creating Change Bottom-Up

In accordance with the logic of the cultural hindrances, integration efforts are likely to be hampered if not professional leadership is promoted in the development of integrated care. According to Ahgren and Axelsson (2007), a disharmony is likely to evolve between a top-down approach to integration and the value system among health care professionals, which may lead to non-integrative actions despite the supportive policy environment. Following Ham (2003), ways have thus to be fund of creating change bottom-up by engagement of physicians in the development of integrated care and thereby legitimise the development work. Without such legitimacy, improvement proposals are likely to meet resistance and be interpreted as threats to the existing organisational and clinical power structure. Furthermore, it is crucial that suggestions for improvement are based on evidence from impartial evaluation and research. This will not only legitimise change, it will also specify what the change process should focus on.

Beside legitimacy, a successful development of integrated health care is characterised by willingness to collaborate, interdependence between service providers, and mutual confidence in each others' integration intentions. In this sense, the development of integrated care seems to be more of an "art" than a predictable outcome from a specific technique or an adequately designed development work. An adequate infrastructure of the development work can be most helpful when the conditions are favourable, but have a low significance when the work is marked by doubts and mistrust (Ahgren and Axelsson 2007).

Development and delivery of integrated health care is a far-reaching change to fragmented health care provision. As in all radical development, determinants with crucial impact on the outcome need to be explored and get special attention. Forming integrated health care is not difficult if everyone recognises and responds to the need of integrating the services. Thus, the success of the development work will to a large degree depend on the capacity of change management to create professional dedication, confidence and legitimacy. The later is fundamental, since it is the starting point for confidence and professional dedication (Ahgren and Axelsson 2007).

Integration of the Patients

The term patient has nowadays a complex meaning and is to an ever increasing extent placed on equal terms with "consumer", "customer" (e.g. Nordgren 2003) or "partner" (e.g. Coulter 1999). In addition, Coulter (2002) proposes the term "autonomous patients", seeing autonomy as the antithesis of dependency. The term *patient empowerment* can be used for this transformation of the position of the patients (Roberts 1999), and this is, in turn, facilitated a common decreased confidence in and respect for authorities, health care professionals included, and by more accessible and transparent information about the cure of diseases.

One patient group being in the frontline of this movement is the diabetics. Their patient organisations have proclaimed that integrated care is about working together of all the people involved, including the dieticians. Moreover, the inclusion of informal caretakers is also of crucial importance in integrated care (Billings 2005). Following von Otter (1996), physicians tend to listen more to patients than to politicians or health care managers. A major breakthrough for patient empowerment may, therefore, imply that existing sets of professional values will be combined with demands emerging from "consumer" behaviour. Thus, political and top management rhetoric of integration will perhaps not be realised until articulated demands from patients and caretakers are channelled to health care professionals, with such conditions it may be possible to develop more of a common culture and similar understandings in a health care system and in this way diminish the cultural fragmentation. If so, it means that integrated health care will not be complete without the integration of patients.

Goodwin *et al.* (2004) argue that well developed integrated health care networks in co-existence with a well developed care consumerism could be an optimum scenario, i.e. a patient-driven health care. According to these analysts, demand-led integrated health care networks will however probably need additional financing and therefore such a scenario may not be sustainable. This kind of conclusion is based on existing providers of health care and limited public financing and, in addition, a growing gap between needs and resources, where additional demands can be regarded as threats to the budget and as increased workload. On the other hand, well developed care consumerism can probably also open up for non-governmental health care providers to be included in integrated health care systems.

The Over-All Challenge

In summation, the challenge of the future is to integrate highly differentiated health care providers among public organisations, supplementary providers, as well as the patients and informal carers as resources. This could be done by simultaneously promoting integrated health care networks, clinical guidelines, patient empowerment and change bottom-up.

In such a context, integrated health care can be defined as:

> the bringing together of the differentiated health care resources of public and non-public health care professionals, patients and informal caretakers, to create required cure and health care.

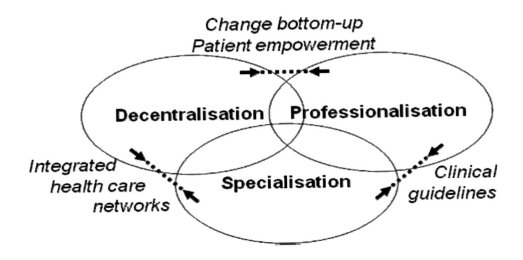

Figure 3. Development approaches of balanced needs for integration and differentiation.

Required cure and health care refers to professional standards as well as patient demands. A definition like this has a holistic perspective and sees integration as a means to ensure that the patients are not lost in a "Bermuda Triangle" of a health care system. It also underlines that integration is needed in differentiated settings, which will be a common situation if patients are included into health care arrangements with their unique competence.

REFERENCES

Abbott, A. (1988). The System of Professions: *An Essay on the Division of Expert Labor*. Chicago: The University of Chicago Press.

Ahgren, B. and Axelsson, R. (2005). Evaluating integrated health care: a model for measurement. *International Journal of Integrated Care*, Vol. 5, August 2005.

Ahgren, B. and Axelsson, R. (2007). Determinants of integrated health care development: chains of care in Sweden. *International Journal of Health Planning and Management*, 2:145-157.

Axelsson, R. and Bihari Axelsson, S. (2006). Integration and collaboration in public health – a conceptual framework. *International Journal of Health Planning and Management* 21: 75-88.

Berrow, D., Humphrey, C. and Hayward, J. (1997). Understanding the relation between research and clinical policy: a study of clinicians' views. *Quality in Health Care* 6: 181-186.

Bertalanffy, L. von (1968). General System Theory: Foundations, Development, Applications. New York: George Braziller.

Berwick, D. (1991). Controlling variation in health care: A consultation from Walter Shewhart. *Medical Care* 12:29-33.

Berwick, D. (1997). Medical associations: guilds or leaders? *British Medical Journal* 314: 1564-1565 (editorial).

Billings, J.R. (2005). What do we mean by integrated care? A European interpretation. *Journal of Integrated Care* 13(5): 13-20.

Brunsson, N. and Sahlin-Andersson, K. (2000). Constructing organisations: the example of public sector reform. *Organization Studies* 21(4): 721-746.

Coulter, A. (1999). Paternalism or Partnership? Patients have grown up – and there's no going back. *British Medical Journal* 319: 719-720.

Coulter A. (2002). The autonomous patient — ending paternalism in medical care. London: Nuffield Trust.

DiMaggio, P.J. and Powell, W.W. (1983). The iron cage revisited: institutional isomorphism and collective rationality in organisational fields. *American Sociological Review* 48(2): 147-160.

Feachem, R., Sekhri, N. and White, K. (2002). Getting more for their dollars: a comparison of the NHS with California's Kaiser Permanente. *British Medical Journal* 324: 135-41.

Glouberman, S. and Mintzberg, M. (2001). Managing the care of health and cure of disease – part II: Integration. *Health Care Management Review* 26: 70-84.

Glendinning, C. (2003). Breaking down barriers: integrating health and care services for older people in England. *Health Policy* 65: 139-151.

Godfrey, M., Hardy, B. and Wistow, G. (2003). Situation in England. In van Raak, A. Mur-Veeman, I., Hardy, B., Steenbergen, M. and Paulus, A. (eds) Integrated Care in Europe. Description and comparison of integrated care in six EU countries. Maarssen: Elsevier Gezondheidszorg.

Goodwin, N. et al. (2004). Managing Across Diverse Networks of Care: Lessons from Other Sectors. Report to the National Co-ordinating Centre for Service Delivery and Organisation R and D (NCCSDO).

Gröne, O. and Garcia-Barbero, M. (2001). Integrated care. *International Journal of Integrated Care* 1(2).

Ham, C. and Brommels, M. (1994). Health care reform in The Netherlands, Sweden, and the United Kingdom. *Health Affairs* 13(5): 106-119.

Ham, C. et al. (2003). Hospital bed utilisation in the NHS, Kaiser Permanente, and US Medicare programme: analysis of routine data. *British Medical Journal* 327: 1257.

Ham, C. (2003). Improving the performance of health services: the role of clinical leadership. *Lancet* 361: 1978-80.

Hardy, B. et al. (1999). Inter-agency services in England and The Netherlands. A comparative study of integrated care development and delivery. *Health Policy* 48: 87-105.

Henriksen, E. (2002). Understanding in Healthcare Organisations – a Prerequisite for Development. Uppsala: Acta Universitatis Upsaliensis.

Jordan, G.L. (1985). The impact of specialization on health care. *Annals of Surgery* 201(5): 537-544.

Johnson, P. et al. (2003). Interagency and interprofessional collaboration in community care: the interdependence of structures and values. *Journal of Interprofessional Care* 17(1): 69-83.

Konrad, E. (1996). A Multidimensional Framework for Conceptualizing Human Services Integration Initiatives. In: Marquart, J and Konrad E (eds) Evaluating Initiatives to Integrated Human Services. New directions for Evaluation. San Francisco: Jossey-Bass.

Lawrence, P.R. and Lorsch, J.W. (1967). Organization and Environment. Managing Differentiation and Integration. Cambridge, MA: Harvard University Press.

Leichsenring, K. (2004a). Developing integrated care and social care services for older persons in Europe. *International Journal of Integrated care* 4: September.

Leichsenring, K. (2004b). Providing Integrated Health and Social Care for Older Persons – A European Overview. In Leichsering, K. and Alaszewski, A. (eds) Providing Integrated Care for Older Persons – A European Overview of Issues at Stake. Aldershot: Ashgate.

Mintzberg, H. (1979). The Structuring of Organizations. Englewood Cliffs, NJ: Prentice Hall.

Mintzberg, H. (1993). Structure in Fives. Designing Effective Organizations. *Englewood Cliffs*, NJ: Prentice Hall.

National Board of Health and Social Welfare (2003). Läkarnas specialistutbildning och strukturen för medicinska specialiteter – en översyn. Stockholm: Socialstyrelsen.

Nordgren, L. (2003). Från patient till kund. Intåget av marknadstänkande i sjukvården och förskjutningen av patientens position. Lund: Lund Business Press.

von Otter, C. (1996). Om den repressiva omtanken och andra tankar om patienternas valfrihet. In: Anell, A. and Rosén. P. (eds). Valfrihet och jämlikhet i vården. Stockholm: SNS Förlag.

Oxford English Dictionary (1989). Second edition. Volume 7. Oxford: Clarendon Press.

Roberts, K.J. (1999). Patient empowerment in the United States: a critical commentary. *Health Expectations* 2(2): 82-92.

Rondinelli, D., Shabhir Cheema, G. and Nellis, J. (1983). Decentralization in Developing Countries: A Review of Recent Experience. *World Bank Staff Working Papers* No.581.

Saltman, R. and Figueras, J. (1997) European Health Care Reform. Analysis of Current Strategies. Copenhagen: World Health Organization. Regional Office for Europe.

Vallgårda, S. (1996). Specialiseringen inom sjukhusväsendet i ett komparativt och historiskt perspektiv. In Sygehusvæsenet mod år 2000. Copenhagen: DIKE.

Weick, K.E. (1979). The Social Psychology of Organizing. Reading, Mass: Addison-Wesley.

Woods, K. (2004) Delivering integrated care: another case of hunting the snark? Paper for keynote address to the IJIC / WHO Conference, 20-21 February 2004, Birmingham, UK.

In: Integrated Health Care Delivers
Editor: Leonie A. Klein and Emily L. Neumann

ISBN 978-1-60456-851-6
© 2008 Nova Science Publishers, Inc.

Chapter 8

IMAGE EXCHANGE BETWEEN A MAJOR HEALTH SYSTEM AND A PRIVATE RADIOLOGY GROUP USING A SHARED IMAGE SERVER

Linda Womack
Sutter Health, Sacramento, CA, USA

INTRODUCTION

How do you deal with exchanging images between sites within our geographic servicing area? When an entity such as a not-for profit health system or radiology group implements PACS, film becomes the least preferred and less cost effective method of image distribution. Unfortunately, at that point there is the possibility of two of these entities storing images in different ways. You must then deal with the issue of how to exchange the images between the two divergent systems. Initially, the advent of burning CDs reduced the cost of printing films, but it still did not reduce the cost of the courier service to deliver the film to the requesting physician's office. In addition, when working in an environment where more and more paper is eliminated in daily routines, the CD created is one more tangible object that had to be shuffled and tracked, which is a time consuming and costly process.

The challenge began when Radiological Associates of Sacramento (RAS), the contracted Radiology group of Sutter Health Sacramento Sierra Region, implemented their own PACS system different from the system implemented by Sutter. Even though we are partners, we compete in the market for outpatient business.

We now had two separate digital storage systems, sharing physician and patient clientele and a continued desire to eliminate paper and shuffling of film from one facility to another. The question remained how do we do it without couriers and hard copy media?

As one of the nation's leading not-for-profit networks of hospitals, doctors, nurses, and additional healthcare services, Sutter Health is also on the leading edge of technology. As the Imaging Systems Team Manager for the Sacramento Sierra Region, which consists of five acute care hospitals, including a trauma center, located in Northern California, my team and I have overseen the implementation of this new technology in radiology, in the form of a PACS system.

PROPOSAL

In this day and age of file sharing using email attachments, shared server locations, and ftp sites, we have the ability to readily share information regardless of file type or size, so it should be just as easy with our images, right? After all, we are all using the same language, DICOM, (DICOM stands for Digital Imaging and Communications in Medicine). It is the standard for distributing and viewing any kind of medical image regardless of the origin. How do you bridge the gap between sites with divergent PACS systems and still meet the HIPAA standards of passing patient information through networks?

Our project scope was to create a single server that provided a storage location for on demand pushing and pulling of images between the Sutter Sacramento Sierra Region and the RAS Outpatient Centers. While we are competing organizations, our physician base is the same and our primary concern is and will continue to be to provide the best patient care possible from the moment the patient walks through the hospital doors to the time that they walk out. In imaging, we can achieve this by compiling the most comprehensive patient file possible to provide a clearer story for the radiologist reading the studies.

We approached Radiological Associates with this idea after I saw a product that I thought we could use. With the help of a neutral vendor and using an ASP model, (application service provider) a plan was developed to create a central storage location that would be used to temporarily store images requested by both Sutter and RAS sites. (An ASP is a business model that provides computer-based services to customers over a network.) Images would be retrieved from the central storage location to the respective PACS system and then purged after 30 days. Physicians, regardless of whether they were working within their outpatient facilities or the hospital, would now have access to the most relevant studies for their patients.

Below is a description of the proposed model for the sharing of images between Sutter and RAS facilities (see also Figure 1):

The Model: On demand pushing and pulling of images from respective site to shared server location.

The Network: Utilizing a previously established pinhole through each site's firewall, images are moved through a secured network connection.

Scenario: Outpatient center schedules exam for Patient A who recently had a study performed at one of the hospital locations.

Outpatient center completes request sheet and faxes to hospital requesting the images.

Hospital receives the request and retrieves the images from their PACS system. Images are then pushed to the central server location which is an established Send and Retrieve destination on the PACS system.

Request form is completed by the hospital and faxed back to the outpatient center along with confirmation that the images have been sent.

Outpatient center receives the completed request sheet and performs a query of the central server 1 location for the images.

Once located, the images are retrieved to the outpatient center PACS system and prepared for comparison reading by the radiologist.

After 30 days, the images are deleted from the PACS system.

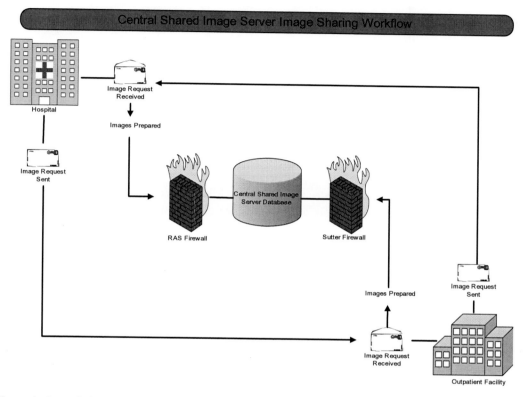

Figure 1. Central shared image server image sharing work flow.

THE PLAN

Sutter and RAS entered into an agreement with a third party vendor to install and implement a centralized server location to store images shared between the two entities. With the third party engaged, the next issue to be dealt with was the ownership of the server. The decision was made that the server would reside on the RAS network and access would be provided using NAT'd (network address translation) IP addresses and pinholes through each sites respective firewalls.

Financially, we decided to split the costs 55% for Sutter and 45% for RAS. Factors in determining this were volumes and how many priors each site retrieves each day.

The implementation of the shared server also provided an opportunity to reduce the amount of man hours associated with locating, pulling and couriering hard copy films (old films filed before PACS) and hard copy media. Sutter and RAS both established designated CSIS (Central Shared Image Server), locations, where all outside film requests were to be handled. If a site required a previous film, they would complete the film request form and fax to their CSIS Central Point of Contact (CPC). The site CPC would then be responsible for processing the image request and notifying the requestor once the images were available. All communication between the two entities was to be handled by the respective CSIS CPCs. The use of the shared server eliminated the wasted time spent tracking down loaned films, the money spent printing the films, and the recurring cost of using a courier service to shuffle films between the sites.

Lessons Learned

While the use of the shared server continues to provide a higher quality of service for our physicians and patients, there were and will continue to be obstacles that present challenges for both Sutter and RAS. The first of these is the workload increase for the designated CSIS site. Previously, the workload was spread across the region with each site requesting their own images, but now that workload is placed upon the one site and existing staff to complete the process. Without the ability to add additional staff, we had to review and make modifications to the expected timelines for turnaround requests. RAS, being an outpatient based practice, often knows days in advance which patients are going to come in for exams. By screening these exams to determine if they had any previous exams performed at a Sutter facility, the RAS sites are able to submit non-urgent requests for the previous exams, thus reducing the number of stat requests received. This practice also allowed time for staff to catch up on requests during the off-peak hours without compromising their other responsibilities.

In addition to the workload associated with processing the request, there is also an additional workload due to the handling of the maintenance associated with storing outside films on our system. RAS and Sutter agreed to store images on each others' systems for 30 days and then they would be purged. This created another process to be completed by the CSIS site and required the storage of the corresponding paperwork to identify those exams that needed to be deleted. It became apparent that while the server eliminated costs, it was imperative to examine the sites current staffing model and then account for increases in workload to handle the additional responsibilities.

Along with the issues surrounding the increased workload, there were also opportunities for growth when it came to communication between the two entities regarding the CSIS processes. Without effective channels of communication, problems such as slow turnaround times or the abundance of stat request would lead to increased staff and physician frustration. To create a clear channel of communication, a supervisor was named to oversee the processes from both RAS and Sutter. Staff presented any issues, problems, or suggestions to their supervisors who, in turn, would take the comments to the supervisor on the other end. Together RAS and Sutter could develop and implement processes to make the CSIS more effective for both parties.

In Summary

To facilitate the flow of clinical information between Sutter and RAS, a third party was utilized to implement the workflow proposed in this solution. This solution bridges the secure exchange of DICOM imaging data to enhance diagnostic workflow while providing compliance with HIPAA guidelines. In addition, the individual institution's PACS are not compromised.

INDEX

A

academic, 37
access, 8, 51, 53, 54, 56, 58, 59, 62, 78, 152, 153
accessibility, 36, 50
accountability, 58, 61
accounting, viii, 35, 37, 38
accreditation, 51
accuracy, 60
achievement, vii, 2, 55
acquisitions, 51, 61
activation, 77
activity level, 37
acupuncture, 105
acute, vii, 4, 8, 37, 50, 51, 56, 118, 119, 151
adaptation, 23, 60, 94, 103
adjustment, 27
administration, 38, 40
administrative, 50, 51, 58, 138, 140
administrative efficiency, 51
administrators, 51, 58
adolescents, 3
adult, 3, 24
adult population, 3
adverse event, 113
advocacy, 2, 8, 9, 10, 11, 12, 15, 16
Africa, x, 115, 116, 117, 118, 119, 120
age, viii, 3, 6, 13, 27, 35, 37, 39, 41, 43, 45, 48, 117, 152
ageing, 68, 129
agent, 123
agents, xi, 11, 116, 119, 121, 126, 138
aging, 17, 51
agriculture, 50
aid, 117
aiding, 98
AIDS, 119, 120, 121, 126, 132

alcohol, 5, 25, 83
alcohol consumption, 83
alternative, 8, 12, 31, 44, 77, 96, 112, 113, 128, 129, 138
alternative medicine, 96, 112, 113
alternatives, 128, 129
Alzheimer, 16, 116
American Psychiatric Association, 10, 15
Amsterdam, 132
anabolic, 54, 65
anabolic steroid, 54, 65
analysis of variance, 38
analysts, 147
anger, 6
animals, 95
ANOVA, 44
antibiotics, 4
antithesis, 147
anxiety, 3, 10
application, 54, 92, 129, 130, 152
Arkansas, 33
arrest, viii, 19, 27, 31, 32
arthritis, ix, 2, 3, 6, 17, 67
arthrodesis, 47
artificial, 44, 79
Asian, viii, 35
Asian countries, viii, 35
assessment, vii, 1, 2, 10, 15, 22, 73, 81, 84, 85, 87, 88, 91, 101, 118, 122, 123, 125, 134
assignment, 32, 130
associations, 149
asthma, 3, 5
Atlantic, 142
atmosphere, 102
attention, 52, 76, 116, 146
attitudes, 100
Aurora, 1
Australia, 116

authority, 53, 55, 56, 58, 117, 118, 119, 139
autonomous, 142, 146, 149
autonomy, 54, 102, 139, 141, 147
availability, 32, 59, 76, 83, 106
aversion, 98
awareness, 138

B

baby boomers, 3
back pain, 36
bacterial, 4
bacterial infection, 4
bargaining, 44, 129
barrier, 86
barriers, vii, 2, 56, 81, 82, 142, 149
behavior, 5, 6, 60, 61, 126, 127, 130
behavioral change, 6, 15
belief systems, 108
beliefs, 6, 14, 25, 60, 94, 98
benefits, viii, 3, 12, 17, 19, 20, 24, 34, 38, 50, 51, 53,
    59, 62, 131
beverages, 13
bias, 106, 108
bilateral, 145
binge drinking, 54, 66
biochemical, 94
biometrics, 10
biopsies, 75, 77
bipolar, 24
bipolar disorder, 24
birth, 54
birth rate, 54
births, 63
blog, 113
blood, 36, 38, 44
blood transfusion, 38
boats, 142
bonding, 52
bonds, 53
bone, 4
bonus, 38
Boston, 17, 62, 63
Botswana, x, 115, 116, 117, 119, 120, 121, 122, 124,
    125, 126, 127, 130, 132, 135
bottom-up, xi, 52, 138, 146, 147
brain, 75
breast, 5, 16, 92
breast cancer, 5, 16
British, 91, 92, 149
broad spectrum, 105
bronchoscopy, 75
Buddhist, 95

buildings, 38
burning, 151
business, 50, 51, 59, 108, 109, 111, 151, 152
business model, 111, 152

C

CAD, 3
California, 47, 133, 134, 149, 151
CAM, x, 93, 96, 97, 100, 101, 102, 104, 105, 106,
    108, 110, 111
campaigns, 5
Canada, 66, 116
cancer, ix, 2, 67, 68, 74, 78, 81, 82, 83, 85, 86, 87,
    89, 90, 91, 92
cancer care, 78, 90, 91, 92
cancer treatment, 89
cancers, 3
capacity, 29, 79, 146
capital, ix, 49, 52, 53, 54, 58, 59, 60, 61, 62, 63, 64,
    65, 66
capital flows, 58
cardiovascular disease, 3, 68, 116
care model, 4, 21, 69, 89
caregivers, 4, 9, 16, 104
case study, 63, 132
cast, 4, 106
casting, 104
Center for Disease Control and Prevention, 3, 16
centralized, 118, 153
cervical, 75, 77
cesarean section, 47
changing environment, 60
channels, 53, 55, 56, 59, 154
chaotic, xi, 137, 145
charities, 52
Chicago, 53, 65, 66, 148
children, 3
China, 49, 66
Chinese, 95
Chi-square, 38
chronic, vii, ix, 1, 2, 3, 4, 5, 6, 7, 8, 9, 12, 14, 15, 16,
    17, 24, 67, 68, 69, 70, 81, 85, 89, 91, 101, 116,
    143
chronic disease, ix, 2, 3, 4, 5, 6, 7, 15, 16, 17, 67, 69,
    85, 89, 91, 143
chronic diseases, ix, 2, 3, 4, 5, 6, 7, 17, 67, 69, 85,
    89, 143
chronic illness, 3, 5, 16, 17, 69, 70, 81, 89, 91
chronic obstructive pulmonary disease (COPD), 3,
    68, 89
chronically ill, 89, 90, 92
cigarettes, 14

citizens, 54, 55
classification, 139
classified, 25, 86
cleaning, 38
clients, viii, 19, 20, 21, 22, 23, 24, 25, 27, 31, 32, 94, 98, 105, 107
clinical, viii, x, xi, 8, 10, 11, 20, 21, 32, 35, 36, 38, 45, 46, 52, 63, 64, 69, 70, 71, 75, 78, 79, 81, 82, 83, 84, 85, 86, 87, 89, 90, 91, 92, 93, 94, 97, 100, 101, 102, 104, 105, 106, 107, 108, 109, 121, 132, 137, 138, 139, 140, 141, 142, 144, 145, 146, 147, 148, 149, 154
clinical trial, 21, 79
clinical trials, 79
clinician, 10, 92
clinicians, 8, 24, 25, 78, 92, 96, 103, 107, 142, 148
clinics, 54, 55, 56, 57, 58, 70, 71, 82, 85, 106, 119, 121
closure, 62
clothing, 119, 121
CNS, 33
coalitions, 24, 144
Cochrane, 88, 91, 101, 112
Cochrane Database of Systematic Reviews, 112
cocoon, 139
codes, 130
co-existence, 147
cognition, 62
cognitive, ix, 4, 6, 7, 11, 15, 17, 49, 53, 60, 61
cognitive domains, 53
cognitive function, 4, 17
cognitive perspective, 61
cohesion, 64
cohesiveness, 121
collaboration, 2, 8, 10, 15, 54, 58, 68, 69, 85, 86, 88, 143, 144, 145, 148, 149
college campuses, 66
colors, 100
Columbia, 116
combination therapy, 75, 76
communication, vii, 2, 5, 6, 9, 10, 11, 20, 52, 53, 55, 58, 59, 60, 74, 78, 86, 92, 116, 119, 123, 125, 154
communication skills, 6, 9, 11, 92
communications channel, 109
communities, 54, 63
community, vii, viii, ix, 6, 20, 21, 22, 23, 25, 32, 33, 34, 49, 50, 54, 58, 64, 65, 66, 69, 70, 88, 118, 119, 121, 122, 125, 149
community care model, 21
co-morbidities, 4
compensation, 53, 61
competence, 65, 148
competency, 60

competition, 86, 139
complementary, 9, 79, 96, 112, 113
complexity, 20, 44, 68, 91, 94, 96, 97, 111, 127, 142
compliance, 4, 7, 11, 15, 24, 70, 71, 72, 77, 155
complications, 36, 37, 46, 47, 48, 122
components, viii, 2, 11, 17, 19, 23, 32, 37, 40, 50, 68, 69, 70, 71, 82, 83, 143
composition, 79, 87, 94, 143
computer, 152
concentration, 139, 145
conceptualization, 107
concrete, 24, 78
conductor, 94, 107
confidence, 6, 7, 11, 146, 147
configuration, 8, 65, 126, 141
conflict, 59, 78, 126
conflict resolution, 59
confusion, 98, 110
congestive heart failure, 88
Congress, 16
consensus, 8, 9, 73, 75
conservation, 43
constitutional, 140
constraints, 20, 32, 133
constructive conflict, 58
consultants, 36
consulting, 98, 104, 108
consumerism, 147
consumers, 77, 101, 111
contingency, 51, 65
continuing, 4, 13, 54, 118, 142, 144
continuity, ix, 21, 67, 68, 70, 74, 85, 119, 121, 144
contracts, 126
control, viii, 14, 17, 19, 20, 22, 23, 27, 54, 55, 77, 88, 126, 127, 130, 133, 144
control group, viii, 19, 20
controlled, 79, 88, 106, 110
controlled studies, 106
controlled trials, 79, 88, 106, 110
coordination, ix, 8, 55, 58, 59, 67, 68, 69, 70, 71, 78, 81, 85, 86, 117, 119, 121, 122, 123, 125, 126, 127, 130, 145
Copenhagen, 150
coronary angioplasty, 47
coronary artery disease, 3
coronary heart disease, 88
corporations, 116, 118
correlation, 23
cost effectiveness, 122
cost saving, 44, 45
cost-effective, 70, 87, 88, 112
costs, viii, ix, 2, 3, 8, 12, 35, 36, 37, 38, 40, 41, 43, 44, 45, 46, 47, 51, 53, 62, 65, 68, 88, 109, 116,

117, 127, 129, 130, 131, 133, 134, 138, 142, 153, 154
counseling, 121
covariate, 27
coverage, 3, 4, 50, 102
covering, 82, 87
CPC, 153
creativity, 91, 122
criticism, 77
cultural, x, xi, 53, 130, 137, 139, 141, 145, 146, 147
culture, 45, 60, 61, 70, 71, 133, 139, 140, 141, 142, 147
curable, 4
curing, 55
customers, 50, 53, 58, 152

D

daily living, 3
data collection, viii, 2
death, ix, 54, 67, 71, 122
death rate, 54
debt, 51
decentralisation, x, 137, 138, 139, 141
decentralized, 118, 120
decision making, 16, 79, 131
decision-making process, vii, x, 1, 93, 101, 102, 107, 108, 110
decisions, x, 8, 9, 69, 107, 115, 116, 127, 130
decompression, 46, 47
deconcentration, 138, 140
defects, 123
deficits, 36
definition, x, 16, 20, 50, 93, 140, 148
degenerative disease, 36
degree, 22, 23, 58, 100, 104, 106, 133, 141, 145, 146
delays, 142
delivery, vii, viii, ix, x, xi, 19, 22, 23, 31, 32, 36, 45, 50, 52, 53, 55, 62, 64, 65, 66, 67, 68, 69, 82, 88, 93, 96, 97, 107, 110, 111, 115, 116, 117, 118, 119, 120, 121, 122, 123, 124, 125, 126, 127, 133, 134, 137, 139, 142, 144, 145, 146, 149
demand, 134, 144, 147, 152
dementia, 5, 16, 133
demographic, 27
demographics, viii, ix, 35, 37, 39, 41, 43, 51
Demonstration Project, 54, 57
Department of State, 19, 27, 33
depreciation, 38, 40, 44
depression, 3, 6, 10
dermatology, 56
designers, 8, 15
desire, 11, 151

deterministic, 133
developing countries, 125
devolution, 138, 140
diabetes, ix, 2, 3, 5, 16, 67, 68, 70, 88, 89, 116
diabetes mellitus, ix, 67, 68, 88, 116
diagnostic, 27, 68, 75, 82, 83, 107, 135, 155
dichotomy, 63
DICOM, 152, 155
diet, 101
dietary, 105
dietary supplementation, 105
differentiation, viii, x, 19, 20, 22, 23, 134, 137, 138, 139, 140, 144, 145, 146, 148
direct cost, 44
direct costs, 44
disability, ix, 3, 17, 67
disabled, 13, 116
discourse, 143
disease progression, 7
diseases, ix, 2, 4, 6, 67
disorder, 20, 24, 28, 34
dispersion, 106
distribution, 45, 53, 151
diversification, 63
division, 116, 117, 130, 145
doctor, 79, 81, 83
doctor-patient, 83
doctors, 119, 151
doors, 152
drug-related, 54
drugs, 25, 38
DSM-IV, 24
dumping, 45
duplication, 7, 15, 121, 123
durability, 132

E

E and W, 46
earnings, 4
eating, 5, 82
economic, 8, 36, 51, 52, 53, 63, 65, 66, 72, 138
economic development, 66
economic performance, 53
economic sociology, 63
economics, 133, 134, 135
economies, 50, 51
economies of scale, 50, 51
economy, 66, 120, 138
education, vii, ix, 1, 2, 5, 10, 11, 13, 15, 16, 49, 55, 62, 67, 70, 71, 94, 97, 105, 110, 112, 125, 130, 132, 139, 144

efficacy, viii, x, 6, 7, 9, 11, 12, 13, 14, 15, 19, 20, 51, 65, 87, 93, 98, 106, 112
elderly, 47, 116
elective surgery, 47
electricity, 10
electronic, 86, 125
email, 152
emotional, 4, 6, 14, 53, 59, 77, 78, 105
emotional distress, 14
emotional reactions, 6
employees, 3, 12, 53, 54, 60
employers, 3, 24
employment, vii, 2, 21, 23, 27, 33, 34
empowered, 7, 9
empowerment, vii, xi, 1, 8, 53, 110, 137, 138, 147, 150
encapsulated, 139
encouragement, 11
endurance, 36
energy, 105
engagement, 23, 24, 25, 27, 54, 146
engineering, 133
England, 50, 88, 92, 118, 133, 134, 149
English, 16, 143, 150
enterprise, 53, 106
entrepreneurial, 62
environment, 4, 51, 62, 122, 143, 146, 151
environmental, 51, 59
epidemic, 55, 120
equipment, 38, 51, 56
equity, 64
ESRD, 17
estimating, 27
ethics, 140
EU, 134, 149
euro, 132, 133
Europe, 88, 117, 118, 119, 134, 149, 150
European, 46, 47, 91, 133, 149, 150
evidence, viii, ix, 7, 17, 20, 31, 32, 52, 67, 69, 70, 71, 73, 74, 77, 78, 79, 84, 85, 86, 87, 88, 89, 90, 91, 112, 116, 141, 146
evidence-based practices, 20, 32
evolution, 20, 66, 101, 109, 111
excuse, 123
execution, 126
exercise, 5, 7, 13, 98, 102
expansions, 50
expenditures, 5, 7
experimental condition, 113
experimental design, 24, 27
expert, 7, 73, 74, 84, 87
expertise, x, 10, 78, 79, 84, 93, 106, 107
experts, 3, 5, 25, 81, 83

exposure, 7, 105
external environment, 51
extraction, 74
eye, 128

F

facilitators, 81, 82
failure, 5, 9, 37, 52, 53, 81, 88
family, vii, 1, 12, 13, 24, 25, 45, 55, 56, 76, 77, 78, 94, 96, 102, 119, 122, 125
family factors, 94
family medicine, 55, 56
family members, vii, 1, 12, 24, 119
family physician, 55
family relationships, 13
farmers, 54
fatigue, 6, 76
faults, 128
fax, 153
FDG, 75
fear, 6
fee, 56
feedback, 12, 71, 75
feed-back, 70
feelings, 94
fees, 36, 40
females, 13
fidelity, viii, 19, 20, 21, 22, 23, 25, 27, 28, 31, 32, 33, 34
film, 151, 153
films, 151, 153, 154
filters, 102
financial difficulty, 10
financing, 55, 147
firearm, 64
firewalls, 153
firms, 53
fixation, 36, 46
fixed rate, 36
flexibility, 12
flow, x, 52, 55, 93, 97, 107, 153, 154
FNA, 77
focusing, 106, 143, 144
food, 98, 119, 121
fragmentation, ix, x, xi, 5, 8, 14, 15, 67, 68, 69, 70, 84, 116, 117, 137, 140, 141, 142, 143, 144, 145, 146, 147
freedom, 25, 54, 55
frustration, 154
funding, 60, 116
fusion, viii, 35, 36, 37, 38, 39, 41, 43, 44, 45, 46, 47, 48

G

gastrointestinal, 37
gender, 37, 39, 41
general anesthesia, 47
general practitioner, 85, 118
general practitioners, 118
generalizability, 32
generation, 126
Geneva, 1
geriatric, 94, 118
goals, vii, x, 2, 5, 6, 7, 8, 9, 10, 11, 12, 15, 59, 60, 81, 93, 109, 117, 131
goal-setting, 92
governance, 52, 64, 65, 66, 135
government, iv, 38, 50, 52, 54, 55, 60, 86, 116, 120
government policy, 116
GPs, 116
group membership, 27
group processes, 91
group size, 21
groups, ix, 3, 22, 27, 44, 50, 53, 67, 68, 91, 92, 109, 116, 117, 118, 119, 121, 126, 138, 139, 140
growth, ix, 49, 53, 63, 65, 154
guidance, 33, 120
guidelines, xi, 11, 69, 70, 71, 72, 73, 74, 77, 78, 79, 84, 86, 87, 90, 120, 132, 137, 138, 145, 147, 155
gut, 131

H

handling, 154
hands, 53
harm, 5
harmful, 7
harmonization, 121
Harvard, 61, 62, 63, 150
head, ix, 67, 68, 74, 81, 82, 83, 86, 89, 90, 92
head and neck cancer, ix, 68, 74, 81, 82, 83, 86, 89, 90, 92
healing, x, 93, 94, 96, 98, 104, 108, 110, 122
health, vii, ix, x, xi, 1, 2, 3, 4, 5, 6, 7, 8, 9, 10, 11, 12, 13, 14, 15, 16, 17, 21, 24, 25, 36, 38, 45, 49, 50, 51, 52, 53, 54, 55, 57, 58, 60, 61, 62, 63, 64, 65, 66, 67, 68, 69, 70, 71, 72, 73, 74, 77, 78, 79, 82, 83, 84, 86, 88, 90, 94, 96, 98, 100, 101, 102, 104, 106, 107, 108, 111, 113, 115, 116, 117, 118, 119, 120, 121, 122, 123, 125, 129, 132, 133, 134, 135, 137, 138, 139, 140, 141, 142, 143, 144, 145, 146, 147, 148, 149, 151
health care, vii, ix, x, xi, 1, 2, 3, 4, 5, 6, 7, 8, 9, 10, 11, 12, 13, 14, 15, 16, 17, 36, 38, 45, 49, 50, 51, 53, 54, 55, 57, 58, 61, 63, 64, 65, 66, 67, 68, 69, 70, 71, 73, 79, 84, 86, 90, 94, 98, 101, 104, 107, 113, 115, 120, 122, 123, 129, 132, 133, 134, 135, 137, 138, 139, 140, 141, 142, 143, 144, 145, 146, 147, 148, 149
health care costs, 2, 3, 7, 8, 11, 12, 15, 51
health care professionals, xi, 9, 70, 79, 84, 90, 137, 141, 145, 146, 147
health care sector, ix, 49, 64
health care system, x, xi, 2, 4, 5, 8, 9, 10, 11, 12, 14, 45, 61, 66, 69, 86, 120, 122, 137, 138, 139, 140, 141, 142, 143, 144, 145, 147, 148
health care workers, 45
health education, 10, 17
health insurance, 3, 118
health problems, 13
health services, 3, 16, 21, 58, 62, 64, 120, 121, 142, 149
health status, 2, 6, 7, 11, 16, 17, 70, 74, 77
healthcare, x, 15, 49, 50, 51, 54, 55, 57, 58, 59, 62, 65, 66, 88, 93, 94, 96, 97, 98, 100, 101, 102, 103, 104, 105, 106, 107, 108, 110, 111, 135, 151
hearing, 4
heart, ix, 2, 6, 16, 67, 68, 77, 88, 94, 97, 101, 107, 112
heart disease, ix, 2, 6, 16, 67, 101
heart failure, 68, 88
hematologic, 37
herbal, 10
heterogeneous, 8, 82
high blood pressure, 3
high scores, 81
higher quality, 154
high-risk, 47
high-tech, 55, 109
hip, 47, 88
hip replacement, 47, 88
HIPAA, 152, 155
Hispanic, 28
HIV, x, 115, 119, 120, 121, 122, 123, 124, 125, 126, 133, 135
HIV/AIDS, x, 115, 119, 120, 121, 122, 123, 124, 125, 126, 133, 135
hives, 105
holism, 100
holistic, 55, 97, 100, 104, 112, 140, 148
holistic approach, 104
holistic medicine, 112
homeless, 23, 33, 34
homes, 50, 116
honesty, 101
horizontal integration, 50
hormones, 7

hospice, 125
hospital, viii, ix, 12, 13, 23, 31, 35, 36, 37, 38, 39, 40, 41, 43, 44, 45, 47, 51, 54, 55, 56, 57, 58, 63, 65, 66, 71, 75, 79, 90, 92, 104, 118, 119, 120, 121, 123, 125, 152
hospital beds, 120
hospital stays, ix, 13, 36
hospitalization, viii, 17, 19, 22, 23, 24, 27, 31, 32, 36, 37, 45, 70
hospitalizations, 5
hospitalized, 22
hospitals, viii, ix, 12, 35, 36, 37, 38, 39, 40, 43, 44, 45, 47, 50, 51, 54, 55, 56, 57, 58, 61, 64, 65, 68, 82, 116, 118, 120, 121, 151
host, 94, 104
housing, 24, 25, 116, 118, 144
human, 51, 53, 54, 55, 62, 64, 79, 95, 96, 104, 120
human capital, 53, 54, 62, 64
human resources, 51, 120
humans, 96
hunting, 150
hybrid, 138
hypertension, 3
hypothesis, 32

I

ICT, 125
identification, 10, 22, 69, 129
identity, 140
idiopathic, 46
Illinois, 1
images, 151, 152, 153, 154
imaging, 152, 155
imitation, 140
immune system, 7, 17
immunology, 95
implants, 44
implementation, viii, x, 19, 20, 21, 22, 23, 25, 34, 68, 70, 71, 81, 82, 88, 90, 115, 116, 117, 120, 125, 126, 127, 128, 129, 130, 133, 143, 152, 153
incentives, 7, 8, 52, 133
incidence, 36, 73, 77, 142
inclusion, 24, 79, 147
income, 63, 64, 109
income inequality, 63, 64
increased workload, 147, 154
independence, 139, 140
India, 116
indication, 47, 97
indicators, ix, 37, 49, 59, 60, 69, 73, 74, 75, 76, 77, 78, 79, 81, 82, 84, 85, 86, 87, 90, 91, 92, 122
indigenous, 108

industrial, 79, 116
industrial sectors, 116
industry, 51, 53, 54, 61, 108
inefficiency, 145
inequity, 54
infancy, x, 115, 120
infection, 36, 44
information sharing, 60, 81
information systems, 8, 59, 69
informed consent, 27
infrastructure, 58, 146
injuries, 4
injury, 4, 10
innovation, 60, 79, 91, 92, 109, 132, 133
insight, 34, 81
insomnia, 76
instability, 36
institutionalized care, 71
institutions, 53, 133, 134, 138, 142
instruments, 25, 38, 40, 43, 44, 68, 77, 85, 94
insurance, 3, 4, 8, 15, 54, 102, 108
integration, xi, 25, 49, 50, 51, 55, 58, 61, 62, 63, 64, 65, 70, 96, 110, 117, 119, 123, 134, 135, 137, 141, 142, 143, 144, 145, 146, 147, 148
intellectual capital, 65
intensity, 21, 145
intensive care unit, 48
intentions, 127, 146
interaction, x, 30, 31, 53, 137, 141
interaction effect, 31
interactions, 5, 58, 62, 126
interagency relationships, 25
interdependence, 58, 70, 146, 149
interdisciplinary, 58, 110
interface, 118
international, x, 115
internet, 89
interpersonal skills, 24
interpretation, 17, 63, 79, 149
interval, 122
intervention, vii, 1, 2, 5, 6, 7, 8, 9, 10, 12, 13, 14, 15, 70, 73, 85, 97
interview, 25, 101, 102, 109
interviews, 25, 82
intraoperative, 38
intuition, 79
investment, 53, 63, 70, 110
IP address, 153
iron, 106, 149
island, 102, 142
isolation, 127
isomorphism, 140, 149
Israel, 112

Italy, 116, 117, 118, 133
iteration, 126

J

JAMA, 46, 47, 89, 90
January, 16, 112, 113, 135
jobs, 91
Jordan, 139, 149
judge, 122
Jungian, 95

K

Kazakhstan, 66
Kirchhoff, 91
knowledge transfer, 53

L

labor, 38
labour, 144
labour market, 144
land, 120
language, 152
laparoscopic, 47
laparoscopic cholecystectomy, 47
lead, ix, xi, 3, 4, 5, 7, 17, 52, 53, 55, 68, 72, 79, 87, 106, 137, 140, 142, 145, 146, 154
leadership, 33, 52, 59, 120, 146, 149
learning, 58, 79, 98, 101, 109
legislation, 116, 125, 126, 127
legislative, 86
lending, 32
life changes, 12
life cycle, 38
life-patterns, 101
lifestyle, 5, 9, 10, 77, 82, 86
lifestyle changes, 5
lifetime, 10
likelihood, 6, 108
Likert scale, 14
limitation, 45
limitations, 3, 4, 9, 104, 111
linear, viii, 22, 27, 35, 38, 129
linear model, 27
linear modeling, 27
linear regression, viii, 35, 38
linkage, 145
links, 10

literature, viii, 2, 20, 23, 36, 56, 68, 73, 74, 82, 83, 96, 100, 101, 102, 103, 104, 108, 110, 111, 116, 129, 143
living conditions, 76
local community, 55
local government, 120
location, 81, 82, 152, 153
London, 61, 62, 149
long period, 143
long-term, 2, 3, 4, 5, 7, 8, 9, 51, 58, 63, 110
losses, 142
low back pain, 37
lower prices, 44
lumbar, viii, 35, 36, 37, 38, 39, 41, 43, 44, 45, 46, 47, 48
lumbar spine, 45, 46, 47
lung, ix, 6, 68, 74, 76, 78
lung cancer, ix, 68, 74, 76, 78
lung disease, 6
lymph, 75
lymph node, 75

M

machines, 38, 44
mainstream, 107
maintenance, 25, 50, 55, 70, 71, 128, 130, 143, 154
major depression, 24
malignant, 146
management, ix, x, 2, 3, 5, 6, 9, 11, 16, 17, 20, 21, 22, 24, 31, 32, 33, 34, 36, 44, 45, 46, 49, 52, 61, 62, 65, 67, 68, 69, 70, 71, 72, 79, 81, 82, 83, 85, 87, 88, 89, 91, 92, 93, 97, 107, 110, 111, 117, 130, 132, 133, 139, 140, 143, 144, 146
manifold, 140
manufacturer, 133
manufacturing, 12, 50
manufacturing companies, 12
mapping, 96, 97, 110, 117
market, 45, 50, 51, 62, 151
marketing, 52, 64, 66, 109, 110
markets, 53, 138
maturation, 104
meanings, 50
measurement, viii, 19, 20, 21, 32, 37, 70, 77, 82, 90, 92, 133, 148
measures, viii, 6, 13, 17, 19, 20, 22, 23, 27, 28, 31, 32, 33, 59, 60, 72, 77, 85, 86, 122
mechanical, iv
media, 98, 151, 153
mediastinum, 77
Medicaid, 24, 47
medical care, 3, 123, 125, 149

medical expertise, 106
medical providers, 51
medical services, 55, 119
Medicare, 5, 149
medication, 5, 7, 9, 15, 24, 68, 123
medications, 4, 5, 6, 8, 9, 10, 13, 142
medicine, ix, x, 55, 56, 57, 67, 69, 78, 79, 83, 84, 87, 89, 91, 93, 108, 112
Medline, 101, 110, 112
membership, 27, 51, 59, 65
mental disorder, 15, 24
mental health, vii, 2, 4, 13, 21, 24, 25, 33, 34, 94
mental illness, viii, ix, 19, 20, 21, 22, 23, 24, 33, 34, 67
mergers, 51, 63, 132
messages, 68, 85
meta-analysis, 71, 72
metaphor, 142
microsystem, 70
middle-aged, 44
mind-body, 100, 102, 104, 108
Mind-Body, 94, 95, 98, 100
Minnesota, 113
modalities, 68, 105
modality, 105
modeling, vii, 1
models, viii, ix, 11, 19, 20, 21, 22, 23, 25, 27, 28, 31, 32, 34, 43, 44, 59, 67, 68, 69, 106, 110, 111, 129
money, 52, 154
morbidity, 36, 72, 77, 143
mortality, 47, 54, 64, 65, 70, 71, 72, 77, 140
mortality rate, 65, 140
motivation, 11, 25, 36, 145
movement, 61, 123, 147
MRI, 75
multidimensional, ix, 49, 53, 58, 61, 64, 143, 145
multidisciplinary, vii, ix, 1, 8, 16, 55, 67, 68, 69, 70, 71, 73, 77, 79, 81, 83, 84, 85, 86, 87, 88, 90, 92, 110, 126, 134
music, 94, 97, 107
musicians, 94
mutual respect, 52, 53
mutuality, 52

N

nation, 151
national, 55, 56, 58, 64, 82, 90, 91, 117, 119, 120, 126
National Health Service (NHS), 118, 132, 143, 149
National Institutes of Health (NIH), 111, 112
natural, 101, 104, 105
nausea, 76

neck, 68, 82, 83, 92
neck cancer, 68, 82, 83
negative consequences, 140
negotiating, 51
negotiation, 129
Netherlands, 67, 68, 77, 82, 88, 115, 116, 117, 118, 129, 132, 133, 134, 135, 149
network, vii, ix, xi, 48, 49, 50, 52, 53, 54, 55, 56, 58, 59, 60, 61, 62, 63, 64, 132, 137, 145, 152, 153
network members, 53, 56, 59, 60, 61
networking, 144
New England, 17, 47
New Jersey, 15
New Mexico, 93
New York, 34, 47, 61, 64, 65, 112, 133, 148
NGOs, 120, 125
nocebo, 113
nongovernmental, 120
nongovernmental organization, 120
non-small cell lung cancer, 90
normal, 44, 100
norms, 53, 58, 60, 63, 132
Norway, 135
not-for-profit, 52, 151
NSCLC, 75, 76
nurse, vii, 1, 8, 38, 40, 70, 71, 76, 78
nurses, 38, 58, 79, 82, 83, 85, 118, 139, 151
nursing, 5, 41, 44, 50, 79, 116, 118, 121, 134, 139
nursing care, 121
nursing home, 5, 50, 116, 118, 134
nutrition, 83

O

obesity, 3
occupational, 53
Ohio, 132
oil, 79
older adults, 16, 47
older people, 118, 143, 149
oncology, 76, 82, 90. 92
opportunism, 65
optimal health, 68, 88
optimism, 25
oral, 125
organic, 144
organization, vii, ix, 22, 49, 50, 51, 53, 58, 60, 64, 67, 69, 70, 72, 82, 84, 86, 87, 117, 118, 119, 133
organizational guidelines, 126
organizations, vii, ix, 49, 50, 51, 53, 55, 58, 59, 62, 63, 79, 116, 119, 121, 134, 152
orientation, 79, 81, 138, 144
osteoarthritis, 5

osteoporosis, 3
outpatient, 21, 88, 119, 151, 152, 153, 154
overproduction, 123
oversight, 94
over-the-counter, 10, 13
ownership, 44, 47, 65, 153
oxygen, 95
ozone, 95

P

PACS, 151, 152, 153, 155
pain, 4, 36, 76, 106, 127
pain management, 106
palliative, 121
palliative care, 121
paper, 2, 33, 89, 125, 130, 133, 134, 160, 151
paradigm shift, 107
paradox, 79
paramedics, 78
parameter, 102
parole, 24
partnership, ix, 7, 49, 60, 118
partnerships, 55, 58, 65, 83, 144
paternalism, 149
pathology, 40
pathways, 70, 71, 82, 83, 84, 85, 86, 144, 145
patient care, 58, 61, 68, 70, 71, 83, 84, 85, 91, 132,
    152
patient-centered, x, 91, 93, 96, 98, 100, 104, 105,
    106, 107, 108, 111
patients, vii, ix, x, xi, 1, 2, 3, 4, 5, 6, 7, 8, 11, 15, 17,
    33, 36, 41, 44, 45, 46, 47, 48, 54, 55, 56, 57, 58,
    60, 67, 68, 69, 70, 71, 72, 73, 74, 75, 76, 77, 78,
    79, 81, 82, 83, 84, 85, 86, 87, 88, 89, 90, 92, 93,
    96, 98, 102, 103, 104, 105, 106, 107, 108, 110,
    111, 112, 115, 118, 120, 121, 122, 123, 124, 125,
    131, 132, 137, 138, 139, 140, 142, 143, 145, 146,
    147, 148, 152, 154
payroll, 3
pediatric, 55
peer, 9, 24
peer support, 24
peers, 6
people living with HIV/AIDS, 120
perceived self-efficacy, 17
perception, 16
perceptions, 11, 13, 16, 105
perceptions of control, 13, 16
performance, 7, 11, 38, 51, 53, 59, 62, 65, 66, 69, 73,
    75, 76, 78, 85, 122, 125, 133, 135, 138, 143, 145,
    149
performance indicator, 59, 122

periodic table, 95, 96, 97, 98, 102, 103, 105, 110,
    112
personal, vii, 1, 7, 9, 11, 13, 15, 53, 55, 79, 94, 96,
    101, 102, 103, 104, 106, 107, 110, 139, 140
personal control, 7, 11, 15
personal relations, 53
personal relationship, 53
personal responsibility, 139, 140
personhood, 96
personnel costs, 44
persuasion, 25
PET, 75
pharmaceuticals, 40, 43
pharmacists, 58
pharmacotherapy, 21
philosophical, 63
philosophy, 110
phone, 10, 71
physical health, 4, 13, 14, 78, 86
physicians, xi, 4, 5, 6, 9, 11, 45, 55, 58, 70, 79, 83,
    118, 137, 139, 146, 147, 152, 154
physiology, 113
physiotherapists, 118
pilot programs, 27
pilot study, 47
pinhole, 152
placebo, 108, 113
planning, 9, 15, 65, 118, 129, 130
play, 43, 45, 58, 60, 83, 86, 123, 143
Poisson, 27
Poisson distribution, 27
policy makers, 77
political, xi, 66, 137, 138, 140, 147
politicians, xi, 137, 147
politics, 134
poor, 22, 52, 100, 123
population, vii, 3, 10, 15, 24, 50, 54, 64, 68, 69, 75,
    76, 106, 111, 120, 142, 143, 145
positive feedback, 11
post-hoc analysis, 38
postoperative, 36, 48
posttraumatic stress, 3
posttraumatic stress disorder, 3
poverty, 120
poverty line, 120
power, 32, 44, 51, 53, 61, 95, 139, 140, 146
prayer, 95, 98
prediction, 3, 27
pre-existing, 27, 31
premiums, 3
preparation, iv
pressure, 3, 4, 44, 120
prevention, 11, 25, 55, 66, 88

primary care, vii, 4, 9, 16, 17, 50, 54, 55, 64, 69, 79, 88, 89, 90, 91, 111, 113, 117, 119
printing, 151, 154
priorities, 8, 60
private, 50, 88, 94, 117, 118, 119, 120
private sector, 50, 120
privatisation, 138
proactive, 69
probability, 27
probation, 24
problem solving, 52
problem-solving, 11
problem-solving skills, 11
procedures, 5, 10, 27, 36, 37, 41, 43, 44, 47, 68, 74, 75, 77, 82, 83, 125, 126, 130, 141
process indicators, 77, 122, 123
production, 50, 57, 62, 122, 138
productivity, 3
profession, 97, 139
professionalism, 139
professionalization, x, 137
professions, 8, 94
profit, 36, 51, 65, 151
profit margin, 37
profitability, 51, 135
profits, 51, 62
program, vii, viii, 1, 2, 6, 7, 8, 9, 10, 11, 12, 13, 14, 15, 16, 17, 20, 21, 22, 23, 24, 27, 32, 34, 50, 55, 127
progressive, 4
promote, xi, 5, 86, 91, 116, 138
protocol, 45, 97, 106
protocols, 4, 25, 126, 130
proximal, 32
psychiatry, 56
psychological, vii, 1, 7, 8, 9, 10, 13, 15, 76, 87, 102
psychological well-being, 13
psychologist, 8
psychology, 17
psychometric properties, 27
psychosocial, vii, 1, 2, 4, 5, 7, 8, 10, 21, 76, 78, 86
psychosocial functioning, 6
psychosocial support, 78
public, viii, ix, 5, 21, 34, 35, 37, 39, 40, 41, 43, 44, 54, 58, 61, 66, 88, 100, 116, 138, 143, 144, 147, 148, 149
public financing, 147
public health, 5, 54, 66, 116, 138, 143, 144, 147, 148
public sector, 149
public support, 21, 34
Puerto Rico, 142
pulmonary rehabilitation, 15
pulmonologist, 75

pulse, 48
purchasing power, 45

Q

quality improvement, ix, 67, 69, 70, 71, 73, 75, 76, 77, 79, 83, 86, 87, 112
quality of life, 2, 8, 15, 16, 23, 70, 72, 73, 77, 78
query, 152
questioning, 105
questionnaire, 14, 79

R

R and D, 149
Radiation, 95
radical, 146
radiologists, 83
random, 106
range, x, 22, 24, 53, 75, 76, 93, 98, 104, 107, 111, 116, 117, 127, 129, 142
RAS, 151, 152, 153, 154
ratings, viii, 20, 27, 32
rationalisation, 138
rationality, 140, 149
readership, x, 115
reading, 97, 152, 153
reality, 36
reasoning, viii, 2
recall, 73
reciprocity, 54, 58
recognition, 25
recovery, 4, 36, 38
reduction, viii, 7, 9, 20, 22, 23, 31, 52, 105, 106, 109, 131
regional, 24, 47, 56, 61, 117, 126, 139
regression, 27, 43
regular, 5, 6, 9, 11, 12, 71, 123, 126
regulation, 140
regulations, 64
regulators, 58
rehabilitation, 21, 33, 56, 81, 92, 101
rehabilitation program, 101
reimbursement, 45, 138
relapse, 25
relationship, 7, 10, 37, 38, 43, 44, 45, 47, 52, 53, 58, 92, 108, 134
relationships, vii, 2, 24, 37, 53, 54, 55, 58, 59, 60, 63, 79, 86, 145
relatives, 52, 81, 98, 123, 125
relaxation, 108
relevance, 79, 106, 117

reliability, 27, 32, 79
religious, 95, 105
religious traditions, 105
remission, 23
renal, 5, 37
renal disease, 5
reputation, 54, 63
reputation enhancement, 63
research, viii, x, 2, 8, 9, 11, 17, 19, 20, 21, 22, 23,
    32, 51, 61, 63, 64, 68, 77, 79, 81, 83, 86, 87, 88,
    90, 93, 94, 101, 102, 103, 104, 106, 108, 112,
    115, 116, 129, 130, 134, 146, 148
research design, viii, 19, 20
researchers, x, 2, 3, 5, 6, 11, 51, 77, 115
residential, 34
resistance, 108, 109, 128, 129, 146
resolution, 63
resource allocation, 63
resources, ix, x, xi, 5, 6, 10, 25, 32, 35, 37, 38, 39,
    40, 41, 43, 44, 51, 52, 53, 54, 55, 56, 58, 59, 60,
    69, 101, 115, 116, 117, 127, 138, 144, 147
responsibilities, x, 9, 53, 58, 72, 83, 86, 137, 138,
    139, 140, 145, 154
responsiveness, 143
retail, 50
retirement, 3
retirement age, 3
revolutionary, 104
rhetoric, xi, 137, 147
rheumatoid arthritis, 68, 89, 116
rigidity, 47
risk, 3, 5, 15, 37, 51, 65, 139
risks, 8, 54, 59
RNs, 107
roadmap, 16
routines, x, 115, 116, 117, 126, 127, 130, 131, 134,
    151
rural, 12, 51, 54, 64, 66, 118, 134, 135
rural areas, 54

S

safety, 25, 70, 79, 81, 89
salaries, 38
salary, 38, 109
sample, 27, 31, 32, 33, 79, 92, 117
sanctions, 126, 130
SARS, 55
satisfaction, 13, 14, 36, 47, 72, 77, 78, 86, 88, 92,
    109
savings, 37, 44
scalability, 96, 104, 106, 107
scalable, x, 93, 106, 107, 108, 110

schema, 111
schizophrenia, 24, 27, 28, 31, 33, 48
school, 12
science, 84, 90, 108
scientific, 68, 73, 78, 85, 89, 108
scientific knowledge, 68
scoliosis, 46
scores, viii, ix, 6, 19, 22, 23, 25, 27, 28, 31, 32, 36,
    45, 75, 76, 77, 81, 86, 87
search, 110, 113, 130
search engine, 113
searching, 75
secretariat, 120
seed, 35
segregation, 145
selecting, 73, 96, 98, 100, 102, 104, 107, 110, 129,
    130
self, 6, 13, 14, 15, 16, 17, 71
self-actualization, 12
self-assessment, 90, 101
self-awareness, 102
self-care, 9
self-confidence, 131
self-efficacy, 6, 7, 8, 9, 11, 12, 13, 14, 15, 17
self-evaluations, 6
self-management, 6, 11, 16, 17, 69, 70, 71, 85, 88
self-monitoring, 11
self-rated health, 54
self-regulation, 139
self-report, 25, 72, 79
semi-structured interviews, 25
series, 14
service provider, 24, 25, 70, 126, 145, 146, 152
services, 4, 5, 7, 8, 10, 13, 14, 15, 16, 21, 22, 23, 24,
    25, 27, 28, 31, 32, 45, 50, 51, 52, 55, 57, 58, 62,
    64, 92, 109, 111, 116, 118, 119, 120, 121, 123,
    125, 132, 135, 138, 142, 143, 145, 146, 149, 150,
    151, 152
severity, viii, ix, 6, 27, 31, 35, 36, 37, 39, 41, 43, 45,
    47, 48, 54
shape, 60, 126
sharing, 53, 103, 119, 121, 151, 152, 153
shelter, 119, 121
short-term, 3, 9, 12, 15
side effects, 4, 5
signals, 77, 86, 87
similarity, 61, 117
simulation, 133
sites, viii, 19, 21, 22, 23, 24, 25, 27, 32, 82, 86, 151,
    152, 153, 154
skills, 6, 11, 21, 24, 25, 44, 71, 79, 109, 139, 145
skills training, 21, 24
smoking, 14, 83

SNS, 150
social, vii, ix, x, 1, 4, 7, 8, 9, 10, 15, 25, 49, 52, 53,
    54, 58, 59, 60, 61, 62, 63, 64, 65, 66, 77, 79, 87,
    91, 94, 115, 116, 117, 118, 123, 125, 129, 132,
    133, 134, 143, 144, 150
social capital, ix, 49, 52, 53, 54, 58, 59, 60, 61, 62,
    63, 64, 65, 66
social care, x, 15, 115, 117, 118, 125, 129, 132, 133,
    134, 143, 150
social cohesion, 58
social control, 52
social development, 54
social integration, 58
social isolation, 4
social network, vii, 2, 54, 61, 66
social norms, 53
social psychology, 91
social relations, 52, 58, 61
social relationships, 52, 58, 61
social services, 79, 116, 143
social structure, 66
social support, 7, 9, 25, 58, 61, 62
social theory, 66
social welfare, 144
social work, 8, 116, 118, 123, 125
socialization, 126
socially, 79
society, 45
socioeconomic, 54
sociology, 66, 133
soil, 120
solidarity, 53
solutions, 68, 90, 129, 145
South Africa, 116, 117, 119, 135
sovereignty, 141
specialisation, x, 137, 139, 140, 141, 144, 145
specialists, 4, 78, 139
specialization, 25, 133, 149
spectrum, 3, 27, 31, 97, 105, 123
speech, 4, 82
spinal cord, 4
spinal cord injury, 4
spinal fusion, 36, 41, 46, 47
spinal stenosis, 36
spine, 36
spiritual, vii, 1, 9, 10
spirituality, 13, 108
spondylolisthesis, 36, 46
SPSS, 38
SSI, 24
stability, 36
staffing, 22, 32, 132, 154
stages, 32, 50, 106

stakeholders, 52, 58, 122
standards, 69, 89, 90, 106, 126, 128, 139, 148, 152
statistical analysis, 38
STD, 119, 121
stenosis, 36, 46
sterilization, 38
steroid, 7
steroid hormones, 7
storage, 151, 152, 154
strategic, 51, 59, 61, 62, 65
strategic planning, 59
strategies, 53, 58, 59, 60, 63, 81, 134, 135, 138, 144
strength, 63, 107
stress, 6, 7, 9, 10, 13, 16, 45, 76, 105
stress factors, 76
stress level, 6, 7
stressors, 17
stroke, ix, 4, 6, 67, 68, 71, 81, 88, 92
structural barriers, 86
structural defect, 36
structural defects, 36
structuring, 58, 110, 111
subacute, 50
substance abuse, 3, 20, 24, 25, 33, 34
substance use, viii, 19, 20, 22, 23, 28, 32, 34
substances, 24
suffering, 2, 5, 105, 119
supervision, 36, 119, 138, 139
supervisor, 38, 154
supervisors, 154
supplemental, 36
supplements, 10, 13
suppliers, 51, 58
supply, 4, 57, 59, 68, 72, 82, 86
supply chain, 59
support services, 25
surgeons, ix, 36, 37, 38, 41, 43, 44, 45, 92
surgeries, 45, 56
surgery, 36, 38, 41, 44, 45, 46, 47, 50, 55, 57, 67, 75,
    95, 112, 122, 149
surgical, 36, 37, 38, 44, 46, 47
survival, ix, 49, 51, 64
surviving, 4
sustainability, 96, 104, 108
Sweden, 64, 137, 139, 148, 149
symptom, 6, 11
symptoms, 6, 10, 23, 76, 87, 105
syndrome, 47
synthesis, 17, 66
systematic, x, 68, 70, 73, 74, 81, 82, 85, 88, 89, 92,
    115, 116, 122
systematic review, 68, 82, 88, 89, 92

systems, xi, 7, 8, 10, 15, 16, 25, 27, 50, 51, 54, 58,
    61, 62, 63, 64, 65, 66, 86, 102, 107, 117, 125,
    126, 133, 137, 142, 143, 144, 151, 152, 154

T

Taiwan, ix, 35, 36, 37, 38, 45, 49, 54, 55, 56, 57, 58,
    61, 62, 64
talent, 106
tangible, 96, 151
targets, 146
taxation, 138, 142
TCE, 133
teaching, viii, ix, 6, 35, 37, 38, 39, 40, 41, 42, 43, 46
team members, 9, 10, 11, 79, 81, 125
technology, viii, 20, 21, 32, 51, 86, 88, 151
technology transfer, viii, 20, 21, 32
telephone, 56, 101
terminally ill, 121
test procedure, 76
Texas, viii, 19, 23, 24, 25, 27, 29, 33
theoretical, 2, 62, 63, 66, 79, 129, 133
theory, vii, 1, 8, 15, 62, 69, 128, 129, 130, 133, 144
therapeutic, 25, 57, 96, 97, 98, 100, 103, 105, 107,
    109, 110
therapeutic approaches, 25, 105
therapeutic interventions, 103, 105
therapy, 21, 76, 83, 105
thinking, ix, 49, 97, 107
third party, 153, 154
threat, 120
threats, 60, 146, 147
time consuming, 127, 151
time periods, 31
timing, 58
tobacco, 5, 14
top management, xi, 137, 146, 147
top-down, xi, 52, 137, 146
total costs, viii, 35, 41, 44
tracking, 110, 154
trade, 52, 58
trade-off, 58
tradition, 60
traditional healers, 119, 122, 126
traditional medicine, 95
traditional practices, 58
training, 21, 25, 44, 55, 70, 88, 92, 103, 107, 125,
    126, 130, 139
training programs, 44, 55
trajectory, 75
transaction costs, x, 115, 116, 117, 127, 128, 129,
    130, 131, 134
transactions, 117, 127, 128, 129, 130

transfer, 45
transformation, 147
transfusion, 38, 40, 44
transition, 9, 10, 11, 12, 17
translation, 75, 79, 153
transparent, 85, 147
transport, 116, 123
transportation, vii, 2
trauma, 10, 105, 151
traumatic brain injury, 4
travel, 102
treatment programs, 20, 22, 23, 24, 27, 32
trend, 3, 70, 71, 72
trial, 17, 87, 134
tribal, 141
triggers, 5
trust, ix, 49, 52, 54, 59, 65
trusts, 52, 53, 58, 60, 132
tuberculosis, 119, 135
tumour, 72, 81, 82, 89
tumour growth, 72, 89
type 2 diabetes, 88

U

U.S. economy, 64
ubiquitous, 106
uncertainty, 59
unilateral, 145
United Kingdom (UK), 53, 62, 80, 92, 116, 117, 118,
    132, 133, 143, 149, 150
United States, 1, 2, 3, 5, 50, 90, 142, 150
UP, 78
urban, 12
US dollar, 56
users, 53, 96, 102, 117

V

validation, 91
validity, 22, 27, 32, 79
values, xi, 52, 60, 61, 122, 137, 140, 141, 146, 147,
    149
variability, 47
variable, 22, 27, 101
variables, 27, 32, 37, 38, 94, 101
variation, 22, 36, 84, 148
vertical integration, vii, 45, 50, 51
village, 119, 121, 122
violent, 54, 64, 65
violent crime, 54, 64, 65
vision, 4, 52, 58, 70, 71, 79, 85

visual, 100
vitamins, 13
vocational, vii, 1, 10, 21, 24
volunteerism, 54

W

wages, 38
waiting times, 82, 87, 89, 142
walking, 36
war, 118, 120, 139
Washington, 15, 16, 87
waste, x, 115, 116, 117, 122, 123, 125, 131
weakness, 45
web, 63
web-based, 63
weight loss, 76
welfare, 118, 119, 121, 125, 144
welfare system, 144

well-being, vii, 1, 2, 8, 9, 11, 12, 15, 54, 66, 78, 86, 123
western countries, 54, 125
WHO, 75, 76, 120, 122, 135, 144, 150
women, 16, 121
workers, 119, 127
workflow, 154
workforce, 138
working hours, 38
workload, 79, 154
World Bank, 150
World Health Organization, 69, 150
world-view, 94, 96, 98, 100, 101, 103, 107, 108, 110
wound infection, 37, 40

Y

yield, 61